Ty Cobb

TY COBB

John D. McCallum

PRAEGER PUBLISHERS
New York

Published in the United States of America in 1975
by Praeger Publishers, Inc.
111 Fourth Avenue, New York, N.Y. 10003

Library of Congress Cataloging in Publication Data
McCallum, John Dennis
    Ty Cobb.
      1. Cobb, Tyrus Raymond, 1886–1961.   2. Baseball.
GV865.C6M32   796.357'092'4 [B]   75–51
ISBN 0–275–22520–8

Printed in the United States of America

To
Corky Corcoran
and
Dave Stidolph
and
Jim Ennis,
.400 hitters in
any league

Contents

Acknowledgments   ix

Introduction   xi

1 The Time, the Place, the Boy   1
2 The Name of the Game   7
3 A Career Ended and Begun   18
4 Time and Trial   28
5 Life in the Big League   34
6 The Tigers Roar   47
7 The Day the Tigers Went on Strike   76
8 At the Peak   94
9 Good-bye Cobbian Era, Hello Ruthian Era   112
10 The Final Fling   131
11 The Passing Show   143
12 "Where's Baseball?"   169
13 The Curtain Comes Down   175
14 Cobbian Baseball   181
Postscript   197

Appendix: Lifetime Record of Ty Cobb   215

SECTIONS OF PHOTOGRAPHS FOLLOW PAGES 82 AND 130.

Acknowledgments

In addition to the material I got from personal interviews with Ty Cobb back in the 1950s, I am indebted to a number of baseball people who shared with me private memories of him. The names include such great ball personalities as the late Connie Mack, Mickey Cochrane, Moe Berg, George Sisler, Cy Young, and Honus Wagner; Earl Averill, still alive and residing in Snohomish, Washington; the late Grantland Rice, Joe Williams, and Harry Grayson—illustrious syndicated sportswriters; the late Ernie Lanigan, beloved historian of the Baseball Hall of Fame at Cooperstown, New York, who opened his files to me; and some of the "more moderns"—Gary Nicholson, trainer of the Chicago Cubs; Wes Stock, pitching coach of the Oakland Athletics; Earl Torgeson, former big league first baseman from Averill's hometown ("the Earls of Snohomish"); and Stan Naccarato, General Manager of the Tacoma Twins (Pacific Coast League), one of the leading executives in minor league baseball; and John Pregenzer, former pitcher for the San Francisco Giants.

I wish to thank especially Praeger editor Léon King, without whose help this book would not have been possible.

ix

Introduction

When baseball's Hall of Fame was dedicated at Cooperstown in 1939, the first memento to be hung in the museum was a pair of shoes with gleaming spikes. "That takes care of Ty Cobb," the judges said. "Now let's see who else belongs in the Hall."

In 1942 a poll was taken among big league managers, ex-managers, and the stars of the century to choose who was the greatest ballplayer of all time. Of the 102 votes cast, Ty Cobb got 60, with the remaining 42 divided among fourteen others. Bowlegged Honus Wagner finished second with seventeen, Babe Ruth got eleven votes, and Rogers Hornsby, the greatest right-handed hitter of all time, was the only other player to get more than one vote. The baseball men who cast their votes for Cobb did not do so because of any love for him, but simply because they knew he really was the greatest of them all.

Indeed, in all of baseball there was no other figure quite like Tyrus Raymond Cobb. In twenty-four major league seasons he scored more runs, made more hits, stole more bases, and set more records than any other man in history. He was, like Babe Ruth, who followed him, a colossus of the diamond, and no other nation on earth was better fitted to harbor, tolerate, love, and hate him than the United States of sixty-five years ago.

The rise, the existence, the glory of Ty Cobb were strictly American phenomenan like John L. Sullivan, the Model T, skyscrapers, peanuts, and cracker barrel politics. Cobb's nickname, the Georgia Peach, was so much a part of the national consciousness that the heralding message spelled out in letters three inches high across the top of any afternoon newspaper, "GEORGIA PEACH RUNS WILD," was not journalistic shorthand for "Georgia peaches are selling well on the market" but a very simple presentation of the news that Ty Cobb of the Detroit Tigers had another big day on the base paths.

Grantland Rice was the first sportswriter to call Ty the Georgia Peach, signifying nothing more than that he came from the State of Georgia and his performance as a ballplayer was as sweet and perfect as the fruit grown in the Peach State. The Georgia Peach, the Phantom Mercury, and Tyrus the Terrible all meant the same person, Cobb, a ballplayer owned by the Detroit Tigers for twenty-two years, whose extraordinary coordination of eye, brain, and muscle, coupled with an enormous drive and the fastest reflexes in the game, enabled him to establish ninety records, more than any other man who has ever played organized baseball.

Playing in 3,033 games, Cobb made 4,191 hits and scored 2,244 runs. His closest rival in hits, Tris Speaker, was 676 behind him. Babe Ruth scored seventy fewer runs than Cobb. Ty's lifetime batting average of .367 was the highest ever compiled by any batter. Three times in his career he finished the season with an average above .400. He won the American League batting crown twelve out of thirteen years. In 1909 he even finished first in home runs. His average was .323 in 1928, his last year of baseball, when he was almost forty-two years old. He stole a career total of 892 bases.

Cobb is a difficult man to explain. Some people, like the late NEA Sports Editor Harry Grayson, whom I worked under in 1950, called him mad. "He's crazy," snapped Grayson one day when we were talking about Ty. "Cobb has always been crazy." Moe Berg, who spent sixteen years in the majors as an infielder and catcher, took the opposite view. "Ty was an intellectual giant," the Princeton graduate told me. "He was the most fascinating personality I ever met in baseball. To him, a ball game wasn't a mere athletic contest. It was a knock-'em-down, crush-'em, relentless war. He was their enemy, and if they got in his way he ran right over them."

Cobb went into every game the way Jack Dempsey climbed into a prizefight ring, full of pent-up fury and blood lust, filled with a deep and burning desire to win at all costs. He had no mercy on rival players or on himself. On the ball field, a pitcher who threw a beanball at Cobb usually wound up in the clubhouse nursing his wounds.

Portions of the Ty Cobb story are about as macabre and sordid as any nightmare-ridden mind could conjure up, and to report his life honestly I must write about the tragedies as well as the triumphs. Now, as I sit at my typewriter, I am reminded of something Ty said to me the last time I talked to him:

"I'm not going to apologize for the life I have lived. It's too late for that." Ty Cobb's eyes were clouded with trouble. They were like the eyes of a man weighed down by his sins. "I have but one regret," he said. "I'll go to my grave regretting that I haven't done any real good for humanity. I suppose I'll be forgotten within a few years."

Then he said, "If you are going to write my story, all I ask is that you tell the truth." This I have tried to do.

1

The Time, the Place, the Boy

The famous Eisenhower grin never shone more brightly. I was chatting with him in connection with researching my book about the six Eisenhower brothers, and President Ike paused long enough to recall a golf story.

"I was playing at the Augusta Country Club under all the handicaps a President of the United States puts up with when playing golf," General Ike recalled. "I'd take a shot, then wait patiently while the familiar army of Secret Servicemen swept down the fairway clearing the way for me. It was slow golf and it was accepted by everybody. That is, everybody but one.

"On the fifth green, I bent over to address my ball, when suddenly the air was shattered by a shrieking voice from back down the course:

" 'Get the hell out of my way, I'm coming through.'

"Well, I paused momentarily and looked around, then resumed my putting stance. Again the sharp command from back down the fairway: 'Do you hear me? Get out of my way!' So I stepped aside—to let Ty Cobb come through. I guess nobody but the great Cobb would have dared drive through the President of the United States."

Almost everything you have ever heard about Ty Cobb is probably true. One of the greatest baseball players the game has ever known, he was at the same time a savage, bitter, and weird personality, hated and feared both on and off the field. If you knew nothing of his background, you might guess that he came from a poverty-ridden ghetto where the fight for life was raw and unceasing, where fists and clubs and obscenities ruled and only the strong survived.

If that was what you thought, then go to the back of the class. The Cobbs were a socially prominent Southern family of comfortable means, one of whose antecedents, Joseph Cobb, had arrived from England in 1611 to settle on the James River in Virginia where "Cobham," his home, became a noted Southern mansion. Since then, the bloodline that produced George Washington blended with the Cobbs in marriage and there was just about everything in the family tree—Indian fighters, Revolutionary War officers, pro- and anti-slavery partisans, and at least one Civil War general. Thomas Willis Cobb, a colonel in the Revolutionary War, emigrated from Virginia to Georgia, where he lived to be 111 years old, with his great-great-great grandchildren at his side. In 1824, his son, Thomas, became United States Senator, and eight years later, Cobbs County, Georgia was named in his honor. Thomas Reade Rootes Cobb was a brigadier general and commander of Cobb's Legion in the Civil War. Years before Ty was born, Cobbs had achieved varying degrees of note in law, the military, medicine, business, and agriculture.

Out of this background came Professor William Herschel Cobb, mayor of Royston, Georgia, state senator, country school commissioner, school teacher and principal, and editor of the Royston *Record*. A big man, stern and strong, with piercing eyes, he was born in North Carolina. He graduated with honors from North Georgia Agricultural College, and while still in his early twenties married Amanda Chitwood, daughter of Captain Caleb Chitwood of Banks County, Georgia, a well-to-do plantation owner.

On December 18, 1886, in the rural community of Narrows, Banks County, Georgia near the North Carolina border, Amanda gave birth to her first child. Professor Cobb, an avid reader of ancient history, had always liked Tyrus of Tyre, who had led his people in resistance to Rome before Alexander slaughtered the population of the ancient Phoenician seaport. So he named his son Tyrus Raymond. Another son, John Paul, was born two years later, and a daughter, Florence Leslie, five years after that.

When Ty was only five and a half years old, the Cobbs moved to Royston. Ty was small for his age, and the other boys in Royston put him through the normal trial for any kid who was small and new in town. They greeted him with cool suspicion and made him feel unwelcome around the backyard games. One boy seemed really out to get him. Bigger and about four years older than the newcomer, he claimed the privilege of cleaning Ty's plow. His name was Joe Cunningham.

One day, when school let out, Ty found him standing with his school books under his arm, looking mean and anxious.

"You and Joe aiming to fight?" a classmate asked Ty.

"He ain't said nothin' about it," Ty said. "Maybe he's not mad no more." A brief scuffle had taken place between them during recess.

"How about it, Joe?" the classmate said. "You still got scrappin' on your mind?" A gang of kids had gathered around them now, and they were watching Joe.

One of the bigger boys slid Joe's books from under his arm. Another took Ty's from him. Ty waited, empty and nervous and knowing Joe was going to try and beat him up. Then it dawned on him: Joe was just as afraid of him as he was of Joe. Why, Joe didn't think he could whup Ty, no more than Ty thought he could whup Joe. *Joe was just like Ty.* It made Ty want to join forces with Joe and whip everybody else.

Suddenly Joe cranked up courage enough to hit Ty in the stomach with his fist. Ty hit him in the nose, causing a pearl of blood to flow. Joe hit Ty again and it hurt and Ty hit him again and that hurt. They rolled on the ground, hitting, biting, clawing, and then, almost as abruptly as the fight began, they stopped, panting hard, glaring at each other.

"Had enough?" Joe said.

"You?" Ty asked.

They shook hands and that was all there was to it. In a low voice Joe said to Ty, "Now you won't have to fight anybody else. The fellows will accept you now." Soon, Joe and Ty found themselves walking home together without realizing it. They soon became the closest of friends.

Once, in a moment of reflection, Joe Cunningham remarked that even as a small boy Ty had something nobody else had. "You saw it the moment you set eyes on him," Joe said. "It was something special, hidden almost. He just seemed to think quicker and run faster. He was always driving and pushing, even in grade school. He once beat up a little fat kid in the fifth grade because he missed a word in a spelling bee, causing the boys to lose to the girls."

Life in Royston in the 1890s revolved from the post office to the general store to the local school house. The people gathered in those places to talk about their families, crops, politics, and all the local news. There was nothing there of grandeur or classicism. The citizens were simply good neighbors airing their views on the state of the union and the state of Georgia, and being listened to with respect.

Someone from Atlanta might have considered life bleak in a community of 2,500, but in Ty's youthful eyes there was a fine simplicity, a dim beauty to the old town. In telling me about Royston one time, he said that its charm was made of a hundred things heard and seen and felt by everybody who was lucky enough to have lived there: the flutter of a dark window shade on a hot afternoon, houses with long, wide porches with rockers and boxes of flowers, big rooms of the houses filled with old furniture, bats fleeing the chimney of the train depot as the sun went down, the sound of balls being racked in the pool hall down the street, the country silence of the streets at night and the voices . . .

Ty had a glorious boyhood. June was always a stirring time of the year for him. School let out for summer vacation, and there was always something to do. Not only house doors and windows, but cellar doors, the attic window, and the great barn door were open now, day and night. Barefoot boys, no longer handicapped by school hours, were free to roam at will, wading streams, peering into squirrel holes, feeding small birds in the hollows of trees, following trails into the pine woods, digging in sandbanks, riding a horse. They swam, fished, cooked over a campfire, told time by looking at the sun, caught frogs, whittled, and caught and cleaned catfish.

For Ty the highlight of the summer vacation was the annual visit to his Grandfather Cobb's farm. Granddad Johnny, as Ty called him, was the squire of a section of the Blue Ridge Mountains, near Murphy, North Carolina, about 100 miles from Royston. A lean man of 5 feet 6, he was a wise and warm-hearted soul with a keen sense of humor and something of a legend throughout the area. Though an antislavery Republican, he had fought for the Confederacy, and he loved to regale people with tall tales about the Civil War.

One of Ty's warmest memories of the old man was of the first real present his grandfather ever gave him. They were sitting around the dinner table one night at the farm when Grandad Johnny reached deep into his front pocket. "I found me a knife this morning," he said. "Picked it up, thinking before the day was done I'd more than likely run across a boy in the need of one. I don't reckon you happen to own a knife, do you, Tyrus?"

"No, sir," Ty said. "I'm always needing a knife, too."

The old man laughed and put it into Ty's hand. The knife was small, but it had a little silver shield embedded in one of the pearl handles. Ty didn't realize it then, but it wasn't any found knife; it was brand-new out of the showcase.

His grandfather said, "You use that knife well, now, Tyrus, y'hear?"

"Yes, sir."

Sixty years later, Ty showed me that knife among his personal possessions.

Whenever they were together, Granddad Johnny was always ready to jump into an adventure with Ty. He loved to track bear and would tell Ty hair-raising yarns of the twenty-five bears and more than a hundred deer he had killed in his time.

"There he was, glaring at me red-eyed," Granddad Johnny would say, dramatizing a past hunt, "a slavering monster, twelve feet tall, fangs as long as corncobs, claws on him the size of a scythe—and me with just a long-rifle."

Ty, all ears, shivered with excitement.

"What happened?" he'd gasp.

Granddad Johnny would light his pipe slowly, allowing the suspense to build up. Then he'd look down at Ty solemnly. "Tyrus," he'd say, "if I'd missed, you wouldn't be here today."

No one ever used up a day like Granddad Johnny. Up at first daylight, he didn't go to bed till good dark. He loved to walk, moving swiftly and vigorously, getting over more ground than anyone would expect. He knew every field, every hill, every stream in the territory, and it was a head-spinning adventure into the wonders of nature for Ty to be with him. His grandfather would stop here and there to listen to a bird singing, to watch a cloud drift over, or to watch a sunset, and sometimes, so it seemed to Ty, just to stand and watch a patch of grass grow. An awareness of nature was one of Granddad Johnny's most enduring legacies to young Ty. Now, through the eyes and soul of the old man, Ty grew to appreciate the solemn twilight and the beauty of the fields, the earthy smells, the faint odors of wildflowers, the sheen of rain-washed foliage, the clatter of drops when the wind shook the pine, the far-off hammering of woodpeckers, crocus in bloom. He could fall under the rich spell of the rolling grassland, its loneliness and peace, with a vast chicken hawk hanging motionless in the sky, its wings spread wide. He loved the sight of blue clusters of grapes hanging among the foliage of vines, and loved their taste and the sweet smell. He could tell when a prize watermelon was ripe, how it tasted when it had been honestly come by, and its taste when acquired by illicit means. Both ways tasted good, but Ty knew which tasted better.

Those were to be the happiest years of his life.

"I felt secure and, like small boys, I harbored big dreams," Ty reflected long afterward. "It's like Grandpaw Cobb said, when you're young you go through life unmindful. You don't value anything until you're about to lose it."

2

The Name of the Game

Turn back the clock to the Gaslight Era of Sports and the effect is curious. John L. Sullivan went around shouting, "I can lick any so-and-so in the house!" Harvard men dominated tennis. Walter J. Travis was the demon of golf. Most speed swimmers used the side stroke. Peach baskets served as basketball hoops. Yale, Harvard, and Princeton were The Big Three of college football. Track athletes won Olympic titles in times that schoolboys would scoff at today, and horse racing experienced a reform movement that closed every track except those in Kentucky and Maryland.

Twenty-five years before the American League was organized, the National League played its first game, on Saturday, April 22, 1876. Boston beat Philadelphia, 6-5. Admission was 50 cents (a dime if you came after the third inning). Jim O'Rourke, of Boston, got the first hit in N.L. history, teammate Tom McGinley the first run, and Ezra Sutton of the losers made the first error. Joseph Borden won that first game—and a month later, against Cincinnati, pitched the big league's first no-hitter.

During the not-so-Gay Nineties, the Boston Braves, managed by Frank Selee, won five pennants; the Baltimore Orioles, with

Neal Hanlon at the helm, won the other five. Kid Nichols was the hotshot of the league. He notched at least 20 victories in each of his first 10 seasons.

John J. McGraw was then a 5 feet 6, 121-pound third baseman, the brain and sparkplug of the Orioles. The feats of the old Orioles became legend. Their skill, their flaming courage and team spirit were the talk of the sports world. Muggsy McGraw played third, Hughie Jennings was at shortstop, Big Dan Brouthers at first, and Heinie Reitz at second. In the outfield were Steve Brodie, Joe Kelly, and Wee Willie (hit-'em-where-they-ain't) Keeler. The Orioles and other big leaguers played exhibition games in Havana, Cuba, and toured with all-star teams throughout the South and Midwest, as baseball made its first serious bid to become our National Game.

At the turn of the century, Organized Baseball was still creaking along on legs as unsteady as a new-born colt's. Fans rode to the ball parks in horse-drawn buses. A ball park was nothing more than a rough, uncultivated lot, a grandstand was a jumble of rickety slats, and a club payroll looked like the wage list of a logging camp. Only one umpire was assigned to a ball game, and it was not uncommon for him to carry a loaded revolver on the job. In a contest between Clifton and Little Falls, New Jersey, one day, a pitcher named Jack Connelly blew up at the way Umpire Jock Mahoney was calling balls and strikes. Connelly got so mad, in fact, that he picked up a bat and started for the plate after Jock. Whereupon Jock whipped out his revolver from inside his coat pocket. He shoved it into Connelly's face, telling him at the same time that if he took one more step he'd blow his nose through his noggin. Mr. Connelly, the press reported, returned at once to the mound.

Another colorful umpire of this period was Jack Sheridan. Jack often had to fight his way out of the ball park after a game. One day a sportswriter met him in a hotel lobby and saw that he was unhappy.

"Lost my pocketknife," said Sheridan. "You know—that long one of mine. Carried it 25 years, and it got me out of many a tough spot. All I had to do was whip 'er out, flick open the long blade, and they cleared a path for me."

Jack Sheridan was one of the original boosters for California.

It was his custom to get in a plug for his hometown (San Jose) whenever he found the slightest opportunity. For a long time he made a practice of throwing in a commercial for the town whenever a batter let a third strike go by. If the ball came zipping across the plate and the batter failed to swing at it, Jack would cry magnificently: "Strike three! San Jose, California! The Garden Spot of America!"

By 1901, the United States was ready for a second major league. Along came Ban Johnson, a former Cincinnati sportswriter, with his soundly organized American League. Ban had raided the National League for talent—of 182 players signed, 111 came from the old league, including Cy Young, Nap Lajoie, Jimmy Collins, and Clark Griffith. Johnson organized the American League on the basis that "honesty and gentlemanliness" was its slogan, and that "umpires are untouchable and must not be kicked, mobbed or spat upon, as is the custom over in the National League."

The sensation of the new league was Lajoie, a French-Canadian hack driver. Larry was such an idol that crowds followed him down streets and kids worshiped him. When he endorsed a certain brand of chewing tobacco, half the kids of the country got sick giving the foul weed a trial, too, in the hope it would make them sluggers just like the great Napoleon Lajoie.

Meanwhile, back in the National League, Bones Ely of the Pittsburgh Pirates complained of a sore finger one day and refused to play shortstop. So Fred Clarke, the manager, turned to a top-heavy, clumsy-looking giant and snapped, "All right, Hans, you play in Ely's place." And Hans replied, "Hell, I'm no shortstop. I've never played it in the majors before." Honus Wagner developed into one of the superstars of his day. He slugged the Pirates to pennants in 1901, 1902, and 1903.

Baseball fans, in 1903, saw their first World Series on record. Deacon Phillippe, pitching for Pittsburgh, defeated the Red Sox three times in the first four games.

Other stars who helped to pack those hatbox-sized eastern ball parks in those days were Connie Mack, Eddie Plank, Cap Anson, Billy Sunday, Charley Comiskey, Old Hoss Radbourn, and Clark Griffith; Big Ed Delahanty, King Kelly, Louis Sockalexis, Turkey Mike Donlin, Jimmy Collins, Happy Jack

Chesbro—and Christy Mathewson, whose big right arm, rising and falling, fashioned one of baseball's greatest records in World Series competition in 1905 as he pitched three shutouts against the Athletics to hang up a record that still stands. Men like gods they were to baseball fans, including young Ty Cobb, who was destined to become the greatest of them all.

Ty was started on his baseball career by a Methodist minister named John Yarborough, a large red-haired man who had attended Richmond Academy, where he had been a hard-hitting catcher. When he was assigned to the church in Royston, brother Yarborough had a great deal of difficulty trying to coax the boys of the town to attend Sunday School more regularly. He finally won them over by agreeing to act as manager of their sandlot ball club. They called themselves the Royston Rompers, and Ty was the shortstop.

At home, all Ty had to practice with was a homemade ball. He had made it by winding yarn around a small core ball, and then, for the price of a few errands, got a local leather-maker to make a cover for it. He practiced hitting it with a broken bat; it was only half a bat, but he swung it over and over again to polish his swing.

Wherever Ty and his boyhood pals happened to be, and when the fancy struck them, they played ball. Someone would raise a hand and yell "scrub one." That meant he would get to be the first to bat. "Scrub two" would be the catcher, "scrub three" the pitcher, and so forth. It was usually too much effort to walk all the way over to the school grounds, so they would merely mark out a home plate where they stood and pick the nearest convenient tree for first base. The only restriction they ever observed was to move a few yards away from any plate-glass windows. The only real problem was finding a ball. They would bat and batter a ball until there was no ball left. When the cover came off, they wrapped it in black friction tape. When it got lopsided, they stopped the game and pounded it back in shape. When it started unraveling, they rewound it. Sometimes it unraveled so much it looked like a golf ball. Then they fused it together with the remains of another ball to make a new one. The players had their own gloves. Ty earned his by doing odd jobs, and he would walk around town with it looped over his belt, like a badge of distinction. If he got caught without it, he had to play in the outfield.

Cow-pasture baseball was the popular kids' game when Ty was ten. They called it "town ball." A kid would sock a leather-covered woolen ball around a cow pasture and then chase madly around the bases while his opponents tried to retrieve it and hit him with it. If a fielder could hit him with the ball, the runner was out. The rules allowed another turn at bat for a home run. If a kid kept hitting homers, he could bat all day.

"Nobody ever *tossed* the ball at the runner," Cobb explained one time. "It was thrown always with full force, and the best fielders were those who could knock the runner down. Getting hit in the head, or even on the arm or leg, hurt like the devil. If you were ever stung on the neck by a bee, or hit in the pants by a shotgun blast, you have some idea of what it meant to be put out in town ball. I never thought much about it, but after becoming a big leaguer it dawned on me that the tricks I learned in town ball didn't change. My style of batting, running, fielding, and bunting were basically the same as they'd been down home."

One day, Ty and a cousin climbed into a buggy and bumped and rattled over a red clay road to Carnesville to play some local kids a game of town ball. When the home team saw only Ty and his cousin they wanted to know where the rest of their team was. "This is it," Ty said. "We're the team." The Carnesville kids didn't want to waste time playing them but finally agreed to a couple of innings. As visitors, Ty and his cousin batted first.

"When the fielders saw I batted left-handed, they shaded toward right field, leaving a big hole down the left-field line," Ty recalled. "I laid some wood on the first pitch and placed the ball over the third baseman's head into the hole. I can still see the left-fielder, shirttail flying in the breeze, scampering after the ball. I easily got around the bases to beat his throw to the plate. According to the rules, it was my turn to bat again. Now the outfielders drifted over toward left field. This time I placed my hit into right field for another homer. That set the pattern, and they never did get us out. After only a half inning, the score was something like sixty to nothing and the game was called off."

Playing baseball was an outlet for Ty's emotions. He did not begin to play with any desire to become a professional. His emotions were very close to the surface then, and the Reverend Yarborough recalled his hot temper, the tears that would come to his eyes, the fury with which he played the game. Ty began to read all he could about baseball. He bought the old *Police Gazette,* which carried baseball news. He questioned the older players who were members of the Royston Reds, the town's semipro team, about rules and technique, and began practicing with a vengeance.

While Ty saw in baseball an opportunity to become more than just another schoolboy, his father's attitude was, "Stop horsing around with foolish games and settle down to your studies." Ty's classroom work was only average, except for a flair for oratory, which earned him several prizes. When he was fourteen, his father encouraged Ty's scholarship by letting him write an editorial for the Royston *Record,* of which he was editor. There was also a brief period when Ty thought about becoming a doctor. He even assisted Dr. Sam Moss, a local general practitioner, in an operation. A white boy had shot a black boy, and the victim was brought to Dr. Moss. Ty served as the anesthetist and discovered, as he applied the dousing mask and chloroform, that the sight of blood did not bother him a bit.

There was no question but that Professor Cobb wanted Ty to be a doctor or a lawyer. There was a barrister over in Carnesville, one of the old-fashioned barristers who grew his hair long. His name was Colonel W. R. Little. There came the day when Colonel Little called Ty into his office. He wanted to acquaint him with Blackstone.

"Come in any time, Tyrus," he said, "and read any of my books you'd like."

Ty was sure his father was behind the invitation, because he and Colonel Little were close friends. Ty cracked those books three or four times and they were terribly dry to him. "I knew then I didn't want to be a lawyer," he said.

The Reverend John Yarborough deserved some of the credit for starting Ty in baseball, but it was Bob McCreary who deserved a greater share. Bob clerked in the Royston bank and was also manager-catcher for the local semipro club, the Reds. Being a brother Mason of Ty's father, he was able after a time to soften Professor Cobb's attitude toward baseball. The elder Cobb gave in to the extent of giving Ty permission to accompany the Reds on a short trip to Elberton, Georgia.

The trip was a personal triumph for Ty. He drove in the winning run in the last inning with his third straight hit and returned to Royston something of a hero. That was his first full game as a semipro, and he was made the regular shortstop and occasional outfielder of the Reds.

"Ty was still a little, skinny, spare-built fellow," Bob McCreary recalled later. "But I thought at the time that he was about the best natural ballplayer I had ever seen."

In spite of the glowing tributes about his son, Professor Cobb still had reservations. In those days, in cultured circles, a ballplayer was looked upon as little better than a hoodlum, only a cut above pool-hall roughnecks.

It wasn't until after the Royston Reds beat Harmony Grove that Ty could sense a tiny thaw in his father's attitude. The game was played at Royston, and Ty saved the day with a dramatic, last-gasp catch of a towering drive in center field, with the bases loaded and two outs. In all his life, Ty never made a catch that thrilled him more. The Royston fans went wild, and in their adulation of Ty they threw coins at him—more than $11 in small change. That was the first money Ty Cobb ever made from baseball.

The Royston *Record* had no regular sports page, but it carried a full account of the game all the same. Ty suspected that his father had temporarily turned baseball reporter.

Ty was sixteen before he first saw a big league ball club in action. There was a bright young reporter named Grantland Rice covering sports for the Atlanta *Journal,* and Ty had fallen into the habit of reading his articles. The Cleveland Indians set up their training camp in Atlanta in the spring of 1902, and, according to Rice, they were really something to see. The star of the team was Ty's hero, Larry Lajoie, and Ty was anxious to watch him play. Ty talked his father into letting him ride the train down to Atlanta.

When he got off at the station in Atlanta, Ty caught a trolley car to old Piedmont Park. It was not clear in Ty's mind whether visitors were allowed in to watch the Indians, but with no guard on duty at the front gate, Ty walked into the ball park. He selected a seat by himself in the left-field bleachers and settled down for an afternoon of baseball under the warm, lazy sun.

Ty didn't notice where he came from, but suddenly a ball-player in a Cleveland uniform stood at the rail looking up at him.

"Hi, kid," he said. "What's your name?"

"Tyrus Cobb."

"Where you from?"

"Royston."

"Where's that?"

"About a hundred miles northeast of here."

"Well, my name's Bill Bradley. Glad to meetcha."

William Joseph Bradley was the Indians' regular third base-man. He had been in the big leagues since 1899. A good hitter, he had a batting average of .296 in 1901.

Bradley noticed the little box camera that Ty held in his lap. "Wanna take my picture?" he asked.

"Sure," Ty said, and he climbed down the steps onto the field. Gripping his big bat, Bradley froze into a typical stance and Ty clicked away. Then Bill called over some of his team-mates and Ty took pictures of them, too.

"After that, Bill Bradley was a hero of mine," Ty said. "I kept those pictures until they turned to dust. It was twenty-six years before I saw him again. We met at a banquet in Philadelphia, shortly before my retirement, and I reminded him of that after-noon in Atlanta. Bill looked at me as if I lied. He wouldn't believe that that timid kid from Royston was me. But it was the truth."

Once exposed to that whiff of big league baseball, Ty had trouble sleeping nights. He often got up and walked through his little town in the late hours. He would look up at the stars and burn with a secret desire to get away. He felt he was being held in some sort of bondage and just had to get out of that town. He decided then and there he would become a professional ballplayer.

Professor Cobb continued to hold his older son down, however. He was frequently critical of the boy, very strict, and Ty had a hard time getting through to him. The father believed that both his boys should learn the value of hard work, and what work was more strenuous than inhaling clay dust behind a plow attached to the family mule? Dressed in a hickory shirt under a pair of bib overalls, Ty found it monotonous, wearing, sweaty work: plowing, hoeing, rows and rows of cotton and corn, ten acres of tillable bottom soil. In a vague way, a certain young lady from high school had attracted Ty. Whenever he saw her coming he hid in the lowest part of the field until she passed. He was ashamed to have her see him doing common labor. Somehow the idea of staring at the rump of a balky jackass while wrestling a plow did not strike Ty as at all romantic.

A turning point of this period in Ty's life came when he gradually changed his frame of mind and began to work at cultivating the crops with a new vigor and spirit of cooperation. What he once regarded as a futile chore now took on new meaning when the first plants he had sowed popped through the soil. He suddenly saw farming in a friendlier light. His father saw the change and started giving Ty full acceptance. He took more time to hear his son's ideas and discuss them with him. They even exchanged opinions. They talked about crop production and about English imports of cotton that competed with their Georgia output. Ty never felt closer to his father than when he asked him, "Tyrus, do you think we should sell now or hold on for a better price?" By this time, Ty was highly familiar with such details as pulverizing the seed bed, drop-seeding, chopping and hoeing, the maturing of the bolls, and picking of the lint. To learn even more about cotton, he got a job with a local commission agent, and added to his knowledge of ginning, baling, grading, and transporting the product to market. (Years later, when post–World War I cotton was short, Ty used his firsthand experience to move into the trading market. The shares he bought gave him a profit of $155,000.)

Professor Cobb was pleased with the change in Ty. His dearest wish continued to be that his older son go on to college, perhaps the University of Georgia or one of the state schools. Maybe even a West Point or Annapolis appointment.

Ty's grades in high school had improved steadily in his senior year. But Ty was not thinking about college. His prime goal was still baseball.

Secretly, Ty began to write letters to the manager of the Augusta team and other clubs in the South Atlantic League, asking for a trial. This was in 1904, and the SAL was then in the process of formation. Augusta was the only club to reply. The letter merely informed him that he was free to join the club in spring practice, with the understanding he would pay all his own expenses. Ty wrote back agreeing to the terms. A week later, an Augusta contract arrived, calling for a salary of $50 a month if he made the team. Ty signed the contract without telling his father. He did tell his mother, though, and she did not try to stop him. "If you must, Tyrus, you must," she told him. "You won't be good for anything else until you get baseball out of your system.

Ty waited until the last night to break the news to his father. The professor was as austere as ever when Ty asked to talk to him, but he gave him his undivided attention. Ty made a full confession to the contract he had signed with Augusta, outlined his reasons for going, and then waited for his father's wrath to burst. It did not. The professor asked Ty to consider his action. He said he was not so much against baseball as he was against the prospect of Ty's becoming sidetracked in life and failing. He didn't want the boy, at seventeen, to become "a mere muscle-worker and throw your future away. I want more for you." As a state senator, the senior Cobb was not without influence. He was fairly certain he could get Ty into one of the service academies. He strode up and down the room, hands behind his back, measuring his words. He knew if he said the wrong thing Ty would be out the bedroom window later that night and hiking the eight miles to the next railroad station. As evidence, Ty's little suitcase was already packed. Ty knew he had to go. It was useless to attempt to hold down the strong-willed boy.

The meeting went on until 3 A.M. Professor Cobb finally tired and gave in. He walked to his desk, sat down, and began writing out a check for $90.

"Well, son," he said, handing Ty the money, "you've chosen. So be it. Go get it out of your system, and let us hear from you once in a while."

Ty left Royston on the morning train scared. What if he broke a leg? What if he severely injured himself? What if he couldn't make the team? His Aunt Norah's parting words kept nagging him: "Tyrus, you're going straight to hell if you defy your father!"

Chin up and chest out, Tyrus Raymond Cobb rode the Southern Railroad spur line south to Augusta.

3

A Career Ended and Begun

The City of Augusta, with all its rich history, was an alien place to Ty. No one met him at the train depot, no one on the street said, "There's Ty Cobb," no one at the ball park had a word for him, except for a groundskeeper, who leaned on his rake and said, "The manager's office is back there, kid."

Con Strouthers barely looked at Ty when Ty walked in. His only response was a nod of the head and a grunt: "Get into the clubhouse and put on your ball suit."

Ty had brought along his bright red uniform of the Royston Reds, and he emerged in it after twenty minutes. He was the only candidate who had paid his own fare to camp and was paying for his room and board. He also had to supply his own uniform until he made the team. No one paid any attention to him, so he kept busy hustling balls in the outfield during batting practice. He was not invited to take his turn at bat. The obvious assumption was that he would be taking the train back to Royston within a few days. Not much was expected of him. Ty wasn't called upon even once through the exhibition schedule.

On the day of the opening game against Columbia, South

Carolina, Manager Strouthers surprised Ty by telling him he was starting in center field. Harry Bussy, the regular first baseman, was in a contractual disagreement with the club, so Strouthers was forced to shift McMillin, the center-fielder, to first base. With a small squad, he had no one but Ty to put in McMillin's regular position.

On Ty's second turn at bat, the Columbia pitcher grooved one and Ty smashed it over the left-fielder's head and tore around the bases as if his pants were on fire for an inside-the-park home run. The next time at bat, he doubled. In his second game, he singled up the middle and stole a base—his first stolen base in organized baseball. After the game, when Manager Strouthers called him into his office, Ty was sure he had won a permanent job on the team. But Strouthers just eyed him coldly and said he was letting him go. Harry Bussy had come to terms and signed his contract. He was rejoining the club the next day. Ty was choked up. "But . . . but I'm hitting the ball," he said. Strouthers waved him away. "I can't use you, kid," he said. "You're a free agent now."

Ty opened his mouth to start to say something, but Strouthers motioned him out the door. All Ty could do was stomp out of the room, hurt and angry. Back at the hotel where he was staying, he ran into Thad Hayes, a rookie pitcher from Mobile who had also been given his release by Strouthers. Thad told Ty not to be downhearted. He said he had a friend who managed a semipro team over at Anniston, Alabama; he had already talked to him by phone, and the team needed a pitcher and another outfielder. Thad asked Ty to go with him. Ty was reluctant to make the trip.

"I don't know if I should," Ty said. "I promised my father that if I didn't make the ball club here, I'd go back and go to college."

"Call him," Thad said.

On the phone, Ty relayed the news of his dismissal in a hangdog voice, and he fully expected his father to order him home. But he was in for the surprise of his life.

"Well, son, what are you going to do now?" Professor Cobb wanted to know. "I hope you're not thinking of throwing in the towel. Quitting is the easy way out, you merely walk away.

But what do you prove? A quitter is trained for nothing but being angry."

"There's still a job open at Anniston. They need an outfielder," Ty told him.

"Then go get it," his father said. "I don't like quitters."

That evening, Ty and Thad Hayes crammed themselves into an upper berth for the train ride to Anniston.

Anniston was a member of the Southeastern League. The team was largely a mixture of Southern college athletes and semipros. Thad and Ty were well up to this level of competition. After the first workout, Ty was offered a $65-a-month contract, plus room and board. He was assigned living quarters with a family named Darden. The father was a steel company executive who set a fancy table. Ty's 150-pound frame began to flesh out.

Ty started out sensationally and was soon driving for the league batting crown. He was a young man in a hurry to get to the big leagues. As the season progressed, he wondered if word of his feats had yet filtered back to Royston. He knew his father was an avid reader of the Atlanta *Journal.* Grantland Rice was by now the sports editor of the *Journal,* and Ty set about organizing a personal campaign to attract his attention. Shortly thereafter, Granny began receiving a barrage of unsolicited letters, postcards, and telegrams from "interested fans." "Tyrus Raymond Cobb, the dashing young star with Anniston, is going great guns. He is as fast as a deer and a true phenom," said a message signed "Mr. Jones." A "Mr. Brown" wrote: "Ty Cobb is a sure-fire big league prospect. You should be the first sportswriter to acclaim him." More letters, cards, and wires followed, signed by Roberts, Smith, and Kelly.

The letters were written in every style of longhand imaginable —round hand, slanting hand, Palmer method, and even a scrawly lefthanded script. Ty was the impostor, of course. Rice ignored the messages for a while, but after weeks of this campaign, he decided to go see this kid Cobb. Years later, he told me, "I was curious. I wanted to see for myself if this hotshot Cobb was as good as my correspondents claimed. Before the game, I talked to him in the dugout. He stood about 5-11 and weighed, he said, 160 pounds. He was hard as nails. When I told him my name was Grantland Rice and that I covered sports for the

Atlanta *Journal,* he said, 'What are you doing way over here at Anniston?' As if he didn't know. I told him, 'I've been hearing a lot about you, Ty.' He said he had heard about me, too."

Granny was impressed by Cobb's self-confidence. He was also impressed by the three hits and two stolen bases made by Ty that day, and he went back to Atlanta and wrote a laudatory column about the new boy wonder.

During the booster campaign, Ty had to ask himself if he wasn't perhaps overrating the Cobb boy, but the obvious reply was that this kid really was a sensation. "I'm no knocker," Ty would tell himself.

Ty was leading the Southeastern League with a .370 average when the Augusta club decided it could use him, after all. For one thing, Con Strouthers had been fired as manager and replaced with old George Leidy, a smart baseball man. George was a much more compassionate man than Strouthers. He had the ideal personality for handling Cobb.

Except for one incident, Cobb and Leidy got along well in the thirty-seven games Ty played at Augusta in 1904. The incident occurred in a game in which Augusta beat Savannah, 2-1, and the Savannah run was scored on a hit past Ty in center field. Ty never forgot the details, because he was eating popcorn when the ball came at him. Manager Leidy said nothing to him after the game, but later in the evening he came to Ty's room and suggested they take a streetcar ride together. Sitting side by side on that trolleycar, George opened Ty's eyes to what baseball should mean to him. He said he wasn't mad at Ty, just disappointed. He went on to say that baseball was a great game, that it offered Ty unlimited opportunities. Eating popcorn in the outfield was okay if Ty thought baseball was just a big joke, he said, but suppose his ambitions were too important for such horseplay?

"Suppose you keep your eye on the ball?" George said. "Suppose you study the game? Suppose you practice and learn to make the most of what nature has given you? Why, you can go to cities that will make Augusta seem like a crossroads. You can be famous. You can earn a fortune. Every boy in America would idolize you. Your name would even go down in history books."

Leidy fell silent for a while, letting it sink in.

"Well, Ty," he said, finally, "how about it? I'll be happy to help you. I know some big-league tricks. I can teach you to bunt. I can help you improve your fielding and baserunning. I have some ideas to help you, providing, of course, you don't focus all your attention on popcorn."

In a way, that sack of popcorn started Ty thinking seriously about baseball. He learned from that embarrassing experience that the game was worth his total understanding, and all the practice he could get. Leidy lived up to his promise, too. He taught Ty to bunt into a sweater. He showed him how to poke a hit-and-run pitch through the hole left by the shortstop or second baseman while holding a runner on at second. He taught him how to lure the third baseman in for a bunt, then slash the ball past him. And on the bases, George turned Ty loose.

Ty managed a modest .237 batting average in the final month of play, and the Augusta fans liked his peppery attitude. He hustled all the time. He was out there every second of a game playing as hard as he could, no matter how many runs his team was ahead. He never let up for a minute, never gave his body a rest from trying. He didn't know what it meant to take it easy and loaf along. He was *always* working.

One day, before a game at Columbia, Ty asked Jim Elliott, one of their players, to show him the hook slide. Elliott was a former big leaguer and was credited with its invention. He gave Ty a ten-minute demonstration at second base. Ty stood right over the bag as Elliott showed him the sliding techniques. It's an ordinary maneuver today, but back in 1904 the hook slide was brand new.

Elliott got up and told Ty to try it. Ty backed away about forty feet and then bolted toward the base, a blurred streak that exploded in a cloud of dust, his spikes gleaming in the sun. As he slid even with the bag, his left toe hooked it and came to a stop. Elliott beamed. He threw both hands up and backed away. Ty bounced to his feet and trotted after him. What had he done wrong?

"Nothing is wrong," Elliott said. "There's not a man alive who could do that—and on the first try, too. After this, son, you be the teacher. I'll take lessons from you."

Cobb played a total of fifty-nine games in 1904, counting the twenty-two at Anniston. He stole ten bases.

Over the winter, Ty's .237 batting average gave him some concern. He wondered if the Augusta management would ask him back in 1905. No one had contacted him. Ty kept busy and in shape by working on his family's farm. He had returned home at the end of the baseball season with $200 and opened his first bank account. His father was impressed. The professor also noticed the way Ty jumped in and helped around the farm.

One day he told Ty that one of the fields had been plowed for early spring sowing, but the corn, wheat, and cotton had not yet been planted. There was a forecast of snow, and the professor was worried because they were short-handed and had to get the grain into the ground before it got too wet.

Without even taking time to change into his farm boots, Ty hurried out to the field, where a team of horses was waiting, fully hitched to a wheat-sower. He went to work and toiled until darkness, and he worked all the next day, too. He worked for three straight days. He felt all aglow at his ability to help out his father. The professor shared that pride. He finally felt successful as a parent.

It was late winter before Ty finally heard from Augusta. They had hired a new manager, Andy Roth, who phoned Ty and reassured him that he felt Ty could cut the mustard in the South Atlantic League in 1905. Ty wanted to know if Con Strouthers still was in the Augusta background any place. He certainly wanted no part of the man who had cut him adrift the year before. Roth guaranteed him that Strouthers was no longer in the picture. Then Ty said he wanted to talk to Bill Croke, the owner of the Augusta franchise. Roth put Mr. Croke on the phone, and Ty told him he wanted the salary offer of $90 a month raised to $125. That was quite a hard bargain for an eighteen-year-old with only thirty-seven games at Augusta behind him, but Mr. Croke agreed to the raise.

Cobb's play continued to improve though the 1905 season. From a .260 hitter early in the season, he climbed to an average of .326, best in the league. Ty roomed with a young pitcher named Nap Rucker, the same Nap Rucker who later won 134 games for the Brooklyn Dodgers. They were the only teenagers in a crowd of oldtimers, and in a mutual stand against the veterans' hazing and practical jokes they became close friends.

Rucker saw immediately that Cobb had something nobody

else had. "He just seemed to *think* faster," Nap said one time. "He was always driving and pushing." Nap said he heard stories about how back in Royston Ty dated a local girl whose father looked down on ballplayers as ruffians and didn't approve of Ty. Nap said he figured that Ty drove himself so hard to prove to the world that ballplayers were okay.

Cobb continued to work on his weaknesses. When he heard that left-handed batters had trouble hitting lefthanders in the big leagues, he made Rucker, a southpaw, pitch to him until Nap thought his arm would drop off. Ty said he wanted to know everything there was to know about left-handed pitching. Then he told Nap to get a bat and hit fly balls to him. He felt he had trouble judging flies, but soon he was hauling them down in all directions. On the bases, Ty did not require much work. "In all the games I saw him play," Rucker recalled, "not once did he let his spikes touch the dirt when he slid." A lot of baserunners made the mistake of digging their spikes in the ground and broke bones, but not Cobb. "He was a whiz," Nap said. "He seemed to be on his way the instant his bat hit the ball, and was halfway to first base before other runners even got out of the box."

When rival infielders saw they could not throw Cobb out, they began creeping in closer and closer from their normal positions; five feet at first, then ten, and finally fifteen feet. That gave Ty a better chance to hit between them. He often aimed at left field to give him more time to beat out soft grounders.

"Ty made a real science of baserunning," Rucker testified. "When he was on base you just knew he would steal the next base or bust. Pitchers tried to stop him but usually messed up. They would hurry their delivery and miss the plate, or worse yet, serve up a fat pitch where the batter could kill it; or the catcher would throw before he was set and throw the ball into the outfield as Ty streaked for the plate. If everybody played just right Ty would still beat the throw, and if they started making errors he would rattle them so much they couldn't get our side out."

Back in 1905, it was a custom in the minor leagues for the ballplayers to dress in their own rooms, not at the ball park, and Ty and Nap made it a habit to tub themselves in the room they shared after every game. There never was much of a problem, because Ty usually got to the room ahead of Nap and was the first into the bath. One afternoon, however, Nap was blasted off the mound early by rival bats and got back to the room first. Ty came in and found him soaking in the tub. While Nap soaked, Ty paced the living room like a caged lion, and when Nap finally emerged, Ty pounced on him. "Have you gone crazy?" Nap cried, holding him off. "What's got into you, a-fussin' and a-fightin' this way? Just because I happened to take a bath first today!" When Ty calmed down, he said, "You don't understand, Nap. I've got to be first—all the time!"

"Ty always claimed that story was pure fabrication," Nap Rucker said later. "He said it never happened. But it did. I was there."

Cobb never lost an opportunity to study the game. One day Augusta had an open date and Ty got permission to travel over to Atlanta to watch a widely heralded semipro pitcher make his debut in organized baseball. His name was Happy Harry Hale, and he came from Happy Hollow, Tennessee. Happy's first appearance was preceded by a big buildup in the press. He stood 6 feet 6, had legs clear to his chest, and boasted a smoldering fastball.

Happy Hale was unbeatable for the first four innings. He had a no-hitter going. Then the opposition stopped swinging from their heels and started choking up on their bats to bunt. Happy had not seen a bunt before. He was very awkward trying to field them. He was all arms and legs. On one play he stumbled in for a bunt, made a pathetic stab at it—and spiked his pitching hand. The not-so-happy Harry Hale ended his career then and there, all 6 feet 6 of him. The big guy had unknowingly taught Ty a lesson about the value of a bunt. "It quickly became an important part of my strategy," Ty recollected.

On his way back to Augusta, Ty fell into a conversation with a fat boy from Milledgeville, Georgia. He said his name was Hardy and asked Ty what his name was. Ty said it was Tyrus Cobb, and the fat boy asked him what he did for a living. Ty told him he played ball for Augusta. Hardy glanced at his slight frame and callow features. "Oh," he said, "you must be the bat boy." Ty blinked. "Bat boy!" he shouted. "Come out to the game tomorrow and I'll show you what I do!"

The fat boy came and Ty, with his pride still smarting, got a home run, triple, double, and single, and stole two bases. As for Oliver Hardy, he and his partner later became legends in Hollywood as Laurel and Hardy.

Cobb felt that Manager Andy Roth was too liberal with his players, which went against Ty's grain. Some of the members did pretty much what they pleased and enjoyed nighttime fun. Sportswriters labeled the ball club "a bunch of joy riders." Ty had liked it better when old George Leidy, now a scout for the team, was manager. The youngster went to Roth and bluntly told him he was holding too loose a rein. They argued. Roth took a strong dislike to Ty, and there were more arguments. Roth decided to unload Ty. He arranged to sell him to Charleston for $25. But Owner Bill Croke got wind of the deal and quickly called it off.

One afternoon after Ty had singled in a game at Macon, the rival first baseman turned to him and said, "Hey, Cobb, there's a rumor going around that you're being sold to the big leagues."

Ty was aware of some scouts from the majors who had been trailing Augusta, but it hadn't dawned on him that *he* was the one they were watching. Heinie Youngman, from Detroit, was one of the scouts. He had been around the dugout asking Ty a lot of questions.

Bill Croke had to make a decision. The Detroit Tigers held spring training in Augusta in 1904, leaving behind Eddie Cicotte, a pitcher, in lieu of certain training expenses. They had an understanding with Croke that, for $500 more, they would get first pick of any Augusta players in 1905. The man they really wanted was Clyde Engle, a versatile infielder-outfielder. However, Bill Byron, one of the umpires in the South Atlantic League, got word back to Owner Frank Navin of the Tigers to hold out for Cobb. "He's your boy," Byron told him. "He's leading the league in batting and stolen bases and is like a wild colt. He needs some polish, but as soon as he gets used to a bridle you'll see the world's greatest ballplayer. He'll tear the American League apart."

Umpire Byron wrote to Bill Armour, the Detroit manager, and advised him the same thing. Meanwhile, Edward Grant Barrow, the Indianapolis manager, started dickering for Cobb's contract. Late in the season, Barrow, renowned during the years 1920–45 as "The Man Behind the Yankees," had a chance to purchase two Augusta players, Cobb and Engel. Bill Croke said he could have either one for $500, or both for $800. Barrow turned the offer down. He later confessed that he had other things on his mind at the time and "this muddled mental state cost me Ty Cobb, the greatest hitter of all time."

Up in Detroit, the selection had narrowed down to Ty and Engle, but Clyde's play slowed down in the dog days of August, while Cobb's .326 batting average and forty stolen bases topped the SAL. The deciding factor, though, was that the Tigers needed outfielders more than infielders. Navin and Manager Armour chose Cobb. So for $500 plus another $250, Bill Croke sold Ty Cobb to Detroit with the understanding that he would report to them in late August. A week after the deal was made, four more major league clubs tried to claim him in the draft.

4

Time and Trial

On the night of August 8, Professor Cobb ate supper as usual with Amanda and their two children, Paul, fourteen, and Florence, eleven. Afterward he went to the barn and hitched up his buggy. He had some business in a neighboring village and did not know definitely what time he would return.

Amanda stood on the porch waving good-bye as the buggy clattered off into dusk. When she could no longer hear the buggy, Amanda went back inside the house.

After finishing the dishes, she moved to the living room and picked up her sewing basket. At 10:30, she grew sleepy and climbed the stairs to change for bed. She was all alone now. Paul and Florence were spending the night with friends. Upstairs in the slant-ceilinged bedroom, she took the garments she had changed from and moved to hang them up in the closet. Then, after double-checking the upstairs windows, she went to bed and dropped into a slow, restless sleep. Some time later the silence was broken by a rustling noise. Amanda sat up in bed and listened intently. She told herself that it was only her imagination, but just to make sure she went to the window and looked out. Finding nothing, she crawled back into bed, after taking a pistol out of a drawer. But sleep would not come. Then she heard it again, that same rustling noise at the lower window of her room. She got up again. This time, she had her pistol clutched between her hands.

Trembling in the darkness of her bedroom, she moved on tiptoe from window to window, checking the latches. She was startled by a sudden sound behind her, but it was only a book that had fallen off her nightstand when she had bumped into it. She had just finished inspecting the last window when she heard an assured, firm footstep on the porch roof outside. Then there was an authoritative, jiggling noise at the lower window. Amanda felt herself go limp, almost hysterical with fear. She wanted to cry out—to scream—but she couldn't. Through the curtain she could make out a silhouette trying the window. Gently. Softly. Soundlessly.

The figure outside slowly and cautiously released his pressure against the lock. Then he crouched and carefully put his shoulder to the windowframe. His feet braced, he strained against it, almost as if he was trying to push it in. The windowframe creaked, and Amanda's nightmarish horror bubbled over in a sound which should have been a cry, but was actually no more than a stifled hoarseness. If the man heard her, he did not show it. He went on prying the window.

Amanda wanted to faint but could not. Instead, she crept to the window, pulled the shade ever so slightly to one side, and peered out.

Then she saw him. In the darkness she could not see what the man looked like; he was crouched down as if to spring, his face hidden. Amanda screamed. As her cry echoed, she heard the crash of shattering glass. Then, suddenly, everything seemed to go dead quiet, and she stood there holding a smoking pistol. Out on the porch roof, a limp figure lay slumped—a bullet in his head and another in his stomach. He was still breathing, but barely.

Amanda flung down the pistol and began screaming.

When Clifford Ginn, a boy next door, rushed into the room he found Amanda ghostly white, twitching and chattering and too incoherent to do anything but wave to the window.

Clifford went to the broken window. He crawled out on the roof. He quickly examined the body.

"Mrs. Cobb—MRS. COBB!" he cried. "It's Mr. Cobb. He's not breathing! I think he's dead!"

The boy ran to get Doctor McCrary, the local physician. By the time Clifford returned with him, Amanda was a shivering, gibbering wreck. She still could not believe this was happening to her. That was no stranger lying out there on the porch roof. That was her own husband, father of Ty, Paul, and Florence. At 1:30 A.M. on August 9, Doctor McCrary declared Professor W. H. Cobb officially dead.

Early that day in Augusta, a message was brought to Ty informing him of the accident. In his sudden grief, baseball didn't seem very important to him now. His only thought was that his father would not be able to share in whatever success was ahead of him.

All Ty knew when he left for Royston was that his father had died in a gun accident. When he arrived he learned some of the ghastly details. But it was difficult to get to the bottom of the tragedy, as there were conflicting stories in town. The Royston *Record* only briefly noted the shooting in a front page article that afternoon:

Ex-Senator and County School Commissioner W. H. Cobb of Royston was fatally shot last night by his wife. It seems that he came home late in the night and was mistaken for a burglar. He was unconscious until his death at 1:30 this morning.

Mr. Cobb was shot twice, one shot taking effect in the head, the other in the abdomen. A coroner's investigation is under way.

Since there had been no witnesses to the actual shooting, no two persons gave the same account of the tragedy. Gossip was rampant. "The professor suspected his wife of being unfaithful to him," claimed one source. "He thought he would catch her in the act, so he came home earlier than announced and tried getting into the bedroom by way of the upstairs window."

Amanda Cobb involved in a clandestine affair? Nonsense, said another neighbor. She was a good woman, a faithful wife and a devoted mother. Yet, according to another source, Professor Cobb actually did get through the window, and when Amanda saw this menacing figure coming at her in the dark, she assumed it to be a robber and instinctively reached for her pistol, which she always kept on her nightstand alongside her bed when she was alone nights. There were also varying opinions of the weapon she used. One gossip said it was a shotgun, another a revolver, and there were even those who claimed it was a knife.

The amateur informants also varied the time of the night when the accident occurred; they differed on how many bullets were fired; they gave different reasons for Professor Cobb's trip out of town; and they couldn't agree on where the Cobb youngsters were at the time of their father's death.

At a coroner's inquest on August 10, Amanda, her composure returned, described the killing in detail. That evening, the *Record* carried a brief account of the hearing. The news story hinted of possible scandal:

The coroner's jury in the case of the homicide of County School Commissioner W. H. Cobb, formed a verdict of voluntary manslaughter against Mrs. W. H. Cobb today and ordered her arrest tomorrow. The warrant was held up until after the funeral today.

Witnesses were introduced who testified that there was a considerable interval between the shots, sufficient time for a person to walk back and forth across the room. Dr. J. O. McCrary, the first physician on the scene, produced a revolver and rock found in the coat pocket of the deceased.

Mr. Cobb had gone to a farm he owns near town and left his buggy and walked through the fields back into Royston. He was seen on the street at about 10 o'clock, but seemed, it is claimed, to hide his identity.

It is said that sensational developments will follow the investigation into the killing of ex-Senator Cobb by his wife. According to statements made in this city today, Mr. Cobb had received notice about two weeks ago that he had better watch his home. Before the night of the tragedy, it is alleged that there had been more than one disagreement between himself and his wife and owing to the various rumors it is expected that sensational developments will follow.

Mrs. Cobb's statements that she mistook her husband for a
burglar are doubted by many. No other person, as far as is known,
was seen at the Cobb home on the night of the shooting.

Professor Cobb's funeral was held on August 11, and Ty
would remember it all his life. The day was hot and sticky. The
undertaker, in frock coat, escorted family and mourners outdoors,
where the hearse and two horses with black trappings were waiting at the curb. Later, when the casket was lowered into the
ground, Ty remembered thinking, "There goes the only man I'll
ever love." His world lay shattered at his feet. It was as if he
blamed the whole human race for the accident and held it in
contempt. He felt only cold loneliness.

The day after the funeral, readers of the *Record* learned that
the Cobb case had become police business, and a warrant for
the arrest of Amanda had been served. The published details were
brief:

Mrs. W. H. Cobb, who was arrested under the coroner's warrant,
charging her with voluntary manslaughter in killing her husband,
whom she allegedly mistook for a burglar, quickly gave the $7,000
bond required by Justice Jordan. The court to which this is return-
able will be held the fourth Tuesday in September.

Paul and Florence Cobb, children of Mr. and Mrs. Cobb, said
in an interview that they were much surprised to see the sensational reports in regards to family differences between their parents. Paul said that the domestic relations between his father and
mother were most pleasant and that rumors to the contrary are
absolutely untrue.

What finally happened to the case is something of a mystery.
There was no further mention of it in the newspapers, except for
a note in the Royston *Record* in late November, 1905, announcing
that the original trial date had been postponed because it was
impossible to find a circuit judge, and the case was being turned
over to the regular term. As near as can be determined, the
matter was quietly dropped. It never did reach court.

Ty spent a week at home before returning to Augusta, where
Bill Croke broke the news to him that he had been sold to
Detroit and was to report to the Tigers on August 29. Ty got

hold of himself and went back to work. He played eight more games for Augusta as though his father were watching. The memory of how he died almost drove Ty crazy. He was like a steel spring with a growing and dangerous flaw in it. If he wound himself up too tightly, he would fly apart. Sometimes that spring reached the breaking point and fists flew. Everything Ty was doing in baseball now, he was doing for his father. The professor would never get to see his son in a big league uniform but in Ty's mind he was up there somewhere watching him. And Ty wasn't going to disappoint him.

5

Life in the Big League

At eighteen, Ty stood 5 feet 11 and weighed 160. He was fair-complexioned with lots of reddish-blond hair, parted in the middle. He arrived in Detroit at 10:30 on the night of August 29 with one suitcase, a uniform roll containing his suit, spare underwear, and dirty laundry, his pancake-style Spalding glove, and several of his favorite bats. The first thing he did was check into a third-class hotel for $10 a week, American plan.

The next morning, he asked the desk clerk how to get to Bennett Field and learned it was within walking distance. Named for Charley Bennett, a popular 1894 Detroit catcher who had lost a leg in a train accident, the Tiger ball park at Michigan and Trumbull avenues seated only 8,500, but it looked awesome to Ty.

At the Tiger office, Ty met Manager Bill Armour and Owner Frank Navin and signed a contract for $1,800 per season. But it was now August 30, and Ty could count on only a month's pay before the end of the season.

The Detroit papers had mentioned the purchase of Cobb several days before, but in doing so they hadn't even bothered to check the correct spelling of his first name. "Cyrus Cobb, outfielder

34

from Augusta, Georgia, was picked up for $750 this week to play for the Detroit Tigers," a one-line report read. Because there was so very little known about him, Manager Armour asked Ty a lot of questions. How old was he? Did he drink? Smoke? Chase girls? What did he hit at Augusta? Ty told him he would be nineteen on December 18, that, no, he did not booze, use the foul weed, or wench around, and that in 104 games in the South Atlantic League he hit .326, scored sixty runs, and stole forty bases. "And I bat left-handed and throw right," Ty added. Significantly, he did not go into the details of how his father died. Because he was still an unknown, news of the tragedy had not reached the Detroit papers. Just as well. Ty preferred to suffer in silence.

Ty was properly impressed with Bill Armour, his new manager. Something of a Beau Brummel, Armour wore a colorful walrus mustache, dressed impeccably, and never bothered to change from street clothes to a uniform for games. He was affable and showed no fear that Ty might be too young or inexperienced for the job he needed done. The Tigers had been hit hard by injuries to their outfielders, and Ty would be starting in center field that very afternoon against the New York Highlanders.

"Jimmy Barrett, my regular center fielder, has a bum knee," Armour explained. "He'll fill you in on our signals."

Ty said he wasn't used to a lot of technical signals.

"Can't I just go out there and play my natural way?" Ty asked.

"Suit yourself," Armour said. But there was a warning in his tone that told Ty he had *better* come through, or else.

In the New York lineup that day were such stalwarts as Wee Willie Keeler, who never hit under .300 in fourteen seasons, and the great Kid Elberfeld, at second base. Jack Chesbro was master of their pitching staff, the original spitballer who had won a record forty-one games in 1904. This was the man against whom Ty would be making his big league debut. When Chesbro cranked up and fired his overhand spitter, loaded with slippery elm, it burst up to the plate like a snake on a hot griddle. "It would fly at you like a standard fastball, but then suddenly it'd dive under your bat," Cobb explained once. "Damndest thing."

Armour made out his batting lineup and had Cobb hitting

fifth. Just before the Tigers ran onto the field, Bill gave Ty some last-minute advice. "Ty," he said, "don't let the size of this crowd scare you. Go out there and be calm and not overawed by these guys. Chesbro has a great spitball so don't try to kill it. Just meet the ball."

At the umpire's cry of "Play ball!" both teams went at it with red-eyed ferocity. On one play, Kid Elberfeld tried to knock Germany Schaefer bowlegged as he raced for third base, and Schaefer retaliated by busting Elberfeld on the noggin. Then "Rowdy" Bill Coughlin, the Detroit third baseman, flew into a rage at Umpire Silk O'Loughlin and was banished from the game. Later, Frank Delahanty, the husky slugger for the Highlanders, tried to stretch a double into a triple and tore the tendons in his ankle on the slide into the bag. He was carried off the field on a stretcher, through for the season.

When Cobb walked up to the plate the first time, Detroit fans scanned their scorecards to find out who he was. A murmur fell over the crowd. His name was not even listed. Ty hunched over the plate and twisted his mouth scornfully, taunting Chesbro with a few derisive words. Chesbro poured two fast strikes past him. Then Ty whacked the next pitch over the head of Eddie Hahn in center field for a double, driving in a run from second. The fans went wild. It was a great way for the rookie to break in. On his next time at bat, Ty drew a walk and was thrown out trying to steal. Detroit went on to beat Chesbro, 5–3, and Ty was pleased with himself. The Detroit *Free Press* summed up his debut in a line: "Cobb, the rookie, may consider a double and a walk a much better career-opener than usually comes a young ballplayer's way." The Detroit *Journal* observed that "the juvenile outfielder from Georgia comes up to expectations."

The two teams battled again the following day and Ty had his "plow cleaned." He worked his way to first base on a walk and then went racing down to second and hit the dirt head first. Kid Elberfeld, a tough old cookie, was waiting with the ball to give Ty "the old teach." He slammed his knee down on the back of Ty's neck and ground his face into the dirt. Silk O'Loughlin went up with the thumb and Ty trudged dejectedly back to the bench spluttering and spitting dirt. He looked back over his shoulder and saw Kid Elberfeld grinning at him.

Manager Armour gave Ty hell. "That was a bonehead play!" Armour shouted at him. "Elberfeld could have broken your neck! That head-first slide might be hot stuff in Augusta, but it's suicide up here in the majors."

While he started off in a flash, it soon became evident that Cobb was not going to be establishing any rookie records. He got two more hits in his second game against New York but went hitless in the third. After that, he was shut out regularly. The only reason Armour played him was that Jimmy Barrett was still hobbled by a sore leg.

In 1905, playing conditions in the majors were far from ideal. Old Bennett Park sprouted grass that had been planted at the wrong time of year and was rutted with holes and soft spots like a cow pasture. Batted balls dropped off and flew in all directions at that part of the infield where the grass and the skin surface came together. Groundskeepers raked the infield only once a week. Drainage was crude, and on wet days the outfield grass was marshy.

Those oldtime clubhouses were no better. The players dressed in primitive quarters, waited in line to use the single shower, and dressed the next day in damp uniforms. Game togs seldom saw a laundry. Train travel was in non-air-conditioned chair cars, and it was an eighteen-hour ride from Saint Louis to Boston. There were no batting cages, no pitching machines, no coaching specialists, no vitamin tablets. If you glanced down a hotel hallway after a game, you would have seen ballplayers wrapped in bedsheets, grimy and sore from the day's battle and unable to find a bathtub anywhere. They were sometimes forced to use public toilets in second-rate hotels to clean themselves up. Ballplayers were still shunned by most of society. The best hotels refused even to lodge them, and those that did would not boast of it. Hotel dining room hostesses shoved them back in a corner so they wouldn't be too conspicuous. Waiters waited on them reluctantly.

Life in the majors was still an improvement over the minor leagues. Ty had not forgotten that most of the ball parks had no dressing rooms at all. Players changed in and out of their uniforms back at their hotels. Often when time was short they went straight to their train from the ball field in their uniforms.

Since laundering facilities were scarce, it was necessary for the players to wash their own uniforms aboard the train. Each man carried his equipment in a "uniform roll," and at the start of a trip he unfurled it and shook out the garments, soaked with sweat and saturated with dirt. The custom was then to raise a window and hang the suit on the side of the train in the rushing air. It didn't require many miles to dry out the suit and whip a good part of the dust out of it.

Ty often wondered how they survived. The pancake gloves they wore, the washboard fields they played on, the cramped upper berths they climbed into on endless rides over poor road-beds, the need to grapple with their own luggage, the four-men-to-one-bathtub system in hotels, and the crude equipment—how did they do it?

The conditions might not have been the best, but Ty found no fault in fan loyalty. One afternoon, the Tigers squeaked past the Cleveland Indians in the eleventh inning. In the last frame, Umpire Jack Sheridan suddenly turned toward the grandstand and raised his hand for silence. "Is there a Sam Reed here?" he asked. There was. "Sam," Sheridan shouted, "you're wanted at home. Your house is on fire." Sam didn't move. "Well?" Sheridan said. "I've decided to stay for the rest of the game," Sam said. "I couldn't get there in time to do anything now. Let the damn house burn."

In January, 1906, Ty was dubious about getting called back to the Tigers. The way he sized it up, he had stepped into a starting position in his rookie season mostly by forfeit. His .240 batting average for forty-one games during the last month of the 1905 season made it highly improbable that Bill Armour would want him back. But, for some reason Ty never found out, the Detroit manager did want him to return.

Over the winter, the Tigers picked up Davy Jones, a fleet outfielder and expert leadoff man. That meant four candidates would have to fight for the three outfield positions—Sam Crawford, Matty McIntyre, Jones, and Cobb. The battle figured to narrow down to Ty and Matty, who was a good ballhawk but a light hitter. The Tiger veterans, a tightly grouped clique, sided with Matty, and they began a cruel, systematic, carefully schemed campaign to break Ty's spirit and put him on the bench.

At first there were no open clashes. Gradually, however, tension rose as thick as steam. McIntyre and pitcher Ed Killian, his roommate, began by locking Cobb out of the hotel bathroom the players shared, leaving him shivering in the hallway. At batting practice, Ty would be pushed aside and told to go back to the outfield where he belonged. In the dressing room, he'd find his hat crushed out of shape and his bats sawed in half— and he could never prove who the culprits were. It was clear to Ty that the older players intended to chase him off the team and out of the league. It was a constant battle. Ty's support came from Wild Bill Donovan, the pitcher, and several others. They urged him to stick up for his rights. They promised to stand behind him if it came to a showdown. As for Bill Armour, he considered it Ty's personal battle to win or lose and refused to take sides.

Ty felt like a man climbing a steep ladder. Each day was a rung behind him. Each new rung showed an infinite number still ahead, waiting for him to go on, luring him with their apparent safety, waiting for him to reach the one rotten rung that would do him in. Some day he would reach it, and it would crack under him.

What hurt Ty was seeing the cold scorn in the eyes of the older players when they looked at him. Obviously the outfielders regarded him as a threat to their jobs. This was not the way Ty had imagined it was going to be in the majors.

Ty was no bargain himself. He was obviously callow, given to outrageous opinions and rude behavior as the war of nerves settled down for a long run. His critics called him a petty trouble-maker caught up in an all-consuming love affair with himself. Even his friends found him difficult.

Naturally, Ty felt differently. "I was really just a mild-mannered Sunday school kid in those days," Ty told me. "Sam Crawford was the big dog in the meathouse, and I was only a brash rookie." He was sure it was the newspaper publicity he received that the veterans resented. They made his life almost unbearable. Ty blamed his older teammates for the chip on his shoulder. "They hazed me unmercifully," he said. "If I became a snarling wildcat, it was their fault."

"Ty was a very complex personality," Davy Jones recalled

once. "He never did have many friends on the ball club. I played for seven years in the same outfield with him and was probably the best friend he had. I stuck up for him, sat and talked with him on the long train trips, and tried to get to the bottom of his troubles, but, golly, he had such a rotten disposition and antagonized so many people it was hard to be his friend. He wouldn't let you be his friend."

Davy Jones was an intelligent man. He went to law school at Dixon College in Illinois and graduated in 1901. But after he made the big leagues with the Tigers he never did go back to law.

Another of Ty's teammates who had some very definite ideas about him was Samuel Earl Crawford, who preferred to be called Wahoo Sam. He was in the majors for nineteen years and made 2,964 hits. And he could hit with power. He was, in fact, the outstanding power hitter of the dead-ball era.

Unfortunately, Wahoo Sam and Cobb seldom spoke. Ty spent a lot of time telling people how badly Crawford treated him. "He was always crying about how nasty we were to him, how we tried to *get* him," Wahoo said. "Bosh! He brought most of his troubles on himself. We weren't cannibals or heathens. We were just ballplayers trying to get along together. Every rookie gets a little hazing, and most of them take it and laugh it off, but Cobb was always making a federal case out of it. He had a lousy attitude. He was still fighting the Civil War, and as far as he was concerned we were all Damn Yankees. But who knows, maybe if he hadn't had that terrible persecution complex he never would have been about the best ballplayer who ever lived."

Ty was sure that the Tiger veterans had formed a conspiracy against him. He felt their aim was to keep him off the ball club. So he fought back at them. He was determined not to let them defeat him. "Because I fought them so fiercely," Ty said, "I got the reputation of being a headstrong kid. I had to fight, whether I wanted to or not, or be called gutless and yellow. It just became part of my personality eventually."

It was years before Ty realized that all his fighting was useless. He saw too late that his teammates would have worked with him and helped him if he had just given them a chance to see the good side of his nature. It was never a question of courage. They knew he had plenty of that. In June, 1906, for example, both his legs were a mass of raw flesh and he was running a 103 fever after a wild game in New York. A physician was brought to Ty's hotel room. He ordered Ty to bed for four days. Ty ignored the medical advice and suited up the very next day. He got three straight hits and stole three bases, sliding on bruised flesh. Another time, in Chicago, a battered hip bedded him and an electric heater was placed over the wound to draw out the inflammation. Ty belonged in a hospital. The following day he got out of bed and led Detroit to victory over the White Sox.

That 1906 rookie season was particularly rough for Cobb. In late July he was stricken with tonsilitis and suffffered greatly. It pained him even to swallow soup. Afraid that if he told Manager Armour about his sickness he might get benched, Ty played in silence. His tonsils grew worse. Finally he was forced to call a doctor. The physician examined him and said he had an acute case of tonsilitis. "But I'm not a surgeon," the doctor said. "I don't have the equipment to treat them." Ty ordered him to take them out. The doctor probed into the throat. The tonsils were deeply infected, he said. Before he could operate the tonsils required preliminary treatment. Ty said he couldn't wait. There was no time for medication.

"Take them out *now*," Ty commanded. The doctor shook his head.

"It's necessary to first reduce the inflammation," he tried to explain. "You should rest in bed at least a week before surgery."

Ty was obdurate. He insisted they be taken out immediately. The doctor shrugged and told Ty to come back to his office with him.

Working without an anesthetic, the doctor placed Ty in a chair, tipped it back, and began snipping away at the tonsils. He offered Ty some ether to put him to sleep, but Ty waved it away. "It will only make me sick," Ty said. The tonsils were so terribly infected that they had to be removed in sections. Each time a chunk came out, Ty's mouth surged with blood, and he pleaded for the doctor to pause. At fifteen minute intervals, the doctor stepped back and let Ty collapse on the office sofa. The operation lasted for two hours and Ty was as limp as old rags when it was over. Germany Schaefer, who came with him, had to half-carry, half-drag him back to his hotel room.

Courage? Cobb was back in the lineup the following afternoon and played seven innings. Schaefer had gone back and told the ball club about the operation, but they gave Ty no sympathy. "That sawbones had to be crazy to agree to such a primitive operation," Davy Jones said to Ty. Ty wondered about that, too. A month later, he checked up on the doctor and discovered the office closed. He had been locked up in an insane asylum.

There was a rule among athletes in those days never to let your rivals know when you were hurt. If Ty was in physical pain, or if there were any inner tensions busy inside of him, he usually tried to hide them. But when he was fighting mad, he was a frightful sight to see. His face reddened. Sweat broke out. His hair bristled and his breathing was labored. His chest heaved, and the dilated nostrils quivered. His whole body shook. Fiery hate filled his eyes.

The only man on the Detroit roster who could get Cobb to loosen up and smile once in a while was Germany Schaefer, far and away the funniest guy Ty ever saw. Funnier even than Charlie Chaplin. One of Schaefer's zaniest performances happened in Ty's rookie season. The Tigers were in Chicago playing the White Sox, and the score was 2 to 1 in favor of the home team in the last inning. With two out, the Tigers got a runner on first base. Manager Armour called on Schaefer to pinch-hit.

Schaefer got his bat and walked toward the plate. He was just about to step into the batter's box when he stopped, doffed his cap to the grandstand, and made an announcement. "Ladeees and genteelmen," he shouted, "you are now looking at Herman A. Schaefer, better known as Herman the Great, acknowledged by one and all to be the greatest pinch-hitter in the world. I am now going to hit the ball into the left-field bleachers. Thank you."

Schaefer's batting average was only .238, and he had hit only a couple of home runs in his life. The Chicago fans gave him the old raspberry as he took his position in the box. Doc White, a great little southpaw, was pitching. Germany connected with the second pitch and smashed it straight into the left-field bleachers. Germany made the most of his great moment. He stood at the plate until the ball cleared the fence and then tore down to first base and slid head first into the bag. "Schaefer leads at the quarter!" he yelped, jumping up. He then slid into second, yelling, "Schaefer leads at the half!" He did the same at third, and at home plate, where he got up and shouted, "Schaefer wins by a nose!" He brushed himself off, took off his cap again, and told the audience: "Ladeees and Gents, I thank you for your kind attention." Ty and the rest of the Tigers were breaking up with laughter when Germany got back to the dugout.

Despite those rare moments of comic relief, Cobb spent most of his rookie season at Detroit in grim involuntary isolation between games, forced there by the anti-Cobb segment of the Tigers. He ate alone, roomed alone, and walked alone. Movies, radio, and television had not yet been invented, so Ty spent the hours between dinner and bedtime thinking mostly about baseball: how to hit certain pitchers, how to play hitters, and how to steal bases. Spitballer Jack Chesbro, who gave him fits, occupied much of Ty's thoughts. Ty could visualize him wetting the ball with slippery elm, then gripping it with the first two fingers of his right hand. His thumb applied the spin, which was just the opposite of what happened in a normal pitch. Ty finally figured Chesbro out and had his number before the season ended. (Cobb's lifetime average against Chesbro was .364.)

Doc White was another whose wily slants cost Cobb sleep. His favorite pitch was a trick drop. It often caught Ty with his bat on his shoulder. "It nearly drove me out of the league," Ty confessed. Then one night he was sitting in a Chicago hotel room and a flash came to him. He suddenly saw what Doc had been doing to him. He could hardly wait to bat against Doc. The problem was academic. He had simply been standing too close to the front of the batter's box, and Doc's sinker broke toward the dirt just as it reached the plate. In that position, he had no way of checking his swing. The solution was to move to the back of the box, where he could get a whack at the drop *after* it broke. This mere adjustment would enable him to get more wood on the ball.

While the Tigers were in Chicago, Doc White pitched the second game and went to work on Ty immediately with his sinker. Ty let the first ball go so he could watch it from his new position in the rear of the box. It appeared just right for pickling. The next pitch was a ball, and then Doc reared back and fired his sinker at Ty again. Ty leaned into it and lashed it into right field for a single. The spell was boken. "Doc never struck me out again after that," Ty recalled. "I was sorry to see him leave the league."

Cobb, even as a rookie, was always looking for flaws and weaknesses in pitchers. He found a flaw in Big Ed Walsh, another great spitballer, and averaged .307 against him. "Ed tipped me off unconsciously to his spitter," Ty related one time. "I learned from careful observation that when he brought his hands together in front of his mouth at the top of his windup, he would pause slightly to rub the ball against his mouth. Not every pitch was a spitball, of course, but I usually knew when to expect it because Ed had to open his mouth to wet the ball, and that jiggled the bill of his cap. I kept my eye on that cap."

The spitball was the most controversial pitch in baseball in 1906. Arguments for and against it were violent. Even medical men joined the denouncements. Dr. Herman C. H. Herold, the president of the Newark Board of Health, launched a movement to ban the pitch. "A pitcher might have tuberculosis, spit on the ball, and give the disease to other players," he declared. Others demanded that the spitter be outlawed on aesthetic grounds. President Pulliam of the National League attempted to appease the anti-spitball people with special orders to his umpires: "Watch the pitchers carefully and see to it that they do not moisten the ball in an ostentatious and objectionable manner, such as holding it a foot or so from the mouth with one hand and licking the fingers of the other hand preparatory to rubbing them on the ball. If a pitcher prepares his spitter in that vulgar manner, the umpire is to call a balk on him. If there is such a thing as delicacy in the application of spit to a baseball, the time has come to use it." President Pulliam cited Jack Chesbro as an example of a spitballer with a genteel technique. "Mr. Chesbro moistens the ball in a way which is entirely free from coarseness," he pointed out. "The spectators are unable to see him actually doing it."

Pitchers got away with murder. The umpires gave them plenty of freedom. They let them scuff the ball with all sorts of crude instruments; everything from belt buckles to a piece of nutmeg grater stuck in the shirt pocket. Once those rustic methods were exposed, then the burden was passed along to the catcher. The first baseman got in on the act, too. The umpires did their level best to minimize the doctoring, but those oldtime batteries were highly inventive and never stopped trying.

Cy Young, whose 511 victories top the all-time pitching list, admitted to me years ago that the hurlers of his and Cobb's era enjoyed most of the advantages. "The strike zone was wider, the fences longer, the ball deader, and we always pitched a *dark* ball," he said. "We never threw the ball until we had first doctored it; a little tobacco juice and dirt to blacken and liven it up. There were many ways to tamper with it."

The home team always furnished the balls and there was no rule saying that the umpires had to break them out of factory-sealed boxes. A favorite method of tampering was to poke BB shot under the seams of the ball and then flatten it with a wooden mallet. Because he knew just where the weight was thus located, the hometown pitcher would then spin the ball just so and the BBs did the rest. "The extra weight really made a sinker sink," Cy Young said. But all the bewildered visiting pitcher could do under the circumstances was scratch his head and wonder why so many of his pitches were missing the target. The BB shot trick was eventually solved, however, and pitchers had to invent new tricks, such as weighting the seams of the ball with paraffin. The "paraffin ball" worked on the same principle as the BBs and could be done without any suspicion on the crowd's part. The trick was to rub transparent paraffin on the pantleg, sprinkle some talcum powder on it—and, presto, the "shine ball."

Ballplayers also spent a lot of time on the art of stealing a catcher's signals. In Cleveland, the trick was to keep your eyes on an Indian head painted on the outfield fence. When the eyes rolled left, it meant a curve was coming. When they rolled right, a fastball. In Chicago, the White Sox would send a spy to a certain apartment house beyond the right-center-field fence. From there the spotter signaled his batters with the window shade. When the shade was down, look for the curve; when it was up, fastball. The Pittsburgh Pirates designated one of the hands on their scoreboard clock to signal with. The batter could expect a curve if the hand moved, a fastball if it didn't.

When Cobb realized how much cheating was going on, he beefed to Manager Armour. "Forget it," Bill told him. "It's just a case of not going into court with clean hands." The Tigers had some tricks up their sleeves, too. In 1906, they planted one of their people in center field with a pair of field glasses strong enough to bring out the color of the batter's eyes. The spy sat near a huge advertisement on the fence: "The Detroit News, Best Newspaper in the West." If a Detroit batter watched the "B" in the ad closely, he saw tiny slots open and close. If the slot was open in the top half of the B, it meant that the spotter had picked up the signal for a fastball. If the slot in the bottom of the B opened, then the batter would brace for a curve.

"I don't know how much good that ad does for *News* circulation," Cobb told Davy Jones one day, "but it sure is doing a great job for our batting averages."

Ty finished his first full season at Detroit with a .320 average. He got to play in ninety-seven games, and he stole twenty-three bases. But the best was yet to come.

6

The Tigers Roar

Apologists for Cobb's belligerent baseball behavior often blamed it on the rough, devilish reception he received at the hands of his older teammates during the first full season (1906) he was with them. In those days most rookies took a much heavier hazing than they do today. The wise ones accepted their fate with good-natured meekness. Young Ty couldn't and wouldn't take it. The more he was goaded, the more cocky and aggressive he became, returning threat for threat.

Most of the Tigers were from north of the Mason-Dixon line, and they rode the "Cracker" unmercifully. They sawed his bats in half, tied his clothes in knots, cursed him, tried to bully him, heaped on his raging head every indignity their active brains could devise. The more it infuriated Cobb, the more they razzed and hazed him. Ty didn't have one intimate friend on the entire club. What began as playful taunting became serious and resulted in enmities that were to hold on year after year.

If Cobb felt hurt by the way he was badgered and ostracized, he never showed it. Even many years later, he wouldn't admit that it had any other effect beyond infuriating him. His tone of voice when discussing his relationship with other Detroit players was no longer bitter, but it was still guarded.

"The hazing I got from those men," he said, "made me mad. I was just a kid and I vowed I'd show 'em."

Cobb's answer to the treatment he received was to find someone on whom he could release his pent-up wrath. He chose another rookie, a huge, burly catcher named Charlie (Dutch) Schmidt. It was obvious why Ty picked on Charlie. Schmidt was the strongest man in baseball, a powerful giant who had once fought Jack Johnson, the heavyweight champion. Dutch often drove spikes into the clubhouse floor with his bare fists, just for amusement. A genial, likable fellow, he would throw himself on the ground and defy the entire team to hoist him to his feet.

The way Cobb tormented and bedeviled the easygoing Schmidt gained him more newspaper space during his first two full seasons in the major leagues than anything he did on the playing field. Ty would douse Dutch with water, throw things into his food, humiliate and berate him. Schmidt took it with the patience of a saint, bewildered by Cobb's relentless and cruel attacks, doing all he could to avoid a conflict. Finally, unable to get Dutch to strike the first blow, Cobb jumped him one day after a ball game.

It wasn't a fight, it was homicide. Schmidt outweighed Cobb by fifty pounds and gave him a fierce beating. Ty would not quit, even when Schmidt begged him to give up. It finally ended when the Detroit players, unable to stand the slaughter any longer, pulled Dutch off Ty.

A few weeks afterward, Cobb tried it again and suffered another thrashing. For some reason, instead of drawing his teammates' admiration for his sheer guts and capacity for punishment, Ty's actions made him more despised. All their sympathy was with the amiable Schmidt. "I have no heart for these fights," Dutch said. "I'm glad when they pull that kid off me." He was always nervous whenever Cobb was near him.

Cobb had not yet reached full growth and lacked the power and strength to match the power hitters of the American League, so he had to find ways to overcome his deficiency. He began by carrying three bats while waiting in the on-deck circle for his turn at bat. He swung them like roman candles, and kept swinging them until he got to the plate. Then he quickly discarded two of them. Now the one in his grip felt three times lighter. He was the first batter to carry three bats to the plate.

In 1907, a period of emergence began for Cobb. The organized attempt by the Detroit veterans to drive him off the team began tapering off. Hughie (Ee-Yah) Jennings had replaced Bill Armour as manager. The "Ee-Yah" man was a warm-hearted, wise old ex-shortstop whose sideshows in the coaching box delighted the fans. He would suddenly leap into the air, screech "Ee-Yah! Ee-Yah!" pull handfulls of grass from the ground, and carry on like a madman. Any other manager, lacking Hughie's sense of humor and tolerance, would undoubtedly have rid himself of the troublesome, turbulent Cobb in a hurry. As a matter of fact, Hughie did come close to trading Ty away to the New York Highlanders in a deal for pitcher Billy Hogg, a fourteen-game winner. When a reporter asked Jennings why he wanted to get rid of Cobb, he said, "Cobb's a troublemaker. We need peace on this club, not brawling."

It was not possible for Jennings to like Cobb, but he managed to get along with him without using his fists. Ty, in turn, was never particularly friendly with Jennings. It was impossible for him to like anyone in those days, especially anyone from whom he was obliged to take orders. Hughie deserved some sort of medal for his diplomacy during the fourteen years Cobb played under him.

Ironically, it was Hughie Jennings who helped Cobb break the ice with the anti-Cobb faction on the Tigers. Hughie called his players together in the clubhouse and told them: "The feuding and fighting is over. It's no secret what happened on this club last year. That's going to stop. If you guys can't get along, then you won't play for me. I'll have you on the next cattle car out of here."

Hughie stared straight at Sam Crawford, the big outfielder– first baseman, and then at Cobb. Wahoo Sam had not yet eased up on the campaign against Ty. Any amateur Sherlock Holmes could detect that it was Wahoo who had been sicking some of the older players on the Georgian. He made no overt moves himself but agitated in the background.

"You guys deserved to finish sixth last year," Jennings told them. "Navin tells me there was no harmony here. We're going to change that. I happen to think you can be contenders, so patch up your personal differences and play ball."

Freed from the stigma of being a rookie, with a hard shell beginning to form over his emotions, Cobb cut loose at the plate and on the basepaths. He improved steadily. As the season rolled along, his batting average rose above .330. Dutch Schmidt was even giving out interviews to sportswriters around the league praising Ty's clawing, scrapping, determined play. "He's got guts," Dutch told them. "He loses a good pint of blood every time he slides."

Manager Jennings had changed his opinion of Ty, too.

"Cobb has the heart and ability to be the greatest ballplayer in history," he declared. "That's what he'll be within three years."

Led by Cobb's powerful hitting and speed, the Tigers trailed the White Sox by only two games in the wild race for the pennant in July. In Boston, Ty closed the gap to one and a half games with a game-winning eleventh-inning double off Charley Pruitt. Two days later, in New York, he saved a victory for the Tigers when he made a sensational headlong, diving catch to keep a pair of runs from crossing the plate and end a rally.

That 1907 fight for the American League championship was one of the wildest on record. In August, four teams—Detroit, Philadelphia, Chicago, and Cleveland—swapped first place every few days. Jennings had the Bengals thinking every minute, driving their opponents crazy with their daring strategy. The country was in a lather over them. While Cobb had his ways of showing his contempt for rivals, so did Germany Schaefer, their second baseman. Whenever Schaefer felt contemptuous of another team's capabilities, he would show up in the coaching box with a bag of popcorn. There he would stand, munching popcorn and gazing at the skies, pretending he was very bored by the game. One day, as he went into his little act, Umpire Silk O'Loughlin banished him from the field on the grounds that he was detracting from the dignity of the national pastime. Germany Schaefer thus belongs in the record books—the only big-league ballplayer of record ever expelled from a game for eating popcorn.

"Germany had a great reputation for daffiness," Cobb recollected once. "He kept us loose in the heat of the pennant drive."

One day, Schaefer got into an argument with Davy Jones about whether or not the earth revolves.

"It doesn't," Schaefer snapped.

"It does," Jones said.

"I can prove it doesn't," Schaefer said.

"I know you're nuts," Jones said, "but not that nuts."

"I said I can prove it and I can," Schaefer insisted, and they made a bet.

That night, in their hotel room, Schaefer filled a bathtub with water and called Davy in and told him to look at it. When they got up the following morning, Schaefer took Davy by the arm, led him back to the bathroom, and showed him the tub, still filled with water.

"Now," Schaefer said, "it stands to reason that if the earth revolved during the night as scientists claim, then that water would have spilled out of the tub."

"By golly, I never thought of it that way," said Davy, scratching his head. "You win."

Shortstop Charley O'Leary was another nutty member of the club. Now that the Tigers were regarded as important citizens in the American League, he caught the stage fever. In those days, every ballplayer of any consequence had it. Full-fledged dramatic productions were written as starring vehicles for baseball stars, and though O'Leary was hitting only .241 he figured to cash in on his post-season fame if the Tigers got into the World Series. The medium he would choose was vaudeville. He prevailed upon a Detroit newspaperman to write a comedy act for him, and then he went to Schaefer and coaxed him into joining the skit. They spent a good part of their spare moments sitting on the Tiger bench practicing such deathless dialogue as this:

O'Leary: Have you heard the tale of a baseball?
Schaefer: Don't rib me. A baseball hasn't got a tail.
O'Leary: Well, it sure seams sew.
Schaefer: Get to cover.

That is an exact quotation from the script they rehearsed. Television did not kill vaudeville, the team of O'Leary and Schaefer did.

Hughie Jennings had the perfect personality for leading such a mixed-up bunch. He came from a baseball family. The Jennings Nine, consisting of James Jennings and his eight sons, played ball around Wilkes-Barre, Pennsylvania, at a time when the father-manager (first baseman) was seventy-five years old.

The antics of Jennings on the coaching lines brought vast amusement to fans and sometimes got Hughie into trouble with the umpires. History is not clear on the question, but Hughie is supposed to have introduced the fingers-in-the-mouth whistle into the repertoire of baseball coaches. He was also noted for a gymnastic exercise in which he stood on one leg, lifted his arms above his head, and screeched that "Eeee-Yah!" of his. He delivered this cry with such shrill vigor one day against the Highlanders that he was forced to finish the pennant race with a warped vocal apparatus. Finding himself temporarily unable to "Eeee-Yah!" effectively, he turned up on the coaching lines with a postman's whistle. The whistle soon got on Umpire Silk O'Loughlin's nerves. He ordered Jennings to stop the noise.

Jennings flipped an official rule book out of his hip pocket. "Show me, Silk," he said, "where it says anything about blowing a whistle being illegal!"

Hughie kept his whistle and blew it whenever the Tigers had a runner on base, whereupon O'Loughlin bounced him out of the game and suspended him for a week. Hughie took his case to Ban Johnson, but the league president ruled against him. It was then that Hughie started using his two middle fingers to produce sounds that were more ear-piercing than any postman's whistle. The finger-whistle became a Jennings trademark.

"There was nothing sedate about Hughie," Cobb recalled once. "He once survived a running dive into a concrete swimming pool—after the pool had been unexpectedly drained."

The Detroit Tigers were traditionally a fighting ball club. Before the era of Cobb, Crawford, Schmidt, Jones, and the others, there was always a commotion of some sort between the athletes and the team's board of directors. One day, the players were called to the front office, where several club officials made trite speeches. They warned that the players would have to mend their ways or face fines.

The players were in an angry mood when they got back to the clubhouse. Captain Ned Hanlon and pitcher Charley Getzein got into a rhubarb.

"You go to hell," said Getzein.

"That costs you a twenty-five-dollar fine," said Hanlon.

"You got fleas," said Getzein.

"Twenty-five smackers more."

"You're a bastard."

"Another twenty-five."

"You're a son of a bitch."

"Twenty-five bucks more."

It kept going like that until Getzein finally asked: "What's it all add up to now?"

"Two hundred even," Captain Hanlon said.

"All right," Getzein said. "That's all you are."

On August 2, 1907, the Tigers traveled to Washington for a crucial doubleheader. The pennant race had developed into a three-way fight by now among Detroit, Philadelphia, and Chicago, and every game was vital. Manager Joe Cantillon of the Senators selected a big, easy-going rookie named Walter Johnson to pitch the first game for them. It would be his first big league game. All the Tigers knew about him was that he had once pitched for Tacoma of the old Northwest League, was released, and then hooked on in the Idaho State League and pitched seventy-five straight innings without giving up a run.

The Detroit bench began riding Johnson as soon as he walked out of the dugout to warm up. His arms were so long they hung far out of his sleeves. He had an easy sidearm delivery and gripped the ball with large, powerful, big-knuckled hands.

The Tigers poured it on him.

"Hey, Hayseed, where's your pitchfork?"

"Rube! Get back in the barn!"

Up in the bleachers, a spectator asked his companion, "Who's the greenpea warming up for Washington?"

"I dunno—Johnson something."

"He's not even listed on the scorecard."

Walter Perry Johnson, three months from his twentieth birthday, bore down, indifferent to the taunts and gibes of the Tigers. He limbered up very deliberately, like a mechanic sharpening his tools.

Cobb stood leaning on his bat near the Washington warmup lane, watching. When he felt he had seen enough, he walked back to the Detroit dugout.

"What's he got, Ty?" Sam Crawford wanted to know.

"A terrific fastball," Ty said.

"You serious?"

"See for yourself," Ty advised. "The catcher is just knocking the ball down. He can't hold the kid's pitches. That busher is faster than anybody we've seen in the league. If he's wild, watch out. It'll be murder. Look at that motion. The ball comes out of nowhere and it's part crossfire."

The batteries were Siever and Schmidt for Detroit; Johnson and Heydon for Washington. Mike Heydon, a third-string catcher, was starting because both Cliff Blankenship and Mike Kehoe were sidelined by injuries. Michael Edward Heydon was so minor a pawn in the history of baseball that no man living can bring him clearly to mind. No one can be found who remembers when he was born.

But Cobb remembered standing in the batter's box for the first time that day. He remembered watching Johnson take that easy windup—and then something went past him that made him flinch. The ball whizzed by so fast he could barely see it.

"That's no exaggeration, either," Ty told me years later, recalling the scene. "The ball looked like bird shot coming at you."

The game started and the Tigers couldn't touch Johnson. So they waited, expecting him to turn wild and walk a few batters. But after four innings, he hadn't thrown more than fifteen or sixteen balls. The Tigers were most respectful of him by this time—in fact, *awed*—and there seemed to be only one solution to his smoke ball. They bunted. Back in Idaho, Johnson hadn't had to handle many bunts, so in the fifth inning Cobb dropped a perfect slow roller down the third base line and beat it out. Walter's throw to first was wild, and Cobb legged it all the way around to third. He scored moments later on the next batter's bunt.

Scrambling all the way, the Tigers got only six hits off Johnson in the eight innings he pitched. He went out for a pinch hitter in the last of the eighth as Detroit held on to win, 3-2.

Cobb later recalled that "there were only 2,841 fans in the stands that day to watch the greatest pitcher in history make his big league debut. Some thirty-five years later, the Senators invited all those who had been there to sit in a special section at the ball park, and more than 8,000 people showed up, claiming they'd been *witnesses*!"

When the game was over, Cobb clattered down the cement steps leading to the dressing rooms. A big guy leaned over the rail and jeered at him.

"What's the matter, Cobb? That big farmer got your number?"

Ty started to snarl back, then relaxed. He had to be honest about it. "You're right," he said. "He's got plenty of smoke."

With Johnson on the mound, everybody in the ball park knew what was coming. But that didn't do a batter much good. You can't hit what you can't see.

"It helped to know something about Walter," Cobb said. "I knew, for instance, when he *wasn't* going to throw his famous blazer. He'd shake his head at his catcher, a sure tipoff that you'd better be ready for his dinky curve. Most of us looked for the curve—if we were lucky."

Umpire Billy Evans once called a second strike on Ray Chapman, the Cleveland shortstop, and Chapman looked out at Johnson on the mound and started for the dugout.

"Wait a minute, Ray, you have another strike coming," Billy reminded him.

"Keep it," Chapman told him. "I don't want it."

While Cobb had to settle for a bunt single against Johnson in their first confrontation, he told himself that things would be different the next time they met on the ball field. The Senators were booked to come to Detroit in late August, and already Ty was planning a reception for Walter. He was convinced there was a way to beat him.

Meanwhile, word of Walter's extraordinary fastball had spread around the league, and the excitement in Detroit was electric when the papers announced that he would pitch the first game. On the morning of the game, Ty walked alone to the ball park. He preferred to be alone in the hours before a big game. Pennant fever stretched from one end of Michigan to the other, and at times like that Ty hated to be around crowds, with their banal questions and forced joviality:

"How're you feeling, Ty?"

"Did you sleep all right?"

"Are you ready for them today?"

His answers were always the same: "Never felt better. Yes, all right. Ready as I'll ever be." To his replies he would add a little smile which was half-forced and half-honest.

Fifteen minutes before the start of the game Johnson walked out and began warming up with his catcher. Ty watched him with scholarly interest. As good as Walter was, Cobb brimmed with confidence.

"I always studied and *read* every pitcher I ever faced," Cobb told me. "In that way I let the small clues I picked up work to my advantage. As Walter warmed up, I catalogued all of his mannerisms and style and tendencies. I looked for certain give-aways and tipoffs and those indicators that told me how he'd react to various pressures and situations. He might shift his shoulder slightly or move his feet or twist his head or some other little signal that'd make a big difference to me in a close game. On top of this, I'd also done my homework on him by keeping posted through out-of-town papers and asking questions about him throughout the league. The reports I had on him was that he was a generous, easygoing guy almost to a fault; that he was very fearful of killing a batter with his burning fastball; and that once when he beaned a batter he had to retire for the afternoon, because the incident upset him so. Fortunately, he had good control and never intentionally threw at batters."

When a big, boisterous, noisy crowd full of frenzied anticipation and the spirit of combat grows suddenly quiet, look out —something exciting is about to happen: Houdini tied up at the edge of a river, Yale on Harvard's two-yard line, Joe Louis and Billy Conn waiting for the opening bell—and Ty Cobb stepping into the batter's box against Walter Johnson. Ty was on a hot streak now, well on his way to leading the American League in batting (.350), RBIs (116), hits (212) and stolen bases (49).

In the bottom of the first inning, the announcer cried through his megaphone: "Cobb batting," and the echo boomed off the grandstand and the crowd went quiet, absolutely, breathlessly quiet. This was what Detroit fans had come to see: Cobb *vs.* Johnson.

Ty planted his feet in the batter's box. He stood much closer to the plate than usual. He hugged it because he felt he could take liberties with Walter. From his analysis of him Ty was quite certain that Walter was just a big old country boy who wouldn't harm a fly, let alone a rival batter. So Ty hung his arms over the plate. "I didn't want to give him much of a target to shoot at," Ty explained. "If it had been Cy Young or Eddie Plank or Jack Chesbro or one of those other hard-nosed pitchers, they'd have blown me right out of the box. But Walter —I just knew he wouldn't throw at me. It wasn't in his nature to call on the beanball, even when I was so obviously taking advantage of him. My hunch was that he'd pitch wide of the plate to keep from hitting me, and I was right. The count quickly ran to 3 and 0, and now he had only two choices: walk me or come in with a fat pitch. A less ethical pitcher would have brushed me back, but not Walter. He walked me on four straight balls."

On Ty's next trip to the plate, the same thing happened, only on the fourth pitch he dropped a perfect bunt down the third-base line and caught Walter flatfooted. That set the tempo for the rest of the game. The Tigers bunted him to death and won the game, 2–0.

To his credit, Johnson learned from that experience. The next time he faced Detroit bats they tried bunting again, but this was a different Walter Johnson. He had been practicing fielding bunts. He bolted off the mound like a shot, scooped up the ball expertly, and pegged out runner after runner.

"That was the sign of a real student of baseball," Cobb said. "I found out afterward that after beating him, 2 to 0, Walter went back and spent hours working on his fielding. After that, we seldom tried bunting on him."

In late August, Detroit was blowing its top with pennant frenzy. In two decades in organized baseball the Tigers had never won a championship, and their fans could taste it. A Hughie Jennings Fan Club was formed, buttons were worn on lapels, and bright-colored bunting decorated storefronts. Front page headines heralded every game as the Tigers, White Sox, and Athletics stormed down the stretch in a virtual tie. Everyone in Detroit seemed to own a tin whistle to imitate the shattering sounds made by Manager Jennings.

The emotion of the fans caught up Cobb. He often did desperate things that earned him a reputation as a stupid base-runner who took too many foolish chances. Sometimes he would gamble and lose. Jennings understood his thinking, however, and said nothing. He knew that Ty was merely establishing a threat in the minds of opposing players, and that later on they might become victims of their own nerves and commit costly mistakes with Cobb on base. In one contest, Ty was cut down twice in three innings while running pell-mell. But the Tigers won the game by a wide margin. On the other hand, against Cleveland, he scored four runs in one game for the first time in his career, most of them on wild baserunning. Several days later he got away with four steals in a game for still another personal high.

On their last long road trip of the season to the East Coast, the Tigers figured they had to win fourteen of their last sixteen games to win the 1907 pennant. That's the load they carried into New York against the Highlanders.

In the first inning of the opening game, Cobb got a walk. Claude Rossman, the towering first baseman, then sacrificed Ty to second. The bunt was cleanly handled, but on the out at first, Cobb suddenly lit out for third and was safe as Hal Chase, the fancy first baseman for New York, couldn't get the ball out of his mitt. While Chase stood on the edge of the infield shame-faced, trying to anticipate what Cobb would do next, Ty bolted for the plate and was sliding across for a score before Hal realized what was going on. The Tigers roared on to sweep the series.

After that first game, Cobb had walked across the infield for a drink of water. The water cooler was set up just outside the Highlanders' dressing room, and he could hear Hal Chase inside being chewed out by Manager Clark Griffith.

"You big dummy!" Griffith cried.

"But how was I to know what Cobb was going to do?" Chase shouted back.

Then George Moriarty, the New York third baseman, broke in.

"Cobb won't do it again," George vowed. "We'll be watching him tomorrow."

Cobb walked back to the Tiger dressing room full of ideas.

"Hey, Claude," he said to Rossman, "every time I get on first base tomorrow you bunt."

"Why?"

"I've just overheard the Highlanders talking," he said, and then went on and explained what was up his sleeve.

Rossman was never accused by resident geniuses for super intelligence, but Cobb saw him pull some pretty slick stunts.

"A terrific sacrifice hitter," Ty said. "Tall, long-armed, he had an even temper and plenty of moxie. Claude had such a long reach with his bat he could get wood on any ball that came within two feet of the plate. Pitchers couldn't get the ball past him. He really took the pressure off me. He seldom left me stranded on the bunt play, even when it was obvious we were going to use it. Because I felt he could always get at least a piece of the ball, I had lots of confidence in him. That's why I always had third base in mind when taking a lead off first base, I knew I could count on Claude to protect me."

When the teams met the following day, and as Chase and the Highlanders watched and waited to trap Cobb in the act, Ty duplicated his trick of the first game and scored from first base on a sacrifice bunt. The New York infielders had been over-anxious, Rossman timed his bunt just right, and Ty advanced from first to third in a cloud of dust. George Moriarty was so furious he slammed the ball on the ground. By the time he caught the high bounce, Cobb had scored again.

"That was the sort of strategy that made baseball such a challenge for me," Ty said. "I loved knowing I'd made suckers out of my opponents."

Even the New York *World* delighted in the Cobb magic. After the Tigers left town, the paper stated in an editorial:

> With young Cobb in the game, there's never any telling what might happen: whether he's at bat, on base, or in the field, the fantastic, impossible twist is an easy possibility and we sit there like children wondering what miracle he will perform next. There is an infectious diabolical humor about his coups. Cobb, charging home when he was expected to stay on third, seems to derive such unholy joy at the havoc he causes.
>
> The charm of Cobb lies in his head. His eye and arm, heaven knows, are such as most; but when in addition to directing these against the ball, he directs them against men, then we see more than a game—we see *drama*. He is a Br'er Fox of baseball, and Br'er Fox, wherever we see him, is a never-failing source of enchantment.

The 1907 pennant finally boiled down to a three-game series between the Tigers and Athletics at old Columbia Park in Philadelphia. The teams were meeting for a final time in late

September, and the second game was almost impossible to believe. Before he died, Cobb picked it as his all-time thrill game among the 3,033 big league games he played.

The A's led Detroit by a mere three percentage points when the Tigers reached Philadelphia, but Cobb and Company took care of that with a 5–4 victory in the first game. Now they were all but tied. Rain washed out the second game, requiring a doubleheader on Monday, September 30. But only one of the two games was played. Had the second half of the twin bill been attempted, the teams would have had to fight it out in the moonlight.

The largest attendance in the history of old Columbia Park queued up outside the gates hours before the start. At 1:30 the gates were locked with more than 25,000 overflowing the seats; 5,000 more milled outside, cursing the police for not letting them in. At 2 P.M., Jimmy Dygert of the Athletics pitched the first ball, and for the next six innings they skinned the Tigers alive. The Philadelphia rooters gloated over a pennant only three innings away as their boys pounded Wild Bill Donovan for a 7–1 lead. Cobb and his teammates were desperate as they watched the championship slip away.

Tiger bats heated up in the seventh inning, and they got to Rube Waddell, who had relieved Dygert, for four runs to make the score, 7–5. In the ninth inning, however, Detroit still trailed the A's by two runs, 8–6. Sam Crawford led off for the Tigers with a base hit. Cobb was next, and Waddell fired a strike past him. Then came his big curve. Cobb was not known as a home-run hitter, but the situation was perfect, and he tagged one just right. At the impact of bat on ball, he knew it was a fence-buster. He was already around first base and clawing for second when he saw the ball flying over the right-field barrier into Twenty-ninth Street. According to legend, Connie Mack slid right off the Athletics' bench and went sprawling among a pile of bats.

That home run by Cobb tied the game at 8–8. It also marked the great Rube Waddell's last game in Philadelphia in an A's uniform. He pitched only one more game for Connie Mack, on the road, and then was sold to Saint Louis.

After Cobb's clout, Rube was removed in favor of Eddie Plank. Now things grew deadly grim. Each team scored a run in the tenth. In the eleventh, Cobb doubled and then scored on a base hit by Rossman. The Tigers were sure they had it won, but the A's fought back when they came to bat. Simon Nicholls, a .302 hitter, opened the bottom of the inning with a double, moved to third on a wild pitch, and then scored on a long fly by Harry Davis after Socks Seybold had been purposely passed. The bases were loaded when Jimmy Collins popped up to kill the threat.

In the next inning, Detroit filled the bases with two out, but then little Topsy Hartsel doused the fire when he raced back to the flag pole and pulled down Wahoo Crawford's towering fly ball. Hartsel came up for Philadelphia in their turn at bat and doubled, only to be trapped off second base by a quick throw from Cobb. The home crowd moaned.

In the fourteenth, Harry Davis slugged a long fly into the center-field crowd for what seemed a cinch ground-rule double, but the standing-room-only crowd, which had been growing more and more restless with each pitch, suddenly broke bounds, and Wahoo Crawford was interfered with as he jogged back into the spectators to get under the ball. The Tigers immediately rushed the umpires and claimed interference.

Umpire Silk O'Loughlin refused to commit himself, but Tommy Connolly, his colleague, ruled that Davis was out. Monte Cross, one of the Philadelphia infielders, bolted off the bench after Claude Rossman and started throwing punches. Waddell joined him. Soon the field became a tangle of angry players and policemen. Out of the melee, Bill Donovan, who had only been trying to restrain Waddell, found himself placed under arrest. But then Wild Bill was let go and Rossman was taken into custody.

Rossman was quickly released after tempers cooled, and the game resumed. By the seventeenth inning, the score was still deadlocked. Dusk settled over the field so thickly the players could barely see the ball. Nearly four hours after they started, the contest was stopped with both teams limp from exhaustion and the score 9–9.

"That tie made the difference," Cobb said. "We went down to Washington and won four straight games over the Senators, with the Athletics matching us win for win, and we finally took the pennant by the margin of six percentage points. That was cutting it pretty thin."

Detroit fans did not go to bed for two nights, and the rewards of being with a championship team rolled in on Cobb. He was given a gold watch for winning his first American League batting title (.350). From Detroit to Atlanta, Ty was swamped with gold medals, dimes, and dollars in appreciation of his splendid play. He was even offered $200 a week for a vaudeville tour, plus various other inducements, but he declined with thanks and hit the hunting trail.

As 1907 ended, Ty had another reason for avoiding the limelight and going into the Georgia woods. After edging out the Athletics for the title, the Tigers and Ty, especially Ty, fell flat on their faces in the World Series against the Chicago Cubs.

"The Cubs taught me plenty," Cobb confessed. "They swept us off the carpet in four straight games. I batted only .167 in the first three games and finished the Series with a lousy .200 average. Some of the writers labeled me a *bust,* yet in terms of experience I learned plenty. 'A bust, huh?' I told myself later, down home. I vowed I'd go back the next year and make those birds eat crow."

Ty Cobb picked up a check for $1,945.96 for playing in his first World Series. It was within $500 of his season's salary and the biggest lump sum he had yet seen. He was a rich man. Now he was able to furnish his apartment on the outskirts of Detroit with a player piano, bought his first automobile, a two-seat Chalmers with racy lines, and dressed in spiffy suits and wore an elegant derby. He had even been able to afford to bring his mother and sister up north to stay with him during the World Series.

All his life, Cobb was an astute businessman, a shrewd bargainer. Where the dollar was concerned, he could be stubborn. As early as 1908 he began his holdouts for more money. Being only twenty-one and the American League batting and base-stealing champion, he demanded $5,000 in salary, considered an unreasonable amount for those years. Ty also wanted to take away some of Frank Navin's contractual power. A clause in his last contract stated that Navin had the option to release Ty within ten days after giving notice if he chose, and this Ty wanted stricken from his new contract. He refused to report to spring training—threatened even to quit baseball—unless Navin met his demands.

Navin acted as if Cobb had a gun in his back. "Who does Cobb think he is?" shouted the president of the Tigers. "Less than three years in the league and already he's trying to play God. Well, I'm not giving in. Cobb is not bigger than baseball."

The fat was in the fire. After two seasons of working for $1,800 and $2,400 salaries, Cobb did not intend to let Navin push him around. He told Navin that a .350 batting average deserved a bigger raise in salary than the one-year, $3,000 offer that had been made. Ty made no threats, but Navin was full of them.

"Cobb can have his contract back any time he wants it," Navin told the press. "But if he insists on being stubborn, we still have the best outfield in baseball and can get along without him."

Cobb was just a hair away from quitting baseball. His mother urged him to give up his career and do as his father had wanted him to do: go to college. She still looked down on baseball. Navin finally capitulated, however, and offered Ty a $4,000 season's contract, plus an $800 bonus if Ty averaged .300 or better and fielded .900. Ty signed the contract. He thus came within $200 of his original demand.

"I wanted security," Ty said later. "I didn't know when I would be hurt and forced out of baseball. I wanted to give my best to the game, but in return I wanted all that was coming to me. The prospect of being just another muscle-worker did not appeal to me. I had more ambition than that. If Navin hadn't given in, I would have quit baseball and gone to college. Nobody really believed I was serious, but I was."

When the Tigers opened the season at Chicago on April 13, the White Sox crowd of 20,000 rode Cobb with hoots and howls of, "Here comes the World Series lemon!" He quickly silenced the bleachers with a home run, single, and a double. That's the last time he ever heard the word "lemon" applied to him on a ball field. It was also the year that Grantland Rice coined the nickname "Georgia Peach."

For all his growing wealth and prestige, Cobb was still a very lonely young man. His pleasures were few. He loved to fish and hunt, and he spent part of his free time at those recreations. Still, his loneliness gnawed inside him. "I used to tramp around the woods alone for hours," he recalled. Girls? He dated only a few. Manager Jennings asked him why he didn't find himself a nice girl and settle down. "You ought to get married and have a family," Hughie told him. "You're making good money now. You can afford marriage." Ty's only response was to mumble something about how perhaps Hughie was right, and the subject was dropped. But on August 4, 1908, when the Tigers were fighting for first place, Cobb suddenly left the team and caught a train for Augusta to ask Charlotte Lombard to marry him. She was a pretty young woman he had met and dated while he was playing ball there. He proposed, she accepted, and they were married on August 6. Paul H. Bruske, who covered the Tigers for one of the Detroit papers, reported that Ty's actions caused some grumbling among his teammates. "Ty hadn't even gotten permission from the ball club to go to Augusta," Bruske said. "He just went. The bride was ready, and arrangements had been made. A less tactful man than Manager Jennings might have jumped all over Cobb, fined him, but Hughie knew that wouldn't have fazed him. Cobb would merely have gone away to the ceremony just the same, and wouldn't have come back until he got good and ready, if at all. Only Cobb could have gotten away with it."

Cobb actually missed only four games because of his wedding, and when he returned to the team on August 9, he helped beat Washington with a single and a triple. If the Tigers resented his absence, they soon forgot it. The incident is important in any estimate of Cobb, because it illustrates how in three years he had battled his way from the position of a harassed recruit to a status where he could do as he pleased. Jennings knew that there was nothing much more he could teach him, and the only sensible way to handle Ty was to let him do what he wanted.

The 1908 major leagues were featured by the "Bonehead Merkle" play, an event over in the National League that enabled the Cubs to win out over the Giants by one game. In the last Cub visit to New York, the last game of the series was tied with two out in the ninth, with Moose McCormick on third and Fred Merkle on first, when Al Bridwell lashed a clean hit to center. McCormick raced across the plate with the "winning" run, and Giants fans swarmed onto the field. But . . . The big "but" centered around the actions of Merkle, then a 19-year-old substitute first baseman. Noticing Bridwell's drive landing fair, and McCormick scoring with ease, Merkle veered away on his way to second and headed for the clubhouse without first touching the bag.

The throw from the outfield landed near third base, and amid the confusion of people streaming across the field, Giant coach Joe McGinnity grabbed the ball and tossed it into the stands. Floyd Kroh, a Cub pitcher not in the game, retrieved it, and second baseman Johnny Evers was credited with putting out Merkle for the inning-ending force out at second base. As umpire Hank O'Day was led off the field by police, he kept shouting, "The man is out. The game must go on." But there were too many people on the field to resume play, so O'Day called the game on account of darkness.

The game first went into the record books as a Giant victory. Had the ruling stuck, the Giants would have won the pennant by a full game over the Cubs and Pirates. But league officials decided to order the game replayed, and in the play-off Chicago won, 4–2, sending the Cubs to the World Series.

Forty-two years later, on my way to the Florida training camps, I found Fred Merkle living the life of a recluse in the back end of a little tackle shop at Daytona Beach, tying lures. He still lamented the 1908 incident at the Polo Grounds.

"I suppose when I die," he told me, sadly, "they'll put on my tombstone, 'Here lies Bonehead Merkle.'"

He never fully got over it.

The failure of Fred Merkle to touch second base not only set off the game's loudest controversy, but also obscured the fact that in that same year the American League produced a pennant race that was even closer, with Cobb and the Tigers repeating as American League champs by only a half game over Cleveland. Detroit failed to play one of its scheduled games, and had it played and lost, the race would have ended in a tie. Under today's rules, the Tigers would have been compelled to play a makeup game.

There was never a year in which batting was so effectively throttled as in 1908. There were only three regular .300 hitters in the American League: Cobb led the league again, but his average was only .324; Sam Crawford, his teammate, batted .311;

and Doc Gessler of the Red Sox hit .308. The Chicago White Sox as a team hit only three home runs all year. It was strictly a pitchers' league. Chicago's Ed Walsh was the leader with forty wins.

A big leaguer named Bob Unglaub listened to all the complaints about the need for more hitting as a means of increasing public interest in baseball and announced his solution. He proposed that a white line in the form of an arc be drawn on the field, crossing the foul lines eighty yards from home plate, so that the distance from the plate to any point on the arc would be eighty yards. Outfielders would be required to play within that line until the bat hit the ball. Only then could a fielder start running. In other words, outfielders would be forbidden under Unglaub's scheme ever to "play deep" for heavy hitters. The proposal provoked much discussion, but nothing ever came of it.

For Cobb, the season of 1908 was memorable for several reasons. It marked the first time he was run out of a big league game for arguing with an umpire (Silk O'Loughlin); he led the league in batting, doubles (36), triples (20), RBIs (101), total hits (188), and assists (23); and he received his first commercial endorsement offer.

But after winning the pennant by .004 percentage points on the last day of the season, Detroit ran into its World Series nemesis and lost again, four games to one. Manager–first baseman Frank Chance led the Cubs against the Tigers with a .421 Series batting average and five stolen bases. Orvie Overall and Three-Finger Brown both pitched shutouts and figured in two other wins. On the ·other hand, Cobb had the best World Series of his career: .368 batting average, three RBIs, and two stolen bases.

The Tigers won their third straight pennant in 1909, the first team in American League history to do so. Highlighting the season was the spiking of Frank (Home Run) Baker of the Athletics by Cobb. The incident caused an intense furor among baseball fans everywhere. It was a tense late-season game. The A's were battling the Tigers for the pennant, and Baker was their star. Cobb slid into third base with the speed of an express train. When the dust settled, Baker, who had been covering the bag, had a deep gash in his arm. At the sight of the injured Baker, the Philadelphia fans grew murderous. Only alert umpires and ushers kept Cobb from being mobbed. Never a diplomat, and angered by the furious cries of the crowd, Cobb continued to circle the bases as though bent on chewing up the entire Athletic team. The fans grew uglier and uglier.

In the next few days, Ty got some interesting mail. The letter that excited him most read, "Ty Cobb, Detroit Baseball Club. If you play against Philadelphia again, you will be shot from one of the buildings outside the ball park. Now let's see if you are game enough to play in the next series. If you do, you are done."

The newspapers picked up the story, and the fans were gleeful. Half the baseball citizenry, including Cobb, actually believed the writer of the note was serious. "Scared?" Cobb reflected, thinking back about it. "Sure, I was scared. How did I know that damn crank wouldn't try it?"

But when the next game with Philadelphia came due, Ty trotted out to center field and played the ball game as though he were surrounded by loving friends. Only once, in the seventh inning, did he show any sign of fright. A car backfired on the street behind the ball park. Sam Crawford, playing left field, swore Cobb jumped at least two feet.

On the Tigers' final trip to Philadelphia that season, Cobb received a total of thirteen Black Hand letters promising to shoot him dead. One writer warned him that he would be knifed in a melee that was planned for after the last game. Jennings was convinced it could happen.

"Those nuts mean business," he warned Cobb. He demanded special police protection for his star. More than 300 armed officers and a special cordon of bodyguards were stationed in and around Shibe Park for the four games. The Tigers had a three-and-a-half game lead over the A's when they arrived, but Philadelphia narrowed it down to one and a half games by winning three of the games. That's about as close as they got, however. The final league standings found Detroit with a .645 won-loss percentage, while the Athletics had to settle for .621.

Cobb never lived down the Baker incident. To his dying day, he resented charges that he intentionally spiked the Philadelphia third baseman. "Study a photograph of the play—and there is one available—and you'll clearly see that Baker was standing practically on the base," Cobb insisted. "Frank was one of those stationary baseman—heavy, with powerful legs—who anchored one leg in front of the bag and blocked off runners. Baserunners, jockeying around second base, would shout down at him to look out, they were coming down, in an effort to scare that big piano leg off the base. If you will look at the photograph, the evidence shows Frank on the attack, his arms extended to tag me. I am pulling away, but trying to reach the base. Note particularly that my foot has passed his right forearm and the force of the so-called spiking hasn't even moved his arm from its position. Those who covered the game for the papers gave the lasting impression that I knocked Baker's arm clear behind his back, that he was sprawled flat on the ground and smeared with blood, writhing in agony. Study the season records of 1909 and you'll see that Baker never lost an inning of play for the rest of the season. I honestly didn't even know he was hurt by my slide. No one gathered around him. There was no scene. I actually took a bigger chance than he did, for in trying to avoid smashing into him, I risked breaking a leg. Baker was only slightly scratched, just below the elbow, and he walked back to the bench, where the trainer slapped a little plaster on it. He was back at his position the very next inning."

During that final series of the season between the A's and Tigers, Cobb walked over to Connie Mack and said, "You know, Mr. Mack, there's absolutely no truth to those stories that I spiked Baker. He wasn't hurt and you know it. You could have spoken up and stopped all those wild stories in the papers, but you didn't. I'm terribly sorry to see *you,* a true gentleman of baseball, sanctioning such lies."

Mr. Mack just looked at Cobb, said nothing.

"If the positions had been reversed and I'd been playing third," Ty continued, "I'd have told the press it was an accident and that the runner slid in properly. But you didn't do this."

"Now, Ty. Now, Ty," Mr. Mack said.

"From now on," Cobb said, "I'm going to show you some real baseball." His piece spoken, Ty stalked away.

Cobb later conceded that he played rough baseball, but he never considered it *dirty*. "Aggressive but not dirty," Cobb said. "There's a big difference."

It was Cobb's opinion that when he was on base, he had to protect himself. The base paths belonged to him, the runner. The way he interpreted the rules, he had the right of way. He always went into a bag full speed, feet first. He had sharp spikes on his shoes. If the baseman stood where he had no business to be and got hurt, it was *his* fault, not Cobb's. He admitted, however, that twice he deliberately spiked rivals: Once it was Harry Bemis, the Cleveland catcher, and the other time Hub Leonard, who was pitching for the Red Sox. Cobb said he didn't like the way Bemis blocked the plate on him or the names he called him while doing it. "I might have stood for one or the other but not for both," Ty said. So the next time he set out to gun for Bemis. He missed him, but Bemis stopped cussing at Cobb and roughhousing.

The way Cobb figured, it was *his* base. It was *his* game. *Everything* was his. So when Hub Leonard started throwing beanballs at him, Ty fixed his wagon good. It was time to bring his "dissuaders" into action. The opportunity finally came to Ty. The Tigers and the Red Sox were in a scoreless game and Hub was up to his old tricks. His first pitch barely missed Cobb's head, but the second one nicked him on the back of his neck. Cobb's first impulse was to go out to the mound after him, but he checked his temper and walked down to first base in dead silence. Hub had just declared war.

In the fifth inning, Cobb stepped back into the batter's box. He gazed out at Hub with an expression as cold as a snowman's. Hub missed its meaning. On the very first pitch, Cobb deliberately dragged a bunt down the first baseline. The first baseman dashed in, fielded the ball, and tossed it to Leonard, who had gone over to cover the empty base. Cobb was called out, but that didn't stop him. Ignoring the bag, he slid into Hub with spikes flashing, dumped him heels over head and shredded his stockings. Hub Leonard never threw another beanball at Cobb.

Cobb wasn't the only fighter on the Tigers. His teammates were not above taking a poke at an opponent. On their way to the pennant in 1909, the Bengals trailed the Red Sox by a run in the last of the ninth inning at Detroit one afternoon. Two were

out as George Moriarty worked his way around to third, where
he would have to score to tie it up. George got the signal to
steal home. He started down the line. The Boston pitcher fired
the ball to Catcher Rough Carrigan in perfect position to tag
the runner. The umpire called Moriarty out and the game was
over. But Carrigan was so contemptuous of Moriarty's foolish-
ness in trying to steal home that, as George slid past him, he
casually spat in his face.

Moriarty jumped to his feet and started to swing on Carrigan,
but he saw, in time, that Rough still had on his mask, so he
held back his swing and seized the mask with both hands,
jerking it off. Once again he drew back, ready to bust Carrigan,
but by this time Hughie Jennings arrived on the scene and
pulled Moriarty back to the dugout.

The Detroit fans rioted for an hour afterward, surrounding
the visitors' clubhouse with intent to kill Carrigan. The only
way the Red Sox got Rough out of the ball park alive was to
disguise him in a pair of overalls and a coat belonging to
Frank Navin.

Detroit opposed the Pittsburgh Pirates in the 1909 World
Series. The star of the Bucs was Honus Wagner. That season
both he and Cobb won the batting crowns of their respective
leagues. Wagner led the Nationals with .339, while Cobb jacked
up his percentage to .377.

For the third straight year, the Tigers bowed to the National
League, this time losing to the Pirates four games to three.
Wagner always picked the last game of the 1909 Series as the
greatest of the 2,785 games he played in the big leagues. It was
played on October 16, the same day that Jack Johnson, the
heavyweight champion, kayoed Stanley Ketchel, the middleweight
champion, to keep his title.

"It was my finest hour," Wagner said once. "It meant the
end of a great fight against a great bunch of real fighters. Cobb
and the Tigers were holy terrors. But we beat them, four games
to three. Cobb stole a total of two bases, I got six; Cobb got
six hits, I got eight."

The only players Cobb respected were those who were not
afraid of him, and one of these was the squat, chunky Wagner.

Hans was a silent man on the field and absolutely fearless. The great Pirate shortstop was considered as fast as Cobb on the bases, if not quite as reckless and daring.

Cobb was standing on first base after cracking a clean single to right field in the first game, and he cupped his hands and yelled down to Wagner at shortstop, "Hey, Krauthead, I'm comin' down on the next pitch!" Honus didn't say anything, but when Cobb got there he had the ball and he slapped it into Cobb's mouth for three stitches. From start to finish, that was the kind of World Series it was in 1909. Manager Fred Clarke warned his players they had better sharpen their spikes since Detroit figured to, and the Pirates took him at his word.

"We were sorta rough," Wagner admitted. "Cobb surprised us, though. He played an unusually clean Series."

There was no denying that all seven games were head-crunchers. Tom Jones, the Detroit first baseman, was carried off the field after crashing into Chief Wilson. Bobby Byrne had to leave one game early, too, when he tangled with George Moriarty at third base. Several times it appeared that fists would fly. Germany Schaefer always claimed that the second game of the Series was Cobb's greatest single effort of his career.

"Ty was a whirlwind that afternoon," Schaefer recalled, "hitting, running, dancing back and forth, and fighting with all his strength for victory. After making one of the most sensational catches of a low liner I ever saw, followed by a snap throw to third to pick off a runner over there to stop a Pittsburgh rally, he then climaxed the day by stealing home on a desperate, twisting slide around the catcher. Cobb was a bundle of nerves. I kept my eyes glued on him most of the game. He was like a lion in a cage—always moving, jumping into position, shifting, bending, straining, ready to break on each pitch, bolting off on a dead run at the crack of the bat, hustling every second."

Cobb never played in another World Series. Against Pittsburgh, the official averages listed him five stolen bases and a batting average of .231. He was never pleased with the way he performed in those post-season games. "I was too young when that part of my career happened," Ty said. "I regret I never got a crack at a World Series during my peak years."

One of the greatest action pictures ever captured by a camera on the diamond was taken in 1909. It shows Cobb slashing into third base at the finish of a swirling hook slide. For sweeping movement, zest, and intensity of effort, the effect seldom has been matched by any inspired brush. The man who took it was old Charley Conlon, a proofreader on the old New York *Telegram* whose hobby was photography. The strange thing about that photo was that Charley didn't even know he had snapped the play at all.

New York was playing Detroit at the old Hilltop grounds. It was late in the summer, and Cobb and the Tigers were in the thick of the pennant fight. Cobb was running wild on the bases, with a total of seventy-six stolen bases, or almost double his highest previous total. Conlon was a buddy of Jimmy Austin, the New York third baseman, and he spent much of his time in the vicinity of third base chatting with Austin and casually shooting pictures during the game. On this particular day and in this particular game, Cobb worked his way down to second base. There was one out and the batter was trying to bunt. Austin moved in to be in position to field the ball, and as he stood there waiting for the batter to bunt, a sharp, gasping, short-spaced shout arose from the stands. Cobb was off for third. Sensing this, and knowing he had not time to turn, Austin backed into the bag. As he did so, Cobb threw himself into the dirt, spikes first. Conlon's first thought was that his pal Jimmy was going to be cut down by the desperate Cobb. He stood there on the sideline motionless with his box camera in his hands. He saw a blur of arms and legs through a screen of flying dirt. It was a bright day and Charley would always remember Cobb's lips grimly parted and the sun glinting off his clenched teeth.

Jimmy Austin never got his hands on the throw from the catcher. He was knocked over and fell forward on his face. Fortunately, he wasn't hurt, and Conlon was relieved, because Jimmy and he were very close friends. Later, Charley began to wonder if by any chance he had snapped the play. He couldn't remember that he had, but he decided to play it safe and change the plates anyway. It was lucky he did, for that night when he developed his pictures in his little darkroom at home there was the whole scene plain as day.

There's a curious postscript about that historic photo. Modern editors will find it hard to comprehend, but the picture was not printed in the *Telegram*. Not in 1909 at any rate. It made its first appearance in a baseball guide published the following January. Why? Because in 1909 not a great deal of art was used in the sports pages, and baseball did not enjoy the extensive coverage it commands today.

The crusade against Cobb got so out of hand in 1910, only five years after he had started playing, that American League president Ban Johnson had to investigate the situation. It was no secret that rivals disliked his dominance and laid for him. The cry around the league was, "Get Cobb!" He was only twenty-three, and already his fiery reputation had grown into legend. "His trouble is he takes life too seriously," Cy Young told reporters. "Cobb is going at it too hard." The trouble reached its height at the end of the season when Larry Lajoie of Cleveland and Cobb were battling it out for the league batting championship. The Chalmers automobile company had offered to give the batting champion a new car, and the entire league was rooting for Lajoie to beat out Ty.

The Cleveland second baseman was the idol of the day. Kids followed him in the streets the way they later followed Ruth. He was a large, barrel-chested, friendly man, adored by fans and players alike. Cobb had distinguished himself in 1910 by fist-fighting with umpires and charging into players like a fullback. As the season drew toward a close, Cobb was several points ahead of Lajoie. Then, in a final doubleheader, Cleveland against the Saint Louis Browns, all Lajoie did was to collect eight hits in eight times at bat.

The way that game was played was what caused Ban Johnson's investigation. The Browns were accused of merely waving their gloves at the ball every time Lajoie hit. The infield played deep, allowing Lajoie to reach first on bunts that could have been easily fielded. In the first game, Lajoie tripled his first time up, then on his next three times at bat bunted the ball toward Red Corriden, who was occupying an abnormally deep position, and beat it out. All during the game a procession streamed from the grandstand to the press box, asking how each of the bunts had been scored. E. V. Parish, a local newspaperman, was the official scorer.

The farce continued into the second game, with Lajoie making four more hits, all bunts. But in one other time at bat, with a runner on first, Lajoie bunted to Corriden, who fumbled. Parish scored the play as a sacrifice and an error, which was perfectly proper, but Harry Howell, a Saint Louis scout, visited the press box and asked if there were not some way in which the play could be changed to a hit. Parish said no. Later in the game, an usher handed Parish a note: "Mr. Parish—If you can see where Lajoie gets a B.H. instead of a sacrifice, I will give you an order for a forty-dollar suit of clothes—sure. Answer by boy. In behalf of——————, I ask it of you." The note was unsigned, but Parish suspected it was Howell who had sent it.

After the game, Manager Jack O'Connor alibied to reporters that Lajoie had outguessed his Browns. He said that they figured Larry did not have the nerve to bunt every time. "He beat us at our own game," O'Connor said. "I will not send in any of my players to play up close to Lajoie when he tries to bunt."

In the pressbox in Saint Louis that afternoon was Hugh Fullerton, the sportswriter. He smelled something fishy about the manner in which the Indians and Browns finished the season. Information reached the pressbox that the Saint Louis players held a brief pregame conference among themselves and conspired to help Lajoie all they could to beat Cobb for the batting title.

Fullerton, a believer in fair play, went to Cobb a few days later and promised to do something about the cheats. Much to his surprise, Cobb told him to forget it. "I know it's a plot to get me," Ty told him, "but Larry's a nice fellow. I've won the batting title often and will win it again. Forget it, Hugh."

Hugh wouldn't forget it. The official final averages had not as yet been released. He thumbed through his season records and discovered he had been the official scorer in a game between Chicago and Detroit. In that contest, Cobb had beaten out a questionable hit, and after much heated debate the sportswriters up in the pressbox agreed to change it to an error. Now Fullerton suddenly remembered that he still had the official scoresheet of the game. So he changed the error back to the original hit and sent the scoresheet to the American League office. That slight paperwork made the difference. When the final official batting averages for 1910 were published, they showed Cobb with an average of .384944 to Lajoie's .384084. The Chalmers company, happy over the wide publicity given its automobile because of the incident, gave both Cobb and Lajoie new models.

As for Jack O'Connor and Harry Howell, league president Ban Johnson booted both of them out of the major leagues for their roles in the conspiracy.

7

The Day the Tigers

Went on Strike

After winning his fourth straight batting title, Cobb told Frank
Navin that he wanted a salary of $10,000 in 1911, or more than
double what he had been earning per 154 games. Navin said
he would think about it.

Cobb spent the winter on the stage, touring the country in
The College Widow. Ernie Lanigan, who served many years as
historian for the National Baseball Hall of Fame, recalled that
the part Ty played was Billie Bolton. "In those days," Ernie told
me, "Tyrus Raymond still was not a rich man and would do
anything to add to his income." He also started investing in
stocks. His first buy was United Motors (later General Motors),
and there's a story behind that. The Cobbs lived in a house not
far from Bennett Field, and whenever Ty walked to the ball park
he passed a certain house where a young fellow was always
working on this old heap in the basement. Sometimes he would
stop and fan the breeze with the boy about the contraption he
was working on. The boy's name was Louis Chevrolet, and the
"old heap" he was building was actually the forerunner of the
Chevrolet automobile. In later years, Cobb bought a total of
7,500 shares in the Chevrolet Division of General Motors.

To get his raise in 1911, Cobb was forced to hold out again, refusing to report for two weeks that spring. Grantland Rice recalled: "Ty was an established star by this time and the newspaper stories drifting north from the training camps questioned his fitness. Owing to his stage tour, it was felt by those who'd seen him that he appeared tired and not in his best form. One writer reported that Ty was heavy and slow and lacked his old fire and zip. But I never questioned his fitness, when and if he decided to play. I knew that once the gong rang, he would be ready to go. He finally got his pay raise and then joined the Tigers—only one week before the season opened."

While Cobb was holding out, Manager Jennings had to play Oscar Vitt in Ty's position in right field. When the Tigers began to blow exhibition games, the fans back in Detroit hit the roof, and Navin reluctantly surrendered to Cobb's contractual demands.

That year Cobb enjoyed one of the best seasons of his career. As if determined to leave Larry Lajoie and all the other stars behind him, he began smashing the ball at a furious clip, and by July he had a batting average of .444. He hit safely in forty straight games until Ed Walsh of the White Sox halted the spree on the Fourth of July. Cobb went on to finish the season with a .420 average. Of the thirteen records he treasured most, seven of them were made in 1911: batting (.420), runs (147), hits (248), doubles (47), triples (24), runs batted in (144) and slugging percentage (.621).

Actually, Cobb never cared anything about records if the Tigers could win ball games. The team came first. He frequently sacrificed himself to get an extra run across the plate. If there was a runner on third and Ty was on first, he would start for second, even to be thrown out. But the shortstop or second baseman who went over to tag him found himself all tangled up in arms and legs, and there was no chance for a play at the plate.

Ernie Lanigan, baseball editor of the old New York *Press* in those days, told me that when Cobb was young people were always commenting about his nervousness. "He was always kicking at the bags when he was on base," Lanigan said. "It was years before it dawned on anybody that he was kicking the bags a few inches closer to where he might be if he needed to reach them.

Remember Tom Sheehan, who pitched for the Yankees? He told me that Cobb would make a grab at a base with his right hand and when the fielder started to tag his arm, he'd suddenly lash out with his other hand and grab the bag."

As Cobb grew in stature, he became more incorrigible. The Tigers had their hands full. Trouble stuck to Ty like corn plaster. In Chicago, for example, he objected to his hotel room assignment and belted the desk clerk. The room was over a railroad track. Ty complained that the train engines kept him awake. He went to Jennings and asked for another room.

"By god, Hughie, how do you expect me to hit if I can't sleep?"

Jennings tried to calm Cobb down but neglected to have the room changed to a quieter part of the hotel. That night, Cobb packed up his suitcase and returned to Detroit. He missed two games against the White Sox.

Cobb did have respect for the great stars of his day, but he seldom mentioned it during the years he competed against them. He deliberately riled them, scoffed at them, or shunned them. Ty believed it paid off. Sometimes it did. In 1911, Shoeless Joe Jackson served as the perfect foil for the Cobb treatment.

Jackson was an easygoing country boy from South Carolina who picked up his nickname in 1908, when he was with Greenville and got his feet blistered breaking in a new pair of baseball shoes. The blisters forced him to finish out a game in his stocking feet. In the seventh inning, he socked a triple. The game was played in Anderson, South Carolina, where the bleachers hugged the playing field. As Jackson stopped at third base, one of the spectators stood up and shouted: "You shoeless sonofagun, you!" After that, the fans around the league picked up the line and started calling him "Shoeless Joe."

"That was the only day I ever played in my stocking feet," Jackson explained later. "But the nickname stuck for life."

Joe Jackson's lifetime average of .356 is exceeded only by two other hitters, Cobb and Rogers Hornsby. Once, while analyzing the Jackson swing, Cobb said that he was the only truly great hitter who got away with a careless, free-swinging stroke. "He just busted them and hoped for the best," Ty said. "He just did what came naturally."

When Jackson was at the height of his career, he had eighteen bats. He treated them as if they were people, calling them by such names as "Old Ginril" and "Big Jim" and "Caroliny."

"Joe would tell you that each bat had its own special attributes and its shortcomings," Ty said. "Of 'Big Jim' he'd say, 'He's comin' along good for a young feller, but I ain't got too much faith in him. Trouble is he ain't been up agin big league pitchin' fer very long.' Near the end of one season, we were in Chicago for a series and Joe said it was just about time to pack up his pet bats and take them back to South Carolina for the winter. I asked him why he just didn't leave them in the clubhouse, in Chicago, and he replied, 'Why, Tyrus, anybody with any sense knows that bats are like ballplayers. They hate cold weather.' "

A left-handed batter, Jackson stood with his feet close together. He usually marked a line with his bat, three inches from home plate and then drew a line at right angles to it, standing well back in the box. As the ball came at him, Joe took a slow, even stride, starting his swing in unison with the stride. His eyesight was such that he passed his sixty-first birthday without having to wear glasses.

In 1911, Cobb and Jackson were fighting it out for the American League batting crown and only two weeks remained on the schedule. Joe played for Cleveland that season and led Ty by thirty-five percentage points. With fourteen games left, the Tigers traveled to Chicago to play the White Sox, and Ty had breakfast with Ring Lardner. Lardner had brought along a copy of the latest batting averages.

"How do we stand?" Ty wanted to know.

"Jackson's hitting .418 and you're .383," Ring said.

"That means," Ty said, "that it's time for me to get busy and make my move. Just watch me close the gap."

Cobb was never willing to concede anything to anyone. The greater the pressure, the greater he played. Under the tightest, most intense conditions, Ty came up with eighteen base hits in his next twenty-one times at bat and breezed home to win his fifth straight batting championship. Jackson finished with a .408 season average, but Cobb hit .420.

Down the home stretch, Cobb took no chances. He worked

for every advantage. An idea came to him one night while lying in bed. The way he figured it out, he and Jackson were both Southerners and were quite friendly. The Tigers were scheduled to play six games in four days in Cleveland, and Ty knew that Joe would come over to the Tiger bench and greet him prior to the opening game. Ty also knew that old Joe was a nice, simple, gullible fellow.

When the Tigers got to the ball park, Cobb waited back in the visitors' clubhouse until the Indians finished batting practice. Meanwhile, he arranged for the clubhouse boy to come and tell him when Jackson was through taking his swings. Ty wanted to be sure to bump into Joe when the Tigers came onto the field. The plan worked. Joe spotted Ty immediately and walked over to him, a big grin on his face.

"Hello, Ty," he said, cordially.

"Get away from me!" Ty snapped through gritted teeth. Joe's grin slowly faded. He was puzzled, hurt.

"What's eatin' you, Ty? What are you mad about? I ain't done nothin' to you."

"Beat it! Stay away from me, Hayseed!"

Ty turned and walked away, growling under his breath.

Each inning after that Cobb managed to pass near Jackson on the way to his position as the teams changed sides. "What's wrong, Ty?" Joe kept asking. "What did I do to you?" Cobb, a convincing actor, refused to answer. Finally, Joe stopped speaking to him altogether. But it was plain to see he was confused and troubled. Joe brooded and fretted so much that he went hitless in the first three games, while Ty fattened up his average. Ty's mind was on only one thing: base hits. Joe's mind was on a lot of things. By the time the Tigers left Cleveland, Cobb had passed Jackson in the averages.

"But to keep my psychology alive," Cobb once explained, "I had to come up with a new angle. It was vital to keep Joe upset and befuddled for the rest of the schedule. Just before we got out of town, I walked over to Joe and slapped him on the shoulder, pumped his hand, and said, 'Joe, old boy! It sure's been great seeing you. How's the family? How're things down home?' He was really mixed up now. He just stared at me, his mouth open. Then it sunk in: I'd only been putting on an act to throw him

off. His face reddened as it suddenly dawned on him that I'd
hoaxed him. There's nothing more frustrating for an athlete than
admitting he's been taken. So while Joe finished up the season
cussing himself, I beat him out. If he had been relaxed and easy,
I never would have overcome that thirty-five point lead he had,
because he was a great hitter."

He whom the gods would destroy they first made mad, but the
angrier Cobb became, the more sensationally he performed. A
year later, in 1912, he found himself up to his ears in hot water.
By then he seemed to be landing in bizarre situations all the time.

One early morning, Detroit was scheduled to take a train to
Syracuse, where the Tigers were playing an exhibition game the
following day. Ty had his wife drive him to the railway depot
in downtown Detroit. At that time of day the streets were still
dark and deserted. The car had just rolled up to a stop sign, when
three young men suddenly appeared in front of the windshield,
waving their hands and shouting for help. Ty rolled down the
window on his side of the car to find out what the trouble was
—and immediately the men lunged at him. Ty leaped out of the
seat and took one of them on, while the other two circled around
waiting for their chance. Ty would knock one down and then
another would be on him. Fiercely—instinctively—he fought back
like a madman. He was screaming curses at the top of his lungs
and giving way to personal animosity, to hysteria—to all those
animal reactions that are demonstrated in war after war.

While Ty was in this desperate squeeze, one of the attackers
who had been knocked down got back up and slashed at him
with a knife. Ty tried to dodge, but the wielder cut him up the
back. Despite the three-to-one odds against him and a bleeding
five-inch gash in his back, Ty fought back savagely, driving off
two of the thugs. But one of them hung on. He had the strength
of a bucking horse. Ty rushed him and avoided a kick aimed at
his groin. He socked him once, twice, three times, with firmly
planted punches. The thug's face bled like a cut tomato under
the impact of Ty's fists. When Ty finished with him, he lay on
the ground unconscious. By this time, the other two hoodlums
had taken off and had about a fifty-yard head start on Ty. Ty
was in good condition. He turned on the speed and lit out after

them, leaving his wife still in the car. One of them he caught after a short rundown.

Ty was carrying something in his hand—a Belgian-made pistol with a heavy raised sight at the barrel end. He was licensed to have it, because Detroit was a fairly rough town even then. He had tried to use it when the hoodlums first attacked him. He pressed the trigger, but nothing happened. The gun jammed, it wouldn't fire. Now he took it and went berserk, ripping and tearing at the mug's face until it was almost beyond recognition.

Dumbly, Ty looked down on the lifeless form at his feet. There was blood oozing slowly down the scalp and dripping from his chin in bright drops. He was not breathing. In a spasm of blind hatred, Ty spat on him.

"You dirty lice!" he screamed. "Try to kill Cobb, will you! "Nobody can pull that stuff on *me!*"

His hands were still shaking hours later on the train to Syracuse. His roommate, Jean DuBuc, saw that Ty's coat was soaked with blood. The team trainer then came and patched up the knife wound. The next afternoon, Ty played and managed to get a double and triple.

What about the hoodlum he beat to a pulp with his pistol? Did he die? "I never found out," Ty said. "But if he lived, he had plenty of scars to show for it."

The harder Cobb played, the more the fans of rival clubs in the American League seemed to ride him. It all came to a head on the afternoon of May 15, 1912, when Detroit battled New York at old Highlander Park up on 168th Street and Broadway, where the Columbia-Presbyterian Medical Center stands today.

The stands were packed that day, filled with leather-lunged anti-Cobb rooters. There was one entire section of fans behind the wooden rail in the left-field bleachers who devoted all of their attention to riding Cobb. They were led by a one-armed fan named Claude Lueker, a foul-mouthed, beer-bellied type who really got under Ty's skin. Lueker, a pressman, had a foghorn voice and was none too delicate about the insults he hurled at Ty. For years he had made a practice of razzing him.

As the game progressed, Lueker got rougher and rougher in his abuse and Cobb began to smolder inside. He did his best to hold his temper. In the second inning, knowing his turn to bat

Ty was a very private person, but he did give author McCallum this baby picture of himself.

Photo: Courtesy of Ty Cobb

Ty poses with the Royston Reds. Ty is seated at the left.

Photo: Courtesy John McCallum

Three weeks after his father was shot and killed in 1905, eighteen-year-old Ty Cobb broke in as a rookie with the Detroit Tigers.

Cobb was a demon on the bases. He is shown here skillfully kicking the ball out of Lou Criger's mitt in Boston in 1908.

Cobb slashes into third base at the finish of a hook slide in a game between the Tigers and the New York Highlanders at the old Hilltop grounds in New York in 1909. Jimmy Austin is the third baseman. The photograph is by Charley Conlon, proofreader on the old New York *Telegram,* whose hobby was photography.

Photo: Detroit News

Photo: Courtesy John McCallum

Honus Wagner, who won a battle of wits against Cobb in the 1909 World Series.
Photo: N.E.A.

To George McCallum
From one who
fishing to one
I hear also likes same
Ty Cobb
6/12/55

Ty Cobb always considered this his favorite picture of himself. It was taken around 1911.

Photo: Courtesy John McCallum

Ty loved automobiles and used to drive at the Indianapolis Speedway with Barney Oldfield.

The famous Detroit Tiger outfield of 1915: left to right, Bob Veach, Ty Cobb, Sam Crawford.

Photo: United Press International

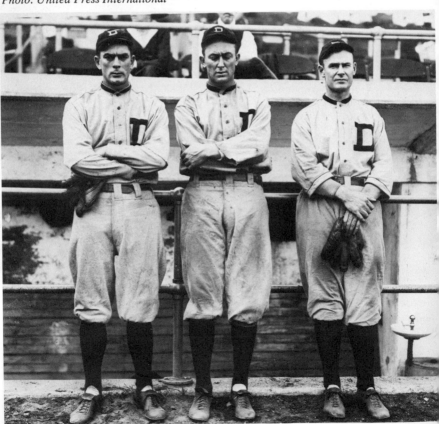

Photo: United Press International

One of Cobb's favorite action pictures of himself batting was taken in 1915, the year he established a base-stealing record of 96. The mark stood until 1962, when Maury Wills broke it with 104. *Photo: Courtesy John McCallum*

Cobb (right) and Walter Johnson in 1918, shortly before Ty went to war. The Big Train mastered most American League batters, but Cobb's lifetime average against him was .335.

Photo: Courtesy John McCallum

Cobb served as a captain in the "Gas and Flame" Chemical Warfare Division in World War I and was sent to France.

Photo: United Press International

would not come up, Ty even stayed out in the field on the side-lines, not trusting himself to pass the rail along the left-field bleachers. But the next inning, on Ty's way into the dugout, Lueker cut loose with some more abusive language.

In the fourth inning, while the Tigers batted, Cobb sat next to Sam Crawford on the bench.

"You goin' to let that bum call you names?" Sam asked.

"I'm doing my best not to explode," Cobb said.

"He's gettin' damned personal," Sam said.

"Let's wait a little longer," Cobb said. "Maybe he'll run down and leave me alone."

"He's got your goat and knows it," Sam said.

Ty nodded.

"Yeah," he said. "I don't know how much more I can take."

Just then Lueker ripped loose with another tirade. "Hey, Cobb!" he shouted. "You're nothin' but a yellow-bellied bastard!"

When the Detroit side was retired and Cobb started back out toward his position, manager Jennings, glancing at him, could tell what was going to happen. "I knew he was going to do it," Hughie said later. "Once I saw the look in his eyes, I was sure of it. But there was no way of stopping him."

Ty trotted down the left-field line. As he turned to go out into center field, Lueker cut loose with another stream of blue sparks. Cobb suddenly swung around and charged. He advanced on the bleachers in the direction of the voice, vaulted over the rail, and shoved his way through the mass of spectators until he reached Lueker. Then he began punching the daylights out of him.

"He hit me in the face with his fists, knocked me down, jumped on me and kicked me in the ear," Lueker told police later.

The New York fans were so amazed and startled that nobody moved a muscle until Cobb had finished with Lueker. Nobody could believe what they had just seen. No ballplayer had ever dared hop into the stands that way. As Cobb finished, they began to rise in rage. Ty had to fight his way back down to the playing field. All his teammates, led by Wahoo Sam Crawford, stood along the field brandishing bats. They were certain the fans would storm on the field and mob Cobb. They almost did.

Cobb was, of course, tossed out of the game. Fred Westervelt,

the plate umpire, gave him the thumb almost apologetically, but
American League rules had been violated and Ty had to go.
When Ban Johnson received Westervelt's report of the incident,
he suspended Ty indefinitely without any sort of preliminary
hearing. The action caused the most incredible series of events
in baseball. The entire Detroit team met in secret a few days later
and agreed to go on strike until Ty was reinstated! All members
of the squad signed a joint ultimatum and sent it by telegram
to League President Johnson. The message read: "Feeling that
Mr. Cobb is being done a grave injustice by your action in
suspending him, we, the undersigned, refuse to play in another
game until such action is adjusted to our satisfaction. He was
fully justified in what he did, as no one could stand such personal
abuse from anyone. We want him reinstated or there will be
no game. If players cannot have protection, we must protect
ourselves."

The Tigers didn't do it out of love for Cobb but because they
knew how much he meant to the team. He was then hitting over
.400. Some of them felt that Lueker had been overly abusive, even
for a fan.

There was a game coming up with the Athletics on May 18
and manager Jennings, unable to reason with the players, wired
owner Frank Navin in Detroit. Jennings said, in effect, "These
guys are not kidding. They won't play without Cobb. It will
cost us $5,000 for every game in which we can't put a team in
the field."

When he received the Tigers' message, Johnson, who was sure
that Cobb was behind the strike threat, rushed to Philadelphia
from Cincinnati, where he had gone to dedicate Redland Feld.
He was furious. "I'll have Cobb's hide for this!" he bellowed. He
then warned the Tigers that unless they were in full uniform the
next afternoon for the game with Philadelphia, he would chase
them all out of organized baseball.

On the day of the game, they went out to the ball park at
1 P.M. and dressed in silence. An hour later, Jim Delahanty,
serving as team spokesman, sought out the chief umpire.

"Has Cobb's suspension been lifted?" he asked.

"No."

"Then we're not playing."

Delahanty went back to the clubhouse and told his teammates. They undressed, put their street clothes back on, and left the ball park. Baseball's first organized strike was on.

Frank Navin was frantic. He knew that the failure to put a team on the field would mean the loss of his franchise and stiff financial penalties. He phoned Jennings and told him to get some sort of team together to go against the Athletics. It was "some sort of team," all right. Hughie hired some Philadelphia semipros, a few sandlot players, and some students from nearby St. Joseph's College—one of whom, Al Travers, pitched the ball game.

"Any ballplayer who could stop a grapefruit from rolling uphill or hit a bull in the pants with a bass fiddle was given a chance of going direct from the semipros to the Detroits and no questions asked," recalled Arthur (Bugs) Baer, one of the standins who later became a renowned humorist. "I was booked to play for the Millville nine in southern Jersey the next day, but I lit out for the Aldine Hotel in time to run into a parade of seven hundred semipros all anxious to fill Ty Cobb's shoes. All seven hundred of us semipros walked single-file past Jennings and he tapped the ones he wanted and that was his team. The first nine he picked got $50 smackers each. Then he picked a couple more for emergency who got $25 just for sitting on the bench. That was almost a full season's salary for a semipro in Philly. I got tapped to sit on the bench."

With manager Jennings that afternoon were two faithful assistants whom he had been using as coaches and scouts; Sugden, whom Baer remembered as a "fatigued old gent who should have spent all his summers pointing out sea shells for his grandkids to pick up," and McGuire, who "had spots before his eyes and had a habit of giving his batter his base on four of them." Jennings, who elected himself captain, manager, and utility infielder, announced that Sugden would play first base for everything except fast grounders and overthrows, while McGuire would catch anything that came near him. A good lightweight fighter named Billy McHarg was picked for third, and Travers, the elected pitcher, was a theology student who later became a priest and teacher at St. Joseph's. When Travers faced the Philadelphia bats, he didn't say, "Let's play ball," but "Let's *pray* ball!"

The fellow who was picked to play Ty Cobb's spot in center was a semipro whose name was so wide that it came out in the papers "L'n'h's'r." Bugs Baer said he never did find out whether his name was Loopenhouser or Lagenhassinger, but he was sure L'n'h's'r's wife called him a liar when he went home that night and told her he played for the Tigers in place of the great Ty Cobb.

Outside of shooing Sugden and McGuire around the bases for old times' sake, the A's bore down all the way like orderlies putting a strait jacket on the star pupil in a laughing academy. "Eddie Collins, the Hall of Fame second baseman, hustled the full nine innings like a long-haired rabbit in a prairie fire," Baer remembered. "The game counted in the standings, too."

A curious, fun-loving crowd of 20,000 Philadelphia spectators watched the Athletics swamp the pick-up team by a score of 24–2. The A's nicked Travers for 25 hits.

Ban Johnson blew his top when he heard about the farce. He cancelled the Monday Philly-Detroit game and called in all the Detroit players. He read them the riot act.

"Unless this team reports for its scheduled game in Washington on May 21," Ban stormed, "I will drive every single one of you out of baseball! Each of you is fined a hundred dollars!"

Ban undoubtedly meant it. Ironically, it was Cobb who suddenly sided with Johnson and urged the players to halt the strike. "Forget about me and go back to work," Ty told them. "You've made our point. With the publicity we've received, the facts are now on record with the public. I don't want you paying any more fines. You've got to go back on the field sooner or later, so do it now. I'll be all right. Johnson will lift my suspension soon."

They finally did. They played the game in Washington, winning 2–0. While Johnson fined practically every player on the team $100, Cobb got off with a $50 fine and a ten-day suspension.

Cobb went right on fighting. He suffered broken ribs, fingers, and thumbs. He fought in and out of the ball parks. One day it would be a husky Detroit butcher-boy whom Ty would take on in a street brawl. The next it would be a player or an umpire. The fight between Cobb and umpire Billy Evans is still rated by oldtime ballplayers and fans who saw it on a par with the Dempsey-

Firpo tiff. It took place under the Detroit stands after a ball game, and it went on for fully an hour. Evans, who knew how to handle his fists, gave Ty a terrific pasting until Cobb got the upper hand by using rough-and-tumble, Indian-fighter tactics.

The year rolled on, and Ty kept in the thick of the smoke. On the Tigers' next trip to Philadelphia he made up his mind to give the fans the batting show of their lives. He felt he had a big score to settle.

Prior to landing in Philadelphia, the Tigers first played seven games in Boston and New York. Ty merely exploded for a total of 18 hits in 28 times at bat.

"But I was only warming up," Ty said later. "I was saving the real fireworks for Shibe Park. We were booked for three straight doubleheaders there."

The A's were fighting neck-and-neck with the Red Sox in a race for the pennant. Ty told the Red Sox that he would polish off Philadelphia for them.

"Big words even for me," Cobb said. "But I haven't forgotten what happened to me the last time we were there. I'm still sizzling."

When the Tigers arrived in Philadelphia, Ty phoned Stoney McLinn, sports editor of the Philadelphia *Press*.

"Stoney," he said, "I'm going to do a job of hitting against your A's on this trip that'll make you blink. I'm going to establish a six-game record for total hits. You'd better come out to the ball park early. Your fans really have me boiling."

Cobb wasn't sure if Stoneyard McLinn believed him.

"Good luck, Ty," was all Stoney said.

"There I was, with my head squarely on the chopping block," Cobb told me later. "It was either put up or shut up. Waiting to clamp a muzzle on me were only three of the greatest pitchers in history: Eddie Plank, Chief Bender, and Herb Pennock."

Manager Connie Mack named Plank to open the series for the A's, but Tiger bats shelled him early and he was forced to give way to Hardin Barry, a rookie. Cobb got four hits in six times at bat. Chief Bender pitched the second game for Philadelphia, and Ty got three hits in five times against him. The Cobb total for the day was seven for eleven.

"I slept like a baby that night," Ty said.

Against Carroll Brown, a lanky righthander, he had a perfect performance, five for five, in the third game, and was two for three against the great Herb Pennock in the fourth game.

In the final doubleheader, Mr. Mack brought Plank and Pennock right back to try and stop Cobb, but the best they could do was hold him to four hits in the two games. That gave Ty a six-game total of 18 hits in 28 times at bat, a .642 percentage, including four doubles, a triple, and two home runs.

"That was the greatest hitting spree of my career," Cobb told me. "It also helped to make good my promise to the Red Sox. Our victories over the A's started them on their downslide and Boston went on to win the pennant."

At the end of the season, an organization calling itself the Players' Fraternity was formed. Its purpose was to serve as a bargaining agency between ballplayers and club owners. The athletes felt that they were held by their leagues in something close to economic bondage—a fact heightened by the Detroit strike when Ban Johnson suspended Cobb. A total of 288 players signed up with the union, with members from every team in both leagues except the two Boston clubs. Cobb served on the board of directors. Among the requests that the union submitted to the club owners were these.

1. The right of each man to have a copy of his contract
2. The right of notification when waivers were asked
3. The right of ten days' notice of unconditional release
4. The purchase of two uniforms for each player by the club
5. The payment of training travel expenses

League officials and a few sportswriters labeled the demands "revolutionary," even "ridiculous." Despite a great deal of stalling and doubletalk, the Players' Fraternity won several concessions.

The Cobb-Johnson tempest also prompted Representative Gallagher of Illinois to introduce a resolution in Congress calling for an investigation of organized baseball as a "predaceous and mendacious trust." This provoked plenty of hell in the press, and baseball owners scurried to Washington to buttonhole their favorite congressmen to stem the movement. Even the man who had led the great Brotherhood of Professional Players strike, John M. Ward, bolted to the defense of the American League President— despite the fact that Ban Johnson had once called him "crooked." Ward accused Cobb of suffering shamefully from a swelled head; what self-esteem had to do with antitrust laws was not immediately made clear. But Ward apparently made his point, because Gallagher's resolution was eventually pigeonholed and the subject dropped. The Players' Fraternity disbanded several years later.

The year 1913 rolled ahead for Cobb and the Tigers. His teammates told of times Ty would get up in the middle of the night to jot down some trick or experiment to try in the next day's game. He knew the weakness of every player in the American League. Most of the time he roamed center field, but one afternoon, when Jennings shifted him to right field, Ty threw out three runners at first base! He would try for any ball, regardless of personal risk. He once executed a back dive into the bleachers, caught his spikes in the rope around the rail, landed on his neck, and still held the ball.

One Philadelphia reporter wrote that he saw Cobb do something that could never be done again on a ball field. After beating out a single to first base, he related, Cobb stole second on the next pitch. "He then shouted that he would steal third, and he did," the sportswriter said. "With two called strikes on the batter, Cobb broke for the plate. The pitch was a little high, and before the catcher could pull it down, Ty slid home. The batter hadn't once swung at the ball, but Cobb had gone all the way around the bases."

The only thing wrong with the story was that it was not the first time Ty Cobb had pulled the stunt. Nor was it the last. Such fine catchers as Paul Krichell and Ira Thomas would actually throw a base ahead of the one Cobb was trying to steal to make sure he couldn't keep on going. It was part of the Cobb strategy to steal bases even when the Tigers were winning by several runs and the extra bases weren't needed. He did it to keep rivals jittery, frantic, on edge. One of his cutest tricks was to overtake a runner ahead of him and follow on his heels right down to home plate.

The older Cobb grew, the more the perfectionist he became.

He often complained bitterly that a lifetime was too short to solve every detail of hitting. "The longer I live, the more I realize that batting is a mental problem rather than a physical stunt," Cobb told one writer. "The ability to grasp the bat, swing at the proper time, take a proper stance, all these things are elemental. Batting rather is a study in psychology, a sizing up of pitcher and catcher and observing little details that are of immense importance. It's like the study of crime, the work of a detective as he picks up clues."

While each season seemed to earn Cobb more enemies around the American League, and his triumphs were often greeted with the sullen hatred reserved for conquerors, small boys of Michigan put him on a pedestal and made him a hero in their youthful eyes. Testifying to this is Homer Post, now eighty-seven, who grew up in Benton Harbor, Michigan, before moving to Tacoma, Washington, where he was my journalism teacher at Lincoln High School. At the University of Michigan he played freshman baseball for coach Branch Rickey. So Homer had a firsthand view of what it was like to grow up in Michigan when the name Cobb dominated the sports pages.

"To Ty, life was a battle, winner take all," Homer recalled. "The fact that he had few, if any, intimate friends in baseball didn't seem to bother him a bit. If it did, he never showed it. We admired him for his independence. He never cried about the shocking punishment he took. There was a definite crusade hatched to chase him out of baseball, and the bigger it got the more we worshiped him. He dominated our thoughts, our conversations. Sure, there were other great stars in those days—Ed Reulbach, Doc White, Three-Finger Brown, Hans Wagner, and the Tinker-to-Evers-to-Chance double play trio—but Ty Cobb was our man. Even though Benton Harbor is only ninety miles from Chicago and the Cubs and White Sox, to us kids, Detroit *was* Michigan— and Cobb *was* baseball.

"Sure, Cobb drew a lot of knocks from his enemies who called his aggressiveness 'dirty ball,' but our answer to that was, 'How can you win if you don't show some fight?'

"That was it to us.

"Ty Cobb was a fighter.

"He played to win, and his fighting spirit filtered down to us schoolboys and we tried to emulate him. Maybe that's why so many of our Benton Harbor High School teams were among the best in the state in those days. Our success paralleled Cobb's. He came up to Detroit for his first full season in 1906—and that was the year we were state football champs. He won his first American League batting title in 1907 with a .350 average— and that fall we won the Michigan West Side football title. Ty won another batting title in 1908—and we finished second in the state football playoffs. We also won in track and baseball.

"More than anything else, Cobb's scrappy spirit took hold of us kids. We really took defeat hard. I remember I sobbed all the way home when the Pirates beat the Tigers, four games to three, to win the 1909 World Series, and I wasn't the only one crying, either.

"Did we fail in our admiration of the great Ty in his troubles? We did not. When he climbed into those bleachers to take a poke at that bum Lueker, who had been calling him unspeakable names, we were 100 per cent behind Cobb.

"What did we think of Ban Johnson, the league president, for fining Cobb? Well, I'm eighty-seven years old—and I still say nuts to Johnson."

While Ty might have been the hero of Michigan youth, his own teammates did not share this adulation. Davy Jones once described him as an "egocentric" and "nasty-tempered" and "domineering."

"Ty brought a lot of his troubles on himself," Davy said. "He was always asking for it. We were playing the Red Sox in Detroit, I recall, and Ty was in a batting slump. Now, when he was in a slump you just couldn't reason with him. He'd be meaner than the devil himself. On this day, Ray Collins was pitching against us and Ty never did hit Collins very well, so the idea of being in a slump and batting Collins, too, didn't go down very well with him. He'd just as soon sit this one out.

"Midway through the game I got on base and Ty came up to bat. I watched him for the hit-and-run sign, like I always did, but he didn't give it. Then, suddenly, after the first pitch, he stepped out of the box and hollered down at me: 'Don't you know what the hit-and-run sign is?' He yelled right at me. Jake Stahl was the Boston first baseman and he said to me: 'Boy, any guy who'd holler down here like that is nothing but a rotten skunk.' But I knew Cobb, so I just ignored him. Those were his ways, that's all. Well, the second pitch came in and curved over for strike two. Was Cobb ever mad then. He went over and sat down on the bench and shouted: 'Anybody who can't see a hit-and-run sign, by God, I'm not going to play with him!' Meaning me, of course. He just sat there and wouldn't play. They had to put in another batter. All he wanted, of course, was to get out of the game because he couldn't hit the pitcher. That's all it was, and I was the fall guy. He placed all the blame on me.

"He was still sulking the next day. He said he wouldn't play. Finally, Frank Navin, the president of the team, called Ty up to the front office and asked him what the trouble was.

" 'I won't play with Jones,' Cobb told him. 'That bonehead can't even see the hit-and-run sign.'

"Mr. Navin said, 'Oh, come on, Ty, suppose he did miss the sign, which the other players tell me he didn't. So what? That's no reason for you not to play. You're just making an excuse because you're not hitting.'

" 'Who told you that?' snapped Cobb. 'Just tell me, who told you that?'

"Navin told him, 'Never mind who told me, that's none of your business. Now, Ty, you are going to play today, and I don't want to hear any more about it. If you still refuse I'm going to suspend you without pay. What's more, it's out of the question to take Jones out of the lineup, so forget it.'

"Mr. Navin personally related that conversation to me later. Which just goes to show you what sort of a guy Cobb could be. Still, despite all this, he was some ballplayer."

As great as Cobb was, the Tigers felt he was stretching it too far when, before a game against Philadelphia in 1913, he went to Manager Jennings and insisted he be given a chance to play second base. It is open speculation as to why he wanted to be switched from the outfield, but Hugh gave in to his star. It was one of the few times Cobb guessed wrong.

"If the Georgia Gem persists in playing second base," wrote one Detroit columnist afterward, "we suggest that he be supplied with the following equipment: one gill net, one dozen sheets of flypaper, one lariat, one pair of shinguards, one setter dog for retrieving purposes, and one map of the infield.

"Eddie Collins, the Athletics' star second baseman, who at first was nervous for fear that a new star might have risen to take his laurels, had hysterics before the afternoon was over, and they had to pound him over the head with a bat before he burst a blood vessel.

"Immediately after the game Collins mailed a dollar to President Navin of the Detroit club, saying that he was ashamed to have all that fun without paying for it. Scouts for the leading vaudeville circuits have been summoned by telegraph and will arrive today with contracts that will net Cobb $15,000 a week to play second base on the stage just as he played it in yesterday's game."

Ty, of course, resumed his career as an outfielder.

8

At the Peak

Each spring Ty went on working out new methods to improve his speed and skill. One day in 1913, when Ty was twenty-six, a newspaperman watched a rookie win a foot race against Cobb in spring training, circling the bases ahead of him. That was news. Nobody had ever been faster on the basepaths than Ty. The reporter wired the story back to Detroit.

When Cobb read the story, a smile came into his eyes. He called the newspaperman and told him to be sure to get out for the practice game the next day. Cobb stole four bases that afternoon, traveling the paths with the blinding speed of old. After the game, he approached the suddenly nervous reporter carrying a pair of baseball spikes.

"Lift these," Cobb said, scowling at the newspaperman.

The reporter took them. They seemed to be three times as heavy as the ordinary baseball shoe.

"Yeah," Cobb told him, "*weighted* shoes, with steel plates in them. That's what I was wearing the day you wrote that story."

Cobb went on to explain that he had thought up the idea of wearing weighted shoes in training because it would make him work harder, make him even speedier when he switched to light shoes. He was using the same principle as when he had become the first hitter to swing three bats when warming up before going to the plate. Fans thought it was a showoff stunt. Cobb's line drives proved they were wrong.

The seasons from 1911 through 1919 were Cobb's peak baseball years. In that span, the fathers of Georgia no longer told their youngsters the traditional bedtime stories. They told them tales about Ty Cobb, Dixie's greatest invention since the cotton gin. Boys and girls in every community in the South learned about the amazing Peach before they could even read. They were told how, in 1911, he had set a new modern batting record of .420. They heard of his startling quickness and tricks on the basepaths, of the 76 bases he stole in 1909, the 83 in 1911, and the record 96 in 1915. He was the King, winner of twelve out of thirteen batting championships in the American League from 1907 through 1919. Sports historians came to refer to those years as the "Cobbian Era."

Youngsters may be forgiven if they think Cobb was baseball's only star, but there were others in the news, too. The Boston Braves, over in the National League, made Manager George Stallings something of a miracle man in 1914, coming from dead last on July 8 to overtake the Giants' bid for a fourth straight pennant and win by 10½ games. Then, to the astonishment of all, they crushed the previously invincible Athletics, four games to none, in the World Series. During that breathtaking stretch drive, the Braves' pitching triumvirate—Dick Rudolph, Bill James, and Lefty Tyler—won 49 games and lost only 10 for a percentage of .831. Rudolph won 20 out of 23, James 19 out of 20, and Tyler 10 out of 16.

In 1915 another Boston team, this time the Red Sox, won the World Series, beating another Philadelphia team, the Phillies, four games to one. Woodrow Wilson was there, thus becoming the first President to attend a World Series. On that Red Sox team was an outfielder named Tris Speaker, a small but durable shortstop named Everett Scott, and a new pitcher up from Baltimore named Babe Ruth, who was destined to become the vaunted Sultan of Swat.

Though Cobb was able to hit him eventually, pitcher Ruth gave Ty fits, at first. One game, Cobb got so all-fired mad at

Babe they almost came to blows. Cobb claimed that Babe was "doctoring" the ball. He was throwing a strange pitch that he called "a sailer," a ball which, when it broke, actually seemed to *sail* away from the bat. Cobb took a cut at it, missed, and demanded to see the ball. Umpire Billy Evans handed it to him, then tossed it out of the game. Cobb took a swing at another one, and missed again. In all, he made Billy Evans throw six balls out of the game. He finally struck out. "You're cheating!" he raged at Ruth. "I'll find out how you do it and run you right out of the league!" But he never did find out Babe's secret.

Grover Cleveland Alexander was the magic name over in the National League in 1915, winner of 31 games. Walter Johnson was still burning them over the plate for the Senators, his pendulum arm propelling the ball like a slingshot. In 1913 he had an earned-run average of 1.15 and was being called the Big Train.

That same season, 1913, Cobb was offered $100,000 and a three-year contract to jump to an "outlaw" organization calling itself the Federal League. James A. Gilmore, a coal magnate, was its president and planned to begin play in 1914. He had a gift of gab and had sold a group of powerful businessmen on the wisdom of turning the FL, still a sectional minor league operating in the Midwest, into a third major league. Gilmore convinced them that it would be good advertising to own a baseball team, which daily made national news. Among the investors he lined up were the Ward baking brothers, who took the Brooklyn franchise; Charles Weeghman, owner of a chain of restaurants in Chicago; oil tycoon Harry Sinclair, who took the Newark franchise; Phil Ball, the Saint Louis ice king; and Otto Stifel, a wealthy brewer.

The first established star to sign up with the new league was the Cubs' Joe Tinker, who was hired to manage the Chicago Whales.

Harry Sinclair made Cobb a fabulous offer. The oil baron promised him permanent security if he would sign with Newark. "If the league should fail," Sinclair told Ty, "you'll still be the highest-priced oil lease man in the history of the Sinclair Company. You can quit baseball and sign up oil lands for us and name your own salary." Cobb later confessed that he was tempted, but he finally rejected the proposal to stay with his

$12,000 salary in the American League. "This is where I made my name and here I will stay," he told Harry Sinclair.

The Federal League went on without Cobb. Eight new ball parks were built within three months, including what is now known in Chicago as Wrigley Field, home of the Cubs. League combat started in 1914 and Indianapolis nosed out the Chicago Whales, while the latter bounced back the following year to shade Saint Louis by one percentage point. The imminence of America's entry into the World War persuaded the FL magnates to fold after only two seasons. Many of the players then went back to the National and American leagues.

For Cobb's loyalty, Frank Navin increased his salary to $20,000 in 1915. It went up to $35,000 in 1920, and finally to $50,000 when Cobb signed on as player-manager in 1921.

The years 1913–19 saw Cobb win the batting crown six of seven times. He was also the periodic leader in stolen bases, hits, and runs.

Judging by the number of games he played, season after season, Cobb watchers never could understand how he kept from getting seriously hurt. He set some sort of record for endurance. How did he do it? The answer was plain enough. "The human body is like a tree," he told a reporter in 1915. "When the trunk goes, everything goes. So I have to take care of myself." He lived by rigid rules and kept himself fit. Without sensible training habits he knew he could not function at his best. He accepted the fact that he would have to stay in shape constantly, because few athletes in history subjected their legs to such strain. Continuous starting and stopping imposed severe stress on his tendons and sinews; and, in 1915, he was going after a new base-stealing record.

Cobb shocked prohibitioners that year when he told a reporter that he saw nothing wrong with an athlete's drinking alcohol. "Alcohol is all right," he said, "if it is taken under certain controlled circumstances. But never as a steady tonic." Cobb did not mean that heavy drinking or getting boozed up and drunk helped a ballplayer's condition. What he meant was that alcohol in moderation was okay. In fact, he took an occasional drink himself. "But the difference is I drink champagne," Ty said. "I love champagne. I drink it for a reason. When I show signs of

slowing down, I drink it to keep from going stale. It takes the
edge off my condition and puts me in better shape than before."

Cobb made a study of his fellow ballplayers and discovered
that nearly all of them imbibed. Most of them were excellent ballplayers, too. His survey revealed that those who drank beer,
ale, and light wine as a preventative for staleness were physically
strong and able to toss off the bad effects quickly. They showed
no negative effects. "As a matter of fact," Ty said, "They seem
to benefit from it."

When Johnny Evers, a nervous, high-strung infielder, neared
the point of explosion and his condition was too fine, Manager
Frank Chance ordered him to load up on beer. "After a couple
of days, he was good as new," Cobb said. The great Christy
Mathewson, however, drank very little and judiciously. Grover
Cleveland Alexander took a swallow whenever he felt like it.
Hans Wagner abhored hard liquor but loved beer. "Run down
the list," Cobb told the newspaperman. "Those who are careful
about their drinking habits will last a long time; those who abuse
it will be chased out of the game."

Whenever Detroit played in New York, Cobb sometimes
visited a little pub over in Brooklyn near the Dodgers' ball park.
The barkeep who ran the place was a favorite of Ty's. It was a
place where the customer said "two up" and got two long beers,
and if he said "two down" he got two short ones. Very tasty, too.
One evening, Ty took a newspaperman friend into the pub with
him and introduced him to Barney, the barkeep.

"I am pleased to make your acquaintance," Barney said,
pleasantly. "I think I seen you somewhere before. Your face is
familiar, but I can't place the body."

The reporter later said it was one of the few times he ever
saw Cobb laugh, a side of the Cobb personality the public
seldom saw.

Barney continued: "Lots of times on rainy days I help the
newspaper boys out with their stories. Like, for instance, a feller
named Fullterton come in here after the Saint Louises had
clipped the Dodgers three in a row. I tell him to say: 'The Cards
is stacked against us.' How's that, hey? Then once when we lost
four straight to the Giants I tell a feller from the *Eagle* to say:
'Clean out the cellar, the Dodgers is comin'.' I am always thinkin'
of things like that, and, in fact, I shoulda been a sportswriter,

but it woulda broke my mother's heart, so I am now in the pub business, which is at least honest."

Quentin Reynolds, the late author, once said he remembered going into Barney's, too, and a gentleman at the end of the mahogany was making a great deal of noise singing a song called "Sweet Analine," or something like that, and old Barney got sore. "Stop that nerse," Barney growled, "or I will inject you outa the joint." Then to Reynolds he said, "The trouble with the Dodgers is they don't live right no more. I hear they go to bed early and do setting up exercises every morning. They is too tense. They is all tightened up like a cop on his night off. They should unlax a bit. The last time they had a contender I usta know a lot of them. After a game they'd come in here and have a few. I remember one big guy who played for 'em. The first time he come in here I say, 'What do ya' want?' He says, 'Three beers and a gin rickey,' and right away I knew he was a real ballplayer. He had a couple more rounds like that an' the next day he hits five for five and gets hisself a fifty-clam bonus."

When Cobb first went to the majors he didn't know very much about physical conditioning. Everything he knew he learned by himself. When he was a youngster, he had reached the stage where small boys flex their muscles and compare arms, and if any kid had a bigger one than he did he started to work to develop one just as powerful. After he got into baseball, he learned conditioning by trial and error. He learned, for example, that the best way for him to get in condition was to keep in condition. He never allowed himself to get fat. He spent as much time as possible on the golf course, walking a lot, and hunting and fishing.

Ty was a much better shot at live birds than at trap shoots. In 1914, he entered a trapshooting contest at the Georgia State Fair. He entered it impulsively—and with a borrowed gun, too. Some of the top marksmen in the South were entered. Ty finished down the list, but never tried to alibi for shooting with a borrowed gun.

"I don't know how to bust these," he finally admitted. "You shoot straight at a live bird, but you have to get a little under these."

Ty often sat in a big easy chair at home, smoke rings curling around his lean head, and dreamed of the big game he was going to hunt in Africa. He talked about an African adventure for years, but he never got closer to the jungles than Canada. Plans were changed and rechanged. Bears, mountain lions, and moose fell before his crack shooting on preparatory trips. He wanted those elephants, crocodiles and rhinos, but something else always came along in his busy life to postpone the expedition. Yet, as it was, he did not do too badly. The walls in his home were covered with prizes he had killed: bear skins, tanned deer hides, and mounted wild mountain goat heads. He prided himself in being able to take young fellows out and "walk 'em down." He hunted for birds on horseback, trailed fox at night, and dropped deer with his rifle from a moving speedboat.

Wild game were not his only trophies. His home was also liberally scattered with statues and photographs of Napoleon. It was no pose. Cobb—historians have often referred to him as "Napoleonic in his play"—was a great admirer of the French leader. "He was a big-leaguer in my estimation," Ty told his friends. "He has a big influence on me. I've read everything I can get my hands on about him."

In the Fall and Winter, Ty exchanged his ball bat for a shotgun. An avid hunter, he was an excellent shot. His two regular hunting partners were from Augusta; Dr. E. M. Wilder, an authority on dogs who could sketch off-hand the progeny of many famous bird dogs without once referring to notes, and Tom Pilcher, a big, whole-souled buster of a fellow who owned a great kennel of setters. Ty, himself, had a champion Gordon setter named "Hoke." He was as proud of "Hoke" as he was of his batting average.

The three men often hunted on a special preserve located about 70 miles from Augusta. There was a small lodge on it with sleeping quarters limited to three. Ty wrote to the keeper that he and his partners were driving up to the preserve on a certain weekend and wanted to reserve the space. The keeper wrote back that the date was already taken by another hunting party. Ty hit the roof. He suspected foul play.

"Those bums knew we were planning to hunt on the preserve that week end," he told Dr. Wilder. "They got in ahead of us just for spite. Well, we'll show them. We will go up there and follow them around and scare up all the birds. I don't care if we don't get a one."

"If they don't watch out," Dr. Wilder added, "I'll miss a bird and bury a little fine shot in their pants."

Those close to the story never did hear how the expedition came out, but since no homicides were reported in the local papers the following Monday, it was assumed that Cobb & Company got their way.

During the season, Cobb's habits were fairly regular. He rose at 9:30 A.M. and was through with his breakfast no later than 11. Then he loafed around the house and read the morning papers for an hour or so, unless he had some business to attend to. For a while he got up earlier to play golf, but he soon found that the game hurt his batting and refrained from playing it during the baseball season. "Baseball was my stock in trade and I refused to do anything that affected my hitting," Cobb said.

He never ate lunch, because he believed it made him listless for baseball. Several of the Tigers ate a light lunch, such as broth or milk and crackers, but they usually got up before Ty did and felt they needed the extra nourishment for strength. Cobb swore by a diet of only two meals per day. "It's easy to adjust to and surely makes you enjoy your dinner a lot more," Ty said.

In 1914, a newspaper friend of Ty's visited him in Augusta, where he and his family spent their winters, and they made arrangements to do some bird hunting. Accustomed to life in New York, the newspaperman loved his lunch. At noon on the first day, Ty said he hoped his friend wasn't counting on lunch. "We don't eat lunch at my house," Ty told him. The newspaperman's jaw dropped. "I'm famished, Ty," he said, so Ty took him to a restaurant, where he tackled enough groceries to last Ty a week. Within several days, however, he had grown accustomed to skipping lunch and displayed more energy and zip than he had known in years. Upon his return to New York he wrote Ty a letter. "I'm sticking to two meals a day and never felt better in my life," he wrote.

While Cobb frowned on lunch, Walter Johnson carried on a love affair with ice cream. He averaged a quart a day. Home Run Baker, who had grown up on a farm, always ate a big lunch before a ball game. Eddie Collins's pregame meal included a large bowl of chocolate ice cream, while Eddie Plank kept his lunch down to a small dish of soup. Christy Mathewson confined his lunches to a bowl of soup and a chocolate eclair.

Cobb shunned cigarettes but did permit himself the luxury of three cigars a day. "They don't seem to hurt me at all," he told his doctor in 1915. Cobb said that most managers allowed their players to smoke. "Within limits, of course," Ty said. He recalled that both the Giants and Athletics smoked if they wanted, but Manager Fred Clarke of the Pirates put the law down in 1913: "No smoking!" He felt cigarettes were bad for the wind. Yet the elimination of them never seemed to help the Bucs—they finished fourth in the standings.

"When Branch Rickey became manager of the Browns," recalled Cobb, "he introduced a novel system to induce his boys to lay off cigarettes. He supplied them with cigars. Any time one of his players wanted a smoke, he went to Branch and asked for a cigar."

In 1915, Cobb led the American League in batting (.369), runs (144), hits (208), and his record 96 stolen bases. But it was not good enough to win the pennant. That honor went to Babe Ruth and the Red Sox, who edged out the Tigers by twenty percentage points. The Babe's eighteen wins helped immeasurably, for Detroit was the first American League ball club to win 100 games and not win a championship.

"Ball clubs really battled in those days," Ruth said later, "and the Tigers and Cobb were one of the great fighting teams of all time. Every time we played them it was war. We finally beat them by winning the last two series. When we went to Detroit to play them for the last time there that year, there was a lot of spiking and rough stuff, and our Boston writers wrote all about it. So when the Tigers came to Boston on their last trip in September, our fans were all riled up and crying for blood. Only one game separated us in the standings and the pennant was at stake. Bostonians really had it in for Cobb, after he'd been accused of much of the spiking and roughhousing in Detroit. The management had to assign a special squad of cops in center field just to protect Cobb."

There was no love lost between Cobb and the Red Sox. Carl Mays, whom Cobb despised, pitched the second game for Boston and in the fourth inning Ty seemed to think that Carl purposely tried to bean him. Cobb fumed and threw his bat at Carl. That started a free-for-all, and Cobb was kicked out of the game. His special squad of body guards swung into action and escorted him out of the ball park to keep him from being mobbed.

At his peak, Cobb moved among lofty circles. He became acquainted with several Presidents on a first-name basis and played a good deal of poker with them. President Woodrow Wilson invited him to the White House one time and said to him, "Baseball is a great game, Ty. I sometimes wish I had gone into it. There are many more worries attached to this job."

"Yes, Mr. President," Ty said, "but don't think there aren't worries in my job when we're fighting for a pennant."

President Wilson nodded.

"You're right," he said. "It's the worry that makes us ambitious and causes us to hustle. A little judicious worrying never hurt anyone."

Cobb also became friends with President William Howard Taft, who adopted Augusta for his vacation home. Ty and his family made their winter residence there, and he and the President met for the first time on the golf course. They chatted briefly, and the President noted, "Baseball is the game for young Americans. Golf is a better game for old Americans."

The Ty Cobb who talked baseball with Presidents and reporters was wholly different from the Ty Cobb who arose each morning to wrestle with the stock market averages and kept his broker busy on the phone in New York. For *that* Ty Cobb was a stock market genius and was anything but eccentric when analyzing the flyspeck quotations appearing in the newspapers. He phoned his business contacts several times a week, checking up on good buys and purchasing in blocks of 500 to 1,000 shares. With a mind that read behind the fluctuations of a dozen different issues, he made much more money in stocks than in baseball salary.

Despite their differences, Cobb gave his teammates tips and urged them to invest their money and plan for the future. Even those sportswriters who panned him came in for financial advice and touting. And if he was in the mood, he gave it to them, too. In Forth Worth, Texas, for example, Cobb told three prominent baseball writers to follow his example and buy a new stock called Coca Cola. They ignored him. If they had followed his advice, each one of them would have made a quarter of a million dollars. Close friends had talked Ty into buying 300 shares of Coke at $1.18 a share. The investment made him a multimillionaire. Before he died, he owned 20,000 shares of it.

While other ballplayers were out for a short beer or horsing around, Cobb usually could be found in his home during the season with his head in a book. When he was younger he seldom picked up a book, but he grew to love literature and could breeze through a volume in several hours and was able to tell all about it in table conversation. An intimate friend of his, newspaper executive John Wheeler, called Ty "an intellectual blotter." He said, "Ty can absorb information rapidly and set down his impressions easily and graphically. He's a born reporter, one who would have been a great journalist." Ty's tastes ran largely to nonfiction: history, biography and the occult sciences, especially physiognomy, the "science" of reading a person's character through a study of his face. When he first discovered the subject of physiognomy, he had many questions to ask himself. "In theory, the science made lots of sense," Ty said. "I figured if there was anything to it, I had to know."

Ty went to the library, talked to professors, and sought answers from his doctor friends. They told him that there was some truth in the theory that the configuration of a person's face, certain shapings and proportions of the features, symbolized his traits of character.

"Now, I had no guarantee of the accuracy of this system," Ty said, "but the subject certainly was fascinating and I was determined to somehow apply it to baseball."

Cobb claimed he first experimented with the science of physiognomy against Walter Johnson in 1907, the first time they faced each other on a ball field. "It takes only a few minutes to know a good deal about a man's character if you can get a close enough look at his face," Ty said. "I knew I could decide on the evidence of his face what sort of guy he was—warm, tough, casual, determined, shy or bold. I went out of my way to walk across to the Washington bench to meet Walter before that first game, just so I could study his face. I figured if I assessed his facial index correctly, I could get his number. All the indicators—wide mouth, warm eyes and large ears—told me he was a generous, easygoing guy. I was right, of course. That's why I was able to take advantage of him."

In a total of sixty-seven big league games, Cobb batted against Johnson 245 times. His .335 percentage included eighty-two singles, fourteen doubles, three triples and a home run. When Cobb first figured Walter's style out, the big righthander could be heard muttering to himself, "Gee whillikins!" Sometimes a Cobb hit drew anger from him, and he'd whisper, "Goodness gracious!" When Cobb made him really mad, he would say, "Goodness gracious, *animal!*" That was the closest Walter came to swearing.

The thing that irritated Cobb most about those duels against the Big Train was when Wahoo Sam Crawford had a good day and Ty didn't. How he would howl then. What Cobb didn't know was that Walter and Wahoo Sam were good friends, and occasionally Johnson would sort of *give* him a hit or two, just for old friendship's sake. But when Cobb came to bat, Walter always bore down extra hard. There was nothing he loved more than to stop the great Cobb.

"If you put the ball on the outside of the plate where he likes it, Ty will drop it into left field," Johnson told reporters. "If you keep it inside, he's liable to kill your first baseman. The only way to fool Cobb is to get the ball up there faster than he can get his bat around."

In 1917, Cobb went right on being the fiery, bull-headed, daring Cobb of old. He remained very much a center of storm and strife. That spring, when the training camps broke up, the Tigers and Giants set out on a tour north. Cobb was very impressed by the way John J. McGraw managed his ball club. In one game, a Giant baserunner found himself suddenly trapped off second base and made a pathetic attempt to avoid the rundown. McGraw was purple with rage. Early the next morning he had his entire squad back on the field for special practice, four hours before the scheduled exhibition game with the Tigers. He ran the man who had been picked off second base until his tongue hung out.

McGraw was teaching him how to lead off base and how to get back to it safely. Then he showed him how to dance back and forth in a rundown. While Muggsy was busy with that, he also polished up his other players, showing them how to nail a base-runner in a rundown. Everybody was busy learning some phase of the game. That was the McGraw pattern. He held 10 A.M. practice almost daily, and only a few hours before a regular game.

At Dallas, fighting broke out between the Tigers and Giants. It all began when Jeff Tesreau unintentionally hit Cobb with a pitched ball on his first trip to the plate. Since the Giants had been taunting Cobb because he appeared on the field just at game time, calling him such things as a ham and a swell-headed stiff, Ty thought big Jeff purposely had nicked him and angrily threatened reprisal. Tesreau, good-humored and not at all afraid of Cobb, laughed at him, then added, "But if you try any funny business with me, I'll knock your brains out."

Charley Herzog at second base and Art Fletcher at shortstop threatened to ram the ball down Ty's throat if he tried to rough anybody on their ball club, and Ty, taking up the challenge, raced for second on Tesreau's second pitch to the next hitter. McCarty's throw to Herzog had him beaten but, riding in high, he ripped Herzog's legs with his spikes.

By the time Ty and Charley were pried apart, the field was swarming with players, cops, and spectators. The players were ordered from the game and, although Herzog went peacefully, Cobb said bitterly to Hughie Jennings, "If I have to leave this field, I'll leave the series."

Jennings, knowing he meant it, tried to intercede for him with the umpire but with no success. Cobb stalked from the ball park and was driven to the Oriental Hotel, where both teams were staying and where they dressed for the game.

John J. McGraw, who had been in the midst of the tangle on the field, hurling imprecations at Cobb, caught up with him in the hotel lobby when the teams returned after the game. There in the hearing of the players and other guests who milled about them, he frightfully abused Cobb, calling him a quitter, daring him to play the following day. Ty managed to restrain himself, although he did tweak McGraw's nose and snarled, "If you were a younger man, I'd kill you." John J., to his dying day, never forgave Cobb for that. Then Ty walked away, pale with anger but ignoring the insults McGraw hurled after him.

"I'll be up to your room at 10 o'clock," Herzog told Cobb, as he was at dinner. "I'll bring one of our players with me and you can have one of yours. You can have Harry Tuttle to referee." Tuttle, brawny and a good street fighter, was the Detroit trainer. Herzog chose Heinie Zimmerman as his second. Not many of the other players knew there was going to be a fight, but Benny Kauff heard of it. Benny wanted to go with Herzog, too. "I'll fight him," Benny said. "I'll murder him."

"No," Herzog said. "This is my fight. And you can't come because I said I would bring only one player and that's all he's going to have."

Cobb and Tuttle were waiting for Herzog and Zimmerman. So were eight other Tigers.

"All right," Herzog said. "If you start anything, Heinie will lick the lot of you."

"Take off your coat and shirt," he said to Cobb.

Herzog's first punch was a right to the jaw that sent Cobb to his knees, but Ty got up and hammered him around the room. The fight ended with Herzog bent over the back of a bed, out on his feet. As he limped dazedly from the room, Cobb shouted after him, "If anyone else wants a score to settle, tell 'em to come right up!"

Herzog showed up the next morning with two black eyes, puffed lips, and a wrenched shoulder. He blamed the shoulder injury on a cop who had yanked him away from Cobb on the field and he didn't seem to mind the bruises on his face.

"Anyway," he said, "I knocked him down."

That seemed to have squared him for the spike wounds.

That was a Sunday. News of the fight at the ball park and the ensuing battle at the Oriental Hotel appeared in the morning papers. The overflow crowd in the afternoon had paid to see not another ball game but another fight. But it had to settle for the ball game. Herzog, because of his bad shoulder, couldn't play, and Cobb wouldn't.

Cobb went as far as the next stop, which was Wichita Falls. He put on his uniform, took batting practice, and even posed for fans who wanted to take his picture. But again he refused to play. The mayor and other civic leaders pleaded with him to change his mind, telling him that hundreds of fans from all over that part of the state had driven in to see him.

"I'm sorry," Cobb said, "but there is no use asking me any more." The Giants watched him silently as he walked from the field. That night he left the tour, having obtained permission to finish his training with the Cincinnati Reds. When the Giants and Tigers finally split up in Kansas City and went their separate ways, the McGraw men sent Cobb a postcard: "It's safe to rejoin your team now," and it was signed by all of the Giants. They thus had the last word—in the only safe manner in which to have a last word with Cobb.

After his series of spats with the Giants, word soon spread through the American League not to rile Cobb. "Ty likes a funny story," said Fielder Jones, manager of the Saint Louis Browns. "When the Tigers come to town, I want you guys to think of some good yarns to tell him. Keep him in good humor."

In 1917, Casey Stengel was an outfielder with the Brooklyn Dodgers. They trained in Georgia that season, and Cobb, a Detroit holdout during the first few weeks as usual, came over from Augusta and worked out with them. At practice, Casey walked up to Cobb and asked him what was his secret to stretching singles into doubles. "I really want to know," Stengel said. He knew he couldn't run like Cobb, but he also knew it wasn't quickness alone which enabled Ty to stretch hits into extra bases. If there was a secret to it, Casey wanted to find out what it was.

Cobb told him that on any ball hit to the outfield, he always rounded first base at full speed. "If the ball is hit to the outfielder's gloved-hand side," Ty explained, "I never break stride but keep right on going. That forces the fielder to turn around to throw." That sounded logical enough to Casey, but he figured there was more to it than that. There was. "If the ball is hit to the outfielder's bare hand," Cobb continued, "I still make my turn at top speed, keeping my eyes on the second baseman and shortstop. If I see either one of them move out toward the outfield to take the throw, that means the throw is short, and I go on to second."

Later that spring, Casey tried the maneuver and was sometimes successful. "But I lacked Cobb's gift for quickness," Stengel said. "Nobody was like him, not even close. When he waggled those wild eyes at a pitcher, you just knew you were looking at the one bird who was unbeatable."

Ty so dominated the Cobb name that few historians even remember that his brother Paul was also a professional ballplayer. Paul Cobb stood 6 feet, weighed 168, and was right-handed all the way. Once the property of the Saint Louis Browns, he spent the years 1907–16 in the minors with such leagues as the Western Association, South Michigan League, Eastern League, Union Association, Three I League, Virginia League, and South Atlantic League. In four of the ten seasons Paul was in organized baseball, he batted above .300: .310 at Lincoln, Nebraska (1910); .306 at Lincoln (1911); .333 at Ogden, Utah (1913); and .331 at Ogden (1914).

An alumnus of the Institute of Technology in Georgia, Paul went to war in 1918 and never returned to baseball.

Ty was a racing car fanatic in those days. He drove the way he ran the bases—very reckless indeed. He had only two speeds, fast and faster. John Wheeler visited Ty in Augusta in 1916 and found him busy at the Georgia-Carolina State Fair, where he was paid $50 a day to serve as starter of the automobile races. The races were quite a big event in the South, and local enthusiasts backed their favorite drivers heavily. "Doped" machines had been imported in the hope of winning prize money. That is, certain devices were applied to increase the speed, such as boring out the piston rods and removing all impediments. It was Ty's duty to make sure each automobile got a fair deal. All complaints were brought to him, and he had to smooth over many disputes. No one questioned his decisions. Some of the drivers even dreamed up arguments as an excuse to talk to the great Ty Cobb.

"That's Ty Cobb," whispered a driver to his mechanic after a lengthy chat with Ty. The auto jockey was from Charleston, South Carolina, and his racer looked like a crab, with its wheels spread far apart. But the theory made sense and it won most of the prize money. It stuck fast on the sharp turns and didn't sling out from the rail.

"They've doped that car for this half-mile track," Cobb told

John Wheeler, quick to pick up the vernacular of the sport. "It's all spread out and will win for sure. Bet your money on it."

Cobb used his influence to have Wheeler appointed as one of the race judges. In one race a driver blew a shoe on a sharp turn and ripped down a hundred yards of fence. He landed on his head and was carried off to the hospital. In no time, Cobb had taken personal charge of the wreck and soon had the races going again. One of the events on the program was called "A Perfect Gentlemen's Race." Every mongrel-bred car in Augusta, most of them antiques, seemed to be entered. Cobb gave them the starting flag and then, fired by that old Cobbian spirit of competition, grabbed Wheeler and jumped into his own car standing nearby and roared after the field, slinging it recklessly around the curves and giving the alarm for everybody to clear the way. The spectators were sure that Cobb and Wheeler would be killed. But who won? "Why, Ty did, of course," John Wheeler said. "It wasn't his nature to lose—at anything."

For a while, Cobb talked about even racing the big death wagons at Indianapolis, but when Frank Navin heard about it back in Detroit he put his foot down. Ty confined himself to amateur racing. One afternoon, he went along on a trial run with a friend of his, a star driver. They hit speeds of 105 mph and Ty said to himself, "This is great. Look at us go." Several days later, his friend was killed in a big race. The car skidded into a bellyroll, did a couple of flips, and smashed into a tree. His friend's death shocked Ty. Only a few days before he had ridden alongside the driver, and now he was dead. That killed Ty's enthusiasm for fast cars. He never raced again.

In 1916, at the urging of the Sunbeam Motion Picture Company, Ty was coaxed out to Hollywood to star in a movie titled *Somewhere in Georgia*. The noted Broadway critic Ward Morehouse, a fellow Georgian, remembered it as "absolutely the worst movie I ever saw." The plot was so thin, Morehouse said, that all he could remember about it was that Cobb was attacked by goons, tied up, and made his escape just in time to race to the ball park on a mule and save the old ball game for the home team. "It was simply awful," Morehouse said.

The years 1913–19 saw Cobb win the batting crown in six of the seven seasons. He was also periodically the leader in stolen bases, hits, and runs. Tris Speaker was the culprit who broke Cobb's string of batting championships. He beat him in 1916 by hitting .386 to Ty's .371. In 1917, when Speaker was sure he finally had caught up with Cobb, he hit .352—but Cobb hit .383.

"Good as I was," Speaker said, "I never was close to Cobb, and neither was Babe Ruth or anybody else. The Babe was a great ballplayer, sure. But Cobb was even greater. Babe could knock your brains out, but Cobb would drive you crazy."

It was an opinion with which you may or may not agree. But it was held by one who played against both Cobb and Ruth when all three were in their prime and who, because of his own remarkable skills on offense and defense ("anybody," he said, "can catch a fly ball"), had a clearer look at them than most ballplayers did because he was on the same level with them.

9

Good-bye Cobbian Era,

Hello Ruthian Era

While the American cinema was surviving *Somewhere in Georgia,* life went on throughout the country. By this time, Henry Ford had more than a half-million Model-Ts on the roads, and he was paying his workers a minimum wage of five dollars a day. The gasoline to make those old flivvers run was selling for 8 cents a gallon. One of the good buys in automobiles was the seven-passenger Abbott-Detroit at $1,195. Franklin Simon was peddling men's overcoats for $15, and fine worsted suits for $21. A ten-room house with a half-acre of property cost $5,500. The favorite cigarettes were Fatima, Sweet Caporal, and Piedmont, although only callow weaklings smoked them.

At Shanley's in Times Square there was a seven-course luncheon for 75 cents, with music. Parades of suffragists demanded the vote for women. Charlie Chaplin traveled to New York from California to stand on the stage of the Hippodrome and conduct Sousa's Band. The British Under Secretary of War announced that Winston Spencer Churchill had been promoted to colonel. Lillian Russell was the sweetheart of musical comedy, Enrico Caruso the magic name of opera, and William Gillette was playing return engagements as Sherlock Holmes. Women were getting the culture bug, and one New York revue had a hilarious song titled "I Belong to the Culture Club of Keokuk, I-A!"

Americans now craved stimulation and excitement to take their minds off of a worsening international situation, following the sinking of the Cunard Liner *Lusitania* off Ireland. The Central Alliance, consisting in the main of Germany and Austria-Hungary, was at war with the *Entente Cordial,* comprising Great Britain, France, and Russia.

The United States was trying to keep out of the fighting. Woodrow Wilson, Cobb's friend, prepared to run for a second Presidential term with the slogan "He Kept Us Out of War," but Congress had already approved a budget of $400 million for national defense and was calling for a standing army of 120,000 men.

Because of the war in Europe, Ty played in only 111 games in 1918 but got in enough times at bat (421) to win his eleventh batting crown with a .382 average. Then, along with other sports stars, he enlisted in the military service. Ty chose the Chemical Warfare Service, where he was given a crash course in defense against and the use of poisonous gas, and was commissioned a captain. He was then shipped to France as an instructor with the "Gas and Flame" Division. George Sisler, Branch Rickey, and Christy Mathewson belonged to the same unit.

They wound up drilling the "damnedest bunch of culls" the World War I army was able to recruit. They were largely rejects from the other services. One of the training exercises involved marching the soldiers into an airtight chamber in which gas was released without warning. At a hand signal, everyone was supposed to snap his mask into position. If they weren't alert and didn't move swiftly, they could be gassed. The stuff the instructors turned loose was the real thing.

One day sixteen doughboys from Cobb's outfit didn't move fast enough, and when the air cleared they were stretched on the ground. Eight of them died.

Other than a shell fragment that narrowly missed his left eye, the war presented Cobb with no further danger. After the Armistice he was on the first ship to the States to rejoin his family and then the Tigers in early summer, 1919.

Detroit was in the thick of another pennant fight when Ty got back. The Tigers moved to within four games of first place in August, before fading and finishing fourth, eight games behind the champion White Sox. Cobb was nearly thirty-three years old, yet batted .384 in 124 games to win his twelfth and final batting title.

It was plain to Tiger-watchers that something was wrong with their ball club. Hughie Jennings had lost his grip. In 1920 the team collapsed to seventh place and Cobb batted .334, his lowest average since 1908, when he hit .324. His fourteen stolen bases made the skimpiest total since his rookie season.

After fourteen seasons at the helm, the once great Jennings, his health and spirit broken, was finished as manager of the Tigers. Ty knew it, too.

"Ty, I don't want to go on," Hughie said at the end of the season. "The pressure is making me sick. You've got to take my place. There just isn't anyone else who knows the situation here in Detroit well enough."

The strain was written all over Jennings. He was only fifty years old and looked seventy. Eight years later he would be dead of tuberculosis.

Cobb did not really want to manage the Tigers. He had accumulated a tidy fortune from such investments as stocks and bonds, cotton shares, real estate, steel and auto stocks, Coca-Cola, and public utilities. So he was not greatly impressed when Frank Navin asked him to drop by the office and discuss the job.

At the meeting, Ty was noncommittal. He told Navin he wanted time to think about the offer. Part of this hesitancy was based on his dislike of Navin. He did not trust him. He was convinced that Navin had been faking his turnstile count in Detroit to cheat the visiting teams and Uncle Sam out of added revenue. So while Cobb weighed his future in the Navin organization, he returned to Augusta to see the family, and then went alone to manage the San Francisco Seals in the California Winter League.

In November, Navin phoned Ty and said the job was still his if he wanted it. Frank made it sound as though he were handing him General Motors or something.

"It's up to you, Ty," Navin said. "All you have to do is say yes."

"No, thanks," Cobb said. "I don't want the job."

"There's a substantial raise in it for you."

"The answer is still no."

Ty thought about his private life. His marriage was stormy. He and his wife often quarreled over how little their four children saw of him. She even mentioned a divorce. He did not want that. And yet he felt a certain amount of loyalty to the Detroit ball club. They needed a manager. In 1920, they had narrowly missed becoming the first Detroit baseball team in history to finish in the American League basement.

When the California Winter League season was over, Cobb returned to his home in Augusta. One weekend Ty went duck hunting at a private club near New Orleans, where he met E. A. Batchelor, a Detroit sportswriter who was down to cover a football game between the University of Detroit and Loyola. Batchelor told Ty that it was his duty to manage the Tigers.

"But why me? Why not Kid Gleason?" Cobb wanted to know.

"I've already told Navin to give the job to Gleason. He's a good baseball man."

"It won't be Gleason," shrugged Batchelor. "If you don't accept the job, it will be Pants Rowland."

"Pants Rowland!" Cobb exploded.

"He's up in Detroit right now meeting with Navin," Batchelor said.

"Rowland!" Ty shouted. The name tasted bitter to his tongue. "I can't play for Rowland! He's never played any big league ball. Pants is merely a puppet."

"Well, Navin's talking to him," Batchelor said.

Charley Comiskey had taken a liking to Rowland and appointed him manager of the White Sox in 1915. Three years afterward he won the pennant and World Series and was celebrated as a Miracle Man. Kid Gleason had been his assistant.

"Hell," Cobb snorted, "everybody knows it was Gleason who was the real brains behind the White Sox."

In 1918, after Chicago dropped from first to sixth in the league, Rowland was fired and Gleason took his place. So when Cobb heard that Pants was a serious candidate to manage the Tigers, he hit the roof.

"You must be joking," he told Batchelor.

"No, I'm not. I'm dead serious."

"This is bad," Ty said.

"Then will you take the job?"

"I have to think about it."

Without another word, Batchelor went to a phone and called Frank Navin. Then he put Cobb on the line and after a brief discussion Ty consented to meet with Navin in New York and talk about the job. Later, Cobb said he regretted going to that conference, for he gave in to Navin's sales pitch. On December, 18, 1920, he signed away his independence as a ballplayer. He always remembered the date, because it was his thirty-fourth birthday. The contract called for a salary of $35,000.

Cobb inherited a seventh-place club with a .265 batting average. During one two-week period, the Tigers dropped thirteen games in a row. Age had corroded the heart of the infield, at shortstop and second base, and George Dauss and Howard Ehmke were the only established pitchers on the entire staff.

Cullen Cain, the Philadelphia sportswriter, forecast nothing but gloom and doom for manager Cobb. After writing that Ty would fail, Cain then hedged: "But let's not bury him too soon. He might surprise us. The key is going to be in his temper and impatience. To win, he'll have to conquer them."

In keeping with the crazy, turbulent Roaring Twenties, baseball was about to begin an abrupt and radical change. It all started when the genial brewmaster of New York, Jake Ruppert, opened his checkbook and bought out the stars of Boston in 1920 from a theatrical entrepreneur—and along came a round, carefree southpaw pitcher out of the deck named George Herman Ruth. He had been working as a pitcher—and what a pitcher!—and as a substitute outfielder up through 1918. His batting average was barely .300 and his home run output was scant. But he had been studying Joe Jackson's method of hitting a baseball and copied it, with a few changes and interpolations of his own.

The Babe had already begun to get control of the home run swing in 1919, although his strikeout record at bat was still above normal. He batted .300 in 1918, .322 in 1919 and .376 in 1920. By then he was no longer merely a fine left-handed pitcher—he was fast becoming the mightiest slugger in the history of baseball.

The Cobbian Era was by now fading away like spent fog.

The Ruthian Attack was the thing.

They built Yankee Stadium for the Babe to hit home runs in. On the road he was becoming an even greater drawing attraction than P. T. Barnum's blood-sweating elephants. His picture was starting to appear in more places than that of Edward, Prince of Wales, and he was well on his way to earning a salary larger than the President's.

Had Abner Doubleday suddenly popped up on the scene, he would not have recognized his century-old recipe. Now it was the broadax instead of the rapier, heavy artillery instead of a fencing match, power instead of skill, flash instead of finessse.

The moguls had to have something to take the place of Cobbian baseball to keep those turnstiles clicking. A new act! Baseball was moving into the circle of business—Big Business. So they invented the livelier ball to make the hits, the Great Bambino's home runs, more exciting to the fans. Larry Lajoie had been a sensation because he hit thirteen homers in one season; in 1908 Wahoo Sam Crawford had been a national idol because he whanged seven, and there were nine by Cobb in 1909. But now the boys were on the verge of clearing the fences twenty, thirty, forty, fifty times a season.

The fans loved it.

Gunpowder destroyed the feudal system, and power batting was destroying the science of baseball. Cobb had to ask himself, where is the hit-and-run, the dragged bunt, the squeeze, the delayed steal? Where is the fielding pitcher, such as Nick Altrock, who got three putouts and eight assists in the first game of the 1906 World Series against the Cubs? Where is the battle of wits, the heart-stopping duels between guys like Wee Willie Keeler at bat and Jimmy Collins playing third base? Except for Cobb and a handful of other veterans who had been weaned on the grand old science, they were gone. All gone.

As player-manager Cobb did his best to make Babe Ruth's life miserable. Whenever the Tigers played the Yankees, Ty would razz the big fellow unmercifully, hurling every name in the Devil's handbook at him. When the teams changed sides between innings, Cobb would trot by Babe with such taunts as, "Somebody stinks like a polecat! G'wan in and strike out, ya worthless bum!"

Babe seldom boiled over. He could take Cobb's ribbing as

well as dish it out. One afternoon at Yankee Stadium, Ruth ran
out on the field to pull one of the New York batters off a Detroit
pitcher. A general melee followed. Cobb rushed in from his
position in right field, grabbed the first man he could reach,
and pushed him away from the fight. Then, realizing it was the
Babe, he said, "Oh, sorry, Babe, I thought you were our pitcher."
In the Yankee dressing room later, the New York players started
baiting Ruth. They told him that Cobb had shoved him around
and called him a son of a bitch. There had been so much confusion, so many punches and hot words thrown around—so many
faces—that Babe wasn't quite certain himself who had done
what to whom. Everything had been a blur.

"You gonna take that from Cobb?" Babe's teammates shouted.

"No, by gum!" roared Babe, and he bolted out of the locker
room. Seconds later he appeared in the Detroit dressing room.
He was glowering.

"Where's Cobb?" he demanded, looking about him.

"Right here," Cobb said. He was seated in front of his locker,
putting on his pants.

The Babe towered over him. "Listen, you old bastard," he
said, "if you ever call me a sonofabitch again, I'll beat the hell
out of you. I don't care how tough you are."

"What's the matter?" Cobb asked, looking up at him calmly.
"Can't you take a little fun?"

"I can take the pushing around," Ruth said. "But I won't
take being called that."

Harry Heilmann walked up to the Babe, an amused smile
on his face. "What did he call you?" he asked.

"He called me a sonofabitch," Babe said.

Heilmann spat a stream of tobacco juice on the floor.

"That's nothing," he said, and walked away.

Cobb said, "You shouldn't mind that after what you called
me yesterday."

"I didn't call you anything yesterday," the Babe said.

"You're a goddamn liar!" Cobb said.

Ruth took a step toward him. A couple of Tigers moved between them. Then Cobb said, "Get out of here before I throw
you out. You have no business here." Startled suddenly by the
tone of Ty's voice, Ruth started for the door. "And remember,

when we get on the field tomorrow," Cobb called at him, "we're playing baseball, not football, you big slob."

Ruth stopped and turned.

"Listen, Ty," he said. "I'm sorry this happened. I don't mind being called a sonofabitch or a bastard, but after this, none of that personal stuff!"

The Tigers howled. The drama had become a comedy.

"Babe didn't really want to fight anyhow," Cobb told his players.

Almost daily now, Cobb could sense the changes in baseball. Power was replacing speed and skill. Baserunning was all but dead. Cobb himself stole only nine bases in 1922, and nine in 1923. They had all but stopped stealing. Now they were waiting for the long ball to drive them across the plate.

As Cobb watched the Babe rocket batting-practice pitches into the Yankee Stadium bleachers one day, he thought to himself, "I guess more people would rather see him hit one over the fence than see me steal second." Cobb felt bad about it, because it wasn't the game he liked to play. The old game was one of skill and speed, of quick thinking and strategy. This game was all power.

"But there will never be another slugger like Babe," Cobb thought, as Ruth sent another ball screaming into the bleachers in right field. "Just watch the ball next year. They will start juicing it up like a tennis ball because Babe has made the home run so popular."

Against the Saint Louis Browns one day, Cobb set out to prove to Babe Ruth and other sluggers in the league that he, too, could hit home runs. He made his point by hitting five home runs in two days. Babe Ruth was unconvinced, however. "Hell," Babe said, "I could have hit .600 myself! But I'm paid to hit homers."

The Babe loved to beat the Tigers after Cobb became manager. In one series, Ty ordered his pitchers to pitch to Ruth and not walk him. All Babe did was hit two into the center field seats on consecutive days. Both balls carried well over 400 feet.

"One of them was off George Dauss, who sure was my *cousin,* as the saying goes," Babe recalled later. "I drove him crazy. No matter where he pitched to me—high, low, inside or outside—I belted it. Long hits off him always gave me a lot of fun, and Ty considered every long hit I made as a personal insult to *him*. He'd run in from center field to tell the pitcher what to throw to me, but that would only make me more determined to slug the ball."

Despite finishing sixth in 1921, Cobb kept the Tigers hustling. It paid off. They crept up to third in 1922, second in 1923, and back to third in 1924. Ty inspired his players by his own feats. During the years 1921–24, his batting average was .389, a fantastic .401, then .340 and .338. Bucky Harris, second baseman and later playing manager of the Washington Senators, said he was impressed by Cobb's fighting attitude. He noticed that Ty would never admit defeat. There was an example of this in 1922. The Senators had a big lead over the Tigers going into the ninth inning. But Cobb refused to quit, and under his driving force Detroit battled back with nine runs in the last inning to win, 11–9. Ty led the way with five hits in six times at bat. "Cobb taught me that a game is never lost until the last man is out," Harris said. "It's the right idea in baseball or in any other game of life."

Fred Haney was a rookie with the 1922 Tigers. Cobb had always been an idol of his. Now he had a chance to observe him up close. Sitting on the bench, Haney would pull down his cap over his face and use one of the eyelets as a telescope, narrowing his vision so that he saw Cobb and Cobb alone. Haney thought, "What a sight he is as he prepares to bat!" The muscles of Ty's jaw were tense; his bright blue eyes blazed; his forehead furrowed into an intense frown. He was working himself up into a fury—a fierce determination to dominate the pitcher, to hit the ball. By the time he stepped into the batter's box, Fred could almost see sparks in the air. "I dare you to pitch to me," Ty seemed to by saying. "I *dare* you." He dared them all. And, one way or another, he hit them all. He continued to drive infielders crazy. If they played back, he dumped one of his unfieldable little bunts. He could practically name the blade of grass where the ball would stop. If the infielders rushed in expecting a bunt, he slashed the ball over their heads to either field. Cobb was thirty-six years old and still playing like a youngster.

One afternoon in Cleveland, Haney was out of the starting

lineup and Jim Bagby pitched for the Indians. Steve O'Neill, the regular catcher for Cleveland, had the day off, and a rookie substituted for him behind the plate. While sitting in the dugout, Haney found he was talking to himself. "Wait a minute," he was saying, "it just doesn't make sense that a star like Bagby is going to let this green catcher tell him what to pitch. He won't be taking signs *from* the catcher. He will be giving signs *to* the catcher." Fred watched closely for three innings, then walked over to Cobb at the end of the bench. "Ty," he said, "I have stolen their signs. I can call every pitch." Ty looked at Fred and said fine, go out on the coaching line and tip off the Detroit batters. The Tigers went on to win the game, and Haney thought to himself, "Great, I helped us win and I wasn't even in the game."

A few days later the Tigers went to Chicago. Catching for the White Sox in the first game was Ray Schalk, a great little hustler. After three innings, Cobb turned to Haney and asked, "Steal any signs today, Fred?" Puzzled, Fred said, "No, I can't spot a one. They're hiding them too cleverly." And Ty said, "Young fellow, I guess you're just not alert enough. The next pitch will be a fast ball. Now a curve. Now . . ." Cobb called seventeen straight pitches correctly as Haney gasped in disbelief.

"No wonder you're a .400 hitter," Haney told him. "You know every pitch that's coming."

"Son," Ty said, "it isn't quite that simple. The tipoff came to me not from intercepting any signals but from something I have learned about human nature. There is always a tendency in this business for a man to get too mechanical. Ray Schalk was a great catcher but he is getting old now and he has let himself fall into a set routine. I have studied him for so long that I even know how he thinks. I merely keep pace with his mental processes and that's why I am able to call all those pitches correctly. I think along the same lines as he does."

Fred Haney saw age catching up with Cobb in 1922 and thereafter. Some days Ty was so stiff and sore he could hardly dress. He would have to go back to his hotel room and to bed to rest his body almost immediately after every game. He often had his meals sent to his bedside and then called his players to the room for strategy conferences. Yet at the ball park, after a long, slow warmup, he was as fierce a competitor as ever, still hitting over .300, still stealing bases. That .401 average in 1922 was his best in ten years, and he also led the American League in fielding (.986) that season.

While Cobb was a tough taskmaster, he never asked his players to do anything he wouldn't do. To keep in shape over the winter, he tramped twenty to thirty miles a day through the Georgia woods, with lead weights attached to the insteps of his heavy hunting boots. He detested athletes who let themselves grow fat and soft or who were "nightwalkers"—curfew violators—in the middle of the season. If a man gave his best, Ty supported him one hundred per cent.

Fred Haney, at 5 feet 6 and 145 pounds, was the smallest man on the Detroit roster. To Fred, his teammates looked like powerful, unbeatable giants. But Cobb stuck by him. One evening, Ty invited Fred over to his house for dinner. Fred expected to hear Cobb tell him that he was shipping him back down to the minors for more experience and to flesh out. He was a gracious Southern host. The dinner was delightful, and then Ty got around to business. He said he liked the way Fred kept hustling. He hoped he would not worry about his size. "Other players even smaller than you have made the grade in the majors," he said. Ty explained that he planned to give Haney every chance to make the team, and he was sure he would succeed. It was an inspiring pep talk for the uncertain youngster to hear. He went back to his hotel room floating on a cloud and determined never to let his manager down. With Cobb's support and sound advice—"Turn your size into an advantage by crouching and making the pitcher come in low with the ball"—Haney hit .352 in his rookie season.

Cobb had all the Tigers playing over their heads in 1922, 1923, and 1924. They did not have anywhere near enough manpower to be contenders, but with Ty's leadership and will to win, they gave it the old college try.

After Cobb took over the Tigers, he made some changes in policy. He abolished skull practice, and he called off morning workouts. But what he couldn't abolish was the frustrations of wanting to be on the field and on the bench at the same time. He realized that a dugout was the hotbed of team hostility, and the manager who could stay there had a big advantage over the player-manager. While team morale was fairly good, there were a few disgruntled and rebellious substitutes who sat on the bench and second-guessed every move Cobb made.

Cobb regarded second-guessing as a disease, "the worst psychological factor in baseball," for on almost every play an act of deliberate judgment occurs. The Tigers, for example, would be nursing a one-run lead. They needed a few insurance runs. Cobb had two men on the bases, and his pitcher, a weak hitter, was the next batter. Ty wanted to get those runners across the plate, but there was a problem. His pitcher had not been hitting well. Should Ty lift him for a pinch-hitter? He decided to go with his pinch-hitter, who came through. Ty looked like a genius—until his relief pitcher got on the mound and was whacked around, and the Tigers lost the game.

That night, Ty couldn't sleep. He just tossed, turned and fretted, *second-guessing* himself. He spent all night stewing and asking himself what might have happened had he not taken out his starting pitcher. Such self-recrimination hurt his spirit. It also hurt his players. One of his pitchers, for instance, might use the wrong judgment on a crucial play and then torment himself for the rest of a game: "Why didn't I do the other thing?" Or the third baseman second-guesses his play on a bunt; or the right-fielder throws to the wrong base.

But the real trouble would start when the Tigers started second-guessing each other: The right-fielder might tell the pitcher where he made the mistake, the catcher would second-guess Cobb, and the shortstop might jump on the second baseman. When that happened, it was all Ty could do to restore peace.

One day a sportswriter asked Cobb what was the hardest part about being a player-manager. "To stand out there in the outfield and watch my pitcher throw the wrong ball to the batter," Ty said. "I have coached him for that hitter over and over, but I can't *throw* the ball for him. So he lays it on the outside when it should have been on the inside, or high when it should have been low, and there goes the old ball game."

Cobb admitted that he found some solace in managing the Tigers, however. Batters like Harry Heilmann were a pleasure to work with. In 1920 Harry hit .309, but Ty knew he could do better. He made him take a lot of extra batting practice.

He moved his hands away from his body to give him a freer swing, and he changed his stance slightly by stationing him deeper in the box. Heilmann soon started tearing up the league. He won four American League batting championship, and during the six seasons Cobb managed him he hit .394, .356, .403, .346, .393, and .367.

Charley Gehringer joined the Tigers in 1924, and Cobb knew immediately he had a great natural hitter on his hands. But after giving him a trial, Ty decided that the rookie second sacker needed more minor league experience. His fielding was all right—when he trapped those grounders it sounded like a catcher's mitt, *thud,* smack in the pocket every time—but Cobb didn't want to make him a regular too soon. He wanted to give Charley more time to work on his hitting, so he farmed him out. Except for moving his feet closer together and lifting his elbows a bit, Ty didn't tinker much with his batting style.

Gehringer did not stay in the minors for long. He returned to Detroit and averaged .320 over the next seventeen seasons. Cobb loved managing him. He called him the "Silent Knight," because Charley never talked much. "He'd say hello at the start of spring training and goodby at the end of the season, and the rest of the time he let his bat and glove do all the talking for him," Cobb recalled.

Paul Krichell, who spent half a lifetime scouting for the Yankees, used Cobb's great reputation in 1923 to pull Lou Gehrig out of low spirits. Gehrig was playing for the Yankees' farm team at Hartford, and Krichell was sent up to Connecticut to talk to him. The problem seemed to be a combination of homesickness and a batting slump, and it appeared as though the Yankees were on the brink of losing a great prospect. When Krichell arrived, Lou was walking around with his chin on his chest. He was surprised to see Paul.

"What are you doing here?" Gehrig wanted to know.

"I came up to see you, you big stiff," Krichell told him. "What's the matter with you, anyway?"

Lou shook his head.

"I don't know," he said. "I just can't seem to get going."

"Well," Paul said, "forget about it for a moment and let's go downtown and see what we can do to a couple of steaks."

They walked down to the Bond Hotel and had a good dinner. They talked about everything but Lou's slump. And then, when Paul had his coffee in front of him and had lighted a cigar, he said, "Now, then, what's this all about?"

Gehrig, more than glad to talk to somebody he knew, poured out his story. Two hitless days. A sleepless night. No hits for two more days. Less sleep. Homesickness. Worry over his job. Humiliation because, having been hailed by the Hartford newspapers on his arrival as the "Great Gehrig" and "Columbia Lou, the Fence Buster," he had failed so miserably.

Krichell listened to him patiently, never interrupting him, letting him spill his somber thoughts as they crowded his mind. It was an old story to Paul. He had heard it from the lips of countless young ballplayers. When at last Lou had finished, Paul said to him, "I know just how you feel. But you've got to get over it. And right away. So you didn't make any hits for two days. So what? Who do you think you are, anyway? The greatest hitters I've ever seen have had two, three, four, five and even six hitless days in a row. Ever hear of Ty Cobb?"

Lou smiled for the first time.

"Who hasn't?" he said.

"A fair country hitter," Paul said. "Well, do you know what Ty told me once when I asked him what he did when he got into a slump? Or does it surprise you, Lou, that even the great Cobb gets into slumps once in a while, too?"

The furrows had left Gehrig's forehead, and he was able to laugh again.

"What did he say?" he asked.

"He said that he didn't worry because he was in a slump. He knew he was a good hitter, that slumps were inevitable, and that he would come out of it in a few days. He figured the reason he was in a slump was that his stroke was off; that instead of hitting straight at the ball he was hitting down or up. So, without even trying to get a base hit, he concentrated on trying to hit the ball back to the pitcher because he knew in that way he would readjust his stroke. And in a couple of days he was hitting like old times again."

"That sounds reasonable," Lou said.

"Reasonable!" Paul said. "Why, it's some of the soundest baseball you ever listened to, you big lug. Feel better now?"

"I sure do. And I'm very grateful to you, Paul."

"Okay," Paul said. "Now let me see you start hitting in a couple of days."

"I will," Lou said.

And he did.

Ironically, once Lou Gehrig became a regular for the Yankees, in 1925, Cobb treated the easygoing first baseman miserably. He seemed to have a special distaste for him. Cobb was the only man in the American League who could arouse Gehrig, and he would bedevil him with the most vituperative language at his command. "You're a bum!" Ty would screech. "You're a thick-headed, no-good Dutchman! Get out of my sight, you lousy Kraut!"

Gehrig stood it for months. Then one day, as he passed the Tiger dugout, Cobb let fly with a barrage of dirty epithets. That did it. Gehrig lowered his head, clenched his fists, and charged down into the dugout to annihilate Cobb, who nimbly stepped out of the way. Gehrig's skull cracked into an iron stanchion and he fell to the ground, stunned. He got up like a punch-drunk fighter a few seconds later and tried to reach Cobb, but the players managed to cool him off. The next day, Cobb and Gehrig shook hands. What Cobb had against Lou he never would say, but he did confess to me years later that he admired him for the way he made himself into a ballplayer.

"When Gehrig first joined the Yankees, he wasn't exactly a model fielder," Ty said. "George Sisler was then a coach for New York, and while he was entranced with Lou's hitting, his finesse around first base embarrassed him. Sisler knew that Gehrig considered him his idol and so he went to work on him. So did Miller Huggins. In the beginning, Lou would commit one bad error a game. Then it got so he made one a week, and then maybe only one a month. In the end, he was trying to keep it down to one a season."

Rogers Hornsby was never able to tolerate Cobb's disposition. In 1923, Hornsby recalled, the Tigers and the Cardinals met in an exhibition game in Augusta. The score was tied when Cobb came to bat and singled. On the very next pitch, Ty tried to steal, and Hornsby, who was playing second base for the Cards, tagged him out. "He was out by a country mile," Hornsby said after the game. But Cobb refused to accept Umpire Cy Pfirman's decision. "I beat the throw!" he stormed. Finally, Steamboat Johnson, the plate umpire, walked out and told Cobb to quiet down so that the game could go on. Cobb ignored the warning and kept it up, screaming, waving his arms, and carrying on like a wild man.

"Ty," Umpire Johnson said, "I'm going to forfeit the game to Saint Louis if you don't shut up and get off the field."

Cobb raged on, and Johnson stuck to his word.

The upshot was that both teams were required to refund all ticket money to a crowd of 6,000. That didn't sit too well with the owners. The players all went back to their hotel and changed into their street clothes. All except Cobb. He remained at the ball park bawling out the umpires. He didn't cool off for an hour. Finally he walked back to the hotel and asked the Cardinals to come back and finish the game. They refused. When Baseball Commissioner Kenesaw Mountain Landis received the report on the game, he fined the Tigers the amount of money the Cardinals lost on their share of the receipts, which was half of the gate.

"Cobb can be an ornery cuss," Hornsby said later. "But he's the greatest player I've ever seen."

Ty was involved in more hot water after the season ended that year. He had promised George Weiss to appear in an exhibition game with the New Haven Colonials against a team from Windsor, featuring a black pitcher named Cannonball Dick Redding. Unbeknown to Cobb, a redneck, the promoters billed the battle as "the greatest major league hitter" versus "the greatest black pitcher." Crowds from all over the countryside filled the ball park. But when Cobb arrived and saw the color of Cannonball's skin, he angrily refused to take the field. The promoters hurriedly huddled with Cobb behind the grandstand. He agreed to play only if he played the first four innings while Cannonball pitched the last five. The black man was used to such idiocies, and the game went on as scheduled. At the end of the fourth frame Cobb went boiling back to Detroit—and Cannonball Redding came in and pitched and batted Windsor to victory.

June 1, 1925, is a memorable date in baseball annals. Lou

Gehrig replaced Wallie Pipp in the Yankee lineup. Thereafter for fourteen consecutive years and 2,130 consecutive games, Columbia Lou was to be installed as Mr. First Base.

The year 1925 also became known as "The Year of the Big Bellyache." That spring at Asheville, North Carolina, Babe Ruth fell victim to the gluttony that beset him for years. Now gluttony with Ruth was not your stuffy napkin-in-collar, bring-me-a-steak-smothered-in-pork-chops kind. The beginning of the stomachache that was felt around the world was engendered by a wayside collation consisting of nine or ten greasy railroad-station frank-furters mounted on papier-mâché rolls, and washed down with some eight bottles of green, red, and yellow soda pop. Anyway, they shipped him up North on a stretcher, and the whole nation trembled with every turn of the wheels that brought him back to New York. He was tucked into a cot in St. Vincent's Hospital, in grave danger of relinquishing his hold upon his great, mortal body, and hung between life and death for many days—on Page One. Bulletins were issued from the sickroom. Little boys brought nosegays, or congregated outside the high walls of the hospital, and looked up at the window of the room wherein lay the stricken hero. The presses lay in wait with pages of obituaries, and editorials announced the impending catastrophe as a national calamity. Even in England, the penny papers watched at his bedside. That *was* fame.

The upcoming years of 1926–28 were about to bring to base-ball the Yankees' fabulous Murderer's Row, commanded by a sharp, dried-up mite of a man named Miller Huggins. Hug was all wisdom and common sense and baseball brains. He had dream pitchers, Herb Pennock, Waite Hoyt, Wiley Moore, and George Pipgras. There were Earl Combs, Mark Koenig, Jumping Joe Dugan, and Poosh-'em-up Tony Lazzeri. All this plus that heart-breaking, fence-busting one-two punch, George Herman Ruth and Henry Louis Gehrig. A wild collection of baseball talent, but how they could play ball.

Starting in 1921, the Giants won four straight National League pennants to bring John J. McGraw's grand total to ten. He also won three World Series. When the Giants and Yankees got ready to square off in the 1921 Series, a reporter from the New York *Times* asked McGraw if the Babe had him worried. "Why should I worry about Ruth?" McGraw grunted. "My pitchers have been throwing to a better hitter all summer." He meant Rogers Hornsby, of course. The Rajah led the National League in batting seven times, six in succession. In 1922 and 1925, he topped both major leagues in home runs, with 42 and 39, and he had the Babe to beat out! From 1919 to 1931, he hit .300 or better every season, nine times .360 or higher.

Though the Tigers failed to win a pennant under Cobb, some of his batting magic rubbed off on them. In 1921, for example, the entire team, including pitchers and subs, batted .316.

"It's murder," Waite Hoyt complained. "You go into Detroit in August and find the entire Tiger outfield hitting .400. Cobb, Heilmann, Manush, and Bob Fothergill can all kill you!"

But Detroit didn't have the pitchers to go with the batters, and when the Yankees faltered in 1924, it was the Senators, not the Tigers, who played Pittsburgh in the World Series. It marked the first time that Walter Johnson—or the Senators—had ever participated in a Series.

In 1925, Cobb was considered, at thirty-eight, a really old ballplayer. He was suffering from a fractured rib, torn ligaments, all the battle scars and aches and pains collected in more than twenty years of ferocious competition. Everyone hinted he was surely through by now. Why didn't he retire? He had proved all there was to prove by now. He held almost all the records. He had a bankful of money. It was high time for the obstreperous old warhorse to quit. Even the fans who hated him the most didn't want to see him go on playing, weakening his record, ruining his reputation. They now had Ruth to love. They no longer needed Cobb to hate. Why didn't he quit?

"I can't quit," Cobb said. "I can't quit as long as I can still run and hit and steal bases."

Cobb was earning some $50,000 a season by this time—a salary he had achieved through a bit of shrewd fakery involving an old friend, George Weiss, owner of the New Haven Colonials. With George in an upstairs room at the Vanderbilt Hotel in New York, Ty was bargaining downstairs with Frank Navin. When Navin made an offer, Cobb would promptly go to a telephone and call Weiss's room. He would tell George the proposed figure, and ask if he could meet it. George, who could no more have matched the offer than he could have bought the New Haven Railroad, would promptly name a higher figure, which Cobb would then repeat for Navin's benefit. In this way, Cobb gradually pushed Navin's offer up to $50,000—the figure Cobb was striving for—and that night Ty and George celebrated his success by doing up Manhattan in ribbons.

Detroit finished fourth and sixth in 1925 and 1926, and Navin was unhappy. He felt Cobb had messed up too many deals for players. One of them was a tall, lean southpaw pitcher from Meeker, Oklahoma, who had been with the Tigers' farm club at Beaumont, Texas. After watching him pitch to the varsity in spring training, Ty recommended that Navin get rid of him. "He'll never make it in the majors," Cobb said. "His big pitch is a screwball, and he's going to throw his arm out with it one of these days. Get rid of him."

Navin followed his manager's advice, and two years later he was picked up by John J. McGraw and the Giants. His name? Carl Owen Hubbell.

"Navin should have shot me," Cobb said later. "One of the greatest pitchers of all time, and I let him go! I just wasn't using my head. I should have remembered that Christy Mathewson threw a screwball, only he called it a fadeaway, and it never hurt his arm. My dumbheadedness cost me my job."

Ty Cobb and Babe Ruth in 1920. Notice Cobb's peculiar split grip on the bat handle. *Photo: United Press International*

Photo: United Press International

Cobb autographs a baseball for kids in San Francisco.

The famous Cobb "fall-away slide" was captured on film in 1921.

Cobb, star outfielder of the 1923 Detroit Tigers,
makes a catch.   *Photo: United Press International*

Photo: Wide World

Cobb as Manager of the Detroit
Tigers in 1924.

Cobb slides in 1925.

Ty takes a good cut for the Philadelphia Athletics in 1927.

Ty and A's Manager Connie Mack show Shibe Park to Thomas Edison, an enthusiastic fan of Cobb's.   *Photo: United Press International*

Cobb slides back to
first on an attempted
pickoff in a 1928
exhibition game.

Cobb and Ted
Williams show
mutual admiration
at spring training
in 1950.

Cobb puts on a batting
exhibition in Seattle in his
sixty-sixth year.

Photo: Seattle Rainiers

Cobb at sixty-nine.

Photo: New York Herald Tribune—Nat Fei

For the last dozen years of his life, Cobb talked about going home to Georgia. He finally made it and built himself a mansion near his hometown.

Ty Cobb and Roger Maris get together before a night game at Yankee Stadium on September 16, 1960.

Before Cobb died on July 17, 1961, he built a mausoleum for himself, his parents, and his sister at Royston, Georgia, his hometown.

10

The Final Fling

Moving up on his fortieth birthday, still scampering around the bases, Ty mowed through the 1926 season with a brisk .339 average as the Tigers wound up exactly where he had found them back in 1906, his first full season in the league—in sixth place. By then, writers and fans alike were ready to believe Tyrus Raymond Cobb would play baseball forever.

Poor old Ty Cobb, still running bases like a kid. Nearly forty, and still dashing for home to win a ball game, crossing up infields, scaring the living hell out of veterans and rookies alike. A worn, tired, battle-happy wreck who, by some magic, was still able to send a screaming double to any field, lay down a perfect bunt, dive into the stands and snare a ball with the same daring he did back when Teddy Roosevelt was President.

How he was able to do it, nobody has ever been able to figure. Thomas A. Edison, the great inventor, was fascinated by Cobb, and when the old gentleman celebrated his eightieth birthday, he asked Ty to tour his laboratories with him. After showing Ty some of his experiments with rubber, he said, "Mr. Cobb, you are involved in a very exact science, too."

At the end of the '26 season, however, Cobb confided to Grantland Rice that maybe it was time to hang up his spikes. He knew he was about as fast as ever, but he feared his reflexes were fading. He sensed he was starting much slower now.

"I don't get that good jump any more," he admitted. "I stole only nine bases this year, and that has to tell you something. I can see the ball as good as ever, but now that quick start from the plate is missing. If I still had my quickness, I'd be a .350 hitter right to the end."

It was the pressure of age, he felt. "With age you get jittery," he said. It was true of ballplayers as it was true of most men his age. "I don't take chances like I used to," Ty added. "The younger player, on the bases, he'll go for that extra base. The older man, he becomes hesitant. A little uncertain, nervous. When it comes to taking chances the younger man, even when driving a car, will take chances that the older man won't."

There really wasn't much reason for Cobb to go on as a player. By now he held most of the records. Hans Wagner's record of batting .300 or better for seventeen straight seasons had become his in 1923. He ran his string to eighteen that season, and to twenty in 1925. He had also caught up with Wagner's 3,430 lifetime hits on the way to a final total of 4,191. In 1924, he had passed Willie Keeler's all-time high of 200 or more hits in each of eight seasons; and in 1926, he topped Wagner's endurance record of playing in 2,785 games with a new record of 2,800. He also now led the majors in lifetime singles, triples, total bases on hits, extra-base hits, stolen bases, and runs scored. Those head-spinning statistics seemed to indicate that Cobb had little more to go on for. The thought galled Ty. It galled him because he resented the pressure put on him by Frank Navin to resign. Navin did not have to draw him a picture. Ty knew that if he did not voluntarily step down, Navin would fire him.

At a news conference in Detroit at the end of the season, Cobb shocked the baseball world by suddenly announcing his resignation. After twenty-two years with the Tigers, he was leaving baseball.

"I'm tired," he told reporters. "I can't take chances any more. It's time to quit. I am going back to Augusta to be with my family."

Cobb was one of six managers either to resign or to be fired from a big league job in 1926. The other five were Bill Mc-Kechnie (Pirates), Art Fletcher (Phillies), Lee Fohl (Red Sox), George Sisler (Browns), and Rogers Hornsby (Cardinals).

Ty was asked if he was breaking all ties with baseball. "I don't know," he said. "I might shop around for a ball club to buy. I am told that Cincinnati is up for sale. I might be interested in the Reds if the price is right."

Metropolitan dailies refused to take the Cobb announcement seriously.

From the New York *Sun*:

Retirements of famous baseball players are like the farewell tours of opera singers in that there is rarely a guaranty that either will be permanent. Doddering and senile as this baseball Methuselah of 40 is, there is still a wallop or two in his bat.

From the New York *Evening Post*:

Ty says he has definitely given up the game, although there will be many who will find it hard to believe that anyone who has loved baseball so fiercely as Ty Cobb can divorce himself from it altogether.

In comparing Cobb with Babe Ruth, the New York *World* editorialized: "The charm of Ruth lies in his eye and arm, but the charm of Cobb is in his head."

Down home, Ty told the Georgia press that he wanted to quit while he was still one of the best. "Ballplayers should retire before they break," he said. "I have known good players who were the idols of fans who finished their careers playing out the string and died broke and broken-hearted. My legs are still good, my eyes are as sharp as ever, but the old fire is gone. I still love baseball. I have lived the game, but I know when to stop."

Cobb was an authentic millionaire, the first man in the history of baseball who accumulated a million without being connected with the ownership of a ball club. Down in quiet, pretty Augusta he would live the life of a small banker, a Georgia squire. His house was on one of the city's finest streets. His family was respected. His oldest son, Tyrus Junior, was headed for college; Ty Senior always envied those with college educations.

Ty told his neighbors that the only plans he had for the present was to do some bird shooting and play a bit of golf. He was going to be a man of leisure. Ty was among the legions of Bobby Jones worshipers, and one day that winter he took it upon himself to accompany the Emperor of Golf around the course during a tournament in Augusta. He was as unlike Bobby as any athlete, or man, could be. Ty was eager to offer advice and moral support. His fellow Georgian accepted the company of his famous fan with grace. On the last three holes of the final round, Jones needed only three pars to get home in 66 and finish eighteen strokes ahead.

After finishing the sixteenth, the fast-playing Jones saw that he had caught up with the match just ahead of him. He sat down for a moment to rest. Cobb began to kick up a storm.

"Get up, get up!" he shouted, rushing over to Bobby. "Move around, keep warm!"

Slightly bewildered, Jones got up and moved around to satisfy his excited compatriot.

"Move faster, don't get cold!" urged Cobb.

Ty's behavior must have upset Bobby, because he lost five strokes on the last three holes with 6-5-6. He still won by thirteen strokes, but after the match, in the locker room, Cobb was still fuming.

"You should have moved around faster," he moaned. "You should have done what I told you to do!"

Jones shook his head. With a sly, sad grin he said, "I suppose you're right, Ty. I'll remember to move around faster next time."

Even in golf, Ty Cobb always bore down.

Ty was just getting adjusted to the life of a country squire when his peaceful world was shattered by newspaper headlines up North. A plot had been hatched to accuse him, Tris Speaker, and Joe Wood, a pitcher, of having "fixed" a game played in 1919 between Detroit and Cleveland, and of having bet money on it. The chief figure in the scandal was Cobb's old enemy Dutch Leonard. Dutch hated Cobb. The game in question was played on September 25, 1919. The Tigers won, 9–5. Leonard alleged that the Indians had agreed to let Detroit win. Dutch was a member of the Detroit pitching staff and claimed he had the facts, but an investigation into his allegations did not support his story.

Leonard then produced letters from Cobb and Speaker that mentioned bets on the game, evidence that was supposed to prove their guilt. Baseball Commissioner Landis found, however, that the letters were merely in reply to requests for information concerning bets—that Cobb and Speaker had not bet and that the game had certainly not been thrown. Speaker, in fact, had a great day for the losers—two triples and a single—and Cobb only had one hit in five times at bat. As for Smokey Joe Wood, he didn't even appear in the game. The witch hunt lasted for two months. "When Judge Landis asked Leonard to go to Chicago to testify against us," Cobb recalled, "Dutch refused. He hid out in his California home."

On January 27, 1927, Judge Landis publicly declared the three men "not guilty." After his full reinstatement, Ty took his dogs and gun and went hunting in the Georgia pine woods. "Landis sure took his time getting to the truth," he said disgustedly. Ban Johnson, after rashly charging Landis with "bungling" the case, was angry enough to resign as President of the American League.

In early February, Dave Driscoll knocked on Ty's door. Dave was an executive for the Brooklyn Dodgers. "This is no social call, Ty," he said. "This is business. We want you to manage the Dodgers."

"But what about Uncle Wilbert Robinson?" Ty asked.

"Robby is getting too old to manage," Dave said. "His contract is not being renewed. It's time for a change in Brooklyn. We like your hustle, and we know you will make the Dodgers hustle, too."

Before Ty could give him his answer, the phone rang. The caller was Connie Mack, phoning from Fort Myers, Florida. He said he had been reading the local papers and gathered that Ty had definitely made up his mind not to play for Detroit in 1927.

"Is that true, Ty?"

"It's true, Mr. Mack. I'm hanging 'em up."

"Ty, nobody who can still hit .339 is washed up. I need your bat. I think we can win another pennant with you in the lineup. How about it, Ty?"

"Give me some time to think about it," Ty said. "I will call you back in a few days."

Cobb went back to Driscoll. "I'm sorry, Dave, but I can't accept your offer. That was Connie Mack on the phone and he needs me. My loyalty still is with the American League."

On February 9, 1927, Ty Cobb signed a contract with the Athletics. The agreement called for a total of $60,000 ($25,000 for signing, another $25,000 in salary, and $10,000 in bonus money at the end of the season).

Ty went on to play two more years for Connie Mack's Athletics, the team that had the distinction of hating him more than any other. On May 10, 1927, some twenty-three years after his first game in the majors, Cobb was again under suspension. All he had done was hit a home run for the Athletics in a game against the Red Sox. It was a ninth-inning homer that would have tied the score. The ball was fair when it sailed out of the park, but a young plate umpire named Ormsby had the temerity to say it curved foul just as it disappeared. Ty pushed him around somewhat. Cobb was still Cobb.

A's fans were always at the ball park early when the club was at home. Cobb batted third in the lineup. They knew that if they were late they would miss seeing him bat the first time around.

The fact that the Athletics finished second behind the Yankees in 1927 was not Ty's fault. He had a great season. In 134 games, he drove in 93 runs, stole 22 bases, and hit .357. He was still the most feared baserunner in the game. One afternoon, Cobb rammed a line shot into right field, where a rookie for the Senators was stationed. Cobb was just making a routine turn at first base when the rookie picked up the ball. Without a flicker of hesitation, the youngster cranked up and rifled the ball to home plate. Ty Cobb wasn't going to score on *him!*

Cobb was no longer a young ballplayer when he reported to the A's for the 1928 season. He was nearly forty-two years old, and his bones ached from twenty-three seasons in the American League. Ty wasn't going to play, at first, but Connie Mack coaxed him into uniform with a $35,000 salary and the reminder that he was very much needed to finish the task of overtaking the Yankees. Mr. Mack had put together some ball club. Seven of its members would one day fill niches at Cooperstown—eight, if you want to include Manager Mack. The seven players were Cobb, Jimmy Foxx, Mickey Cochrane, Tris Speaker, Eddie Collins, Lefty Grove, and Al Simmons. No other big league team has even remotely approached that number of Hall of Fame players in action at the same time.

The Athletics rose swiftly in 1928 to the level of performance that would give them the pennant for the next three years. Their rehabilitation had begun as far back as 1922, after they had finished last seven times in a row, and only the great 1928 Yankees could keep them from winning in that year.

The A's broke fast in 1928 and took the lead. The Yankees quickly snatched it away from them and by July were seventeen games in front and riding easily. Then, practically overnight, New York was riddled with injuries. Herb Pennock's arm was so lame he couldn't lift a ball—and he was New York's best pitcher. Tony Lazzeri's ailing right shoulder had him shuttling in and out of the lineup. Babe Ruth had a bad leg. Earle Combs was so wound in tape he looked like a mummy. It seemed the only able-bodied man on the squad was at first base.

As the Yankees hobbled through one defeat after another, the Athletics put on a terrific finish. On September 8, they lunged past the Yankees into first place. Their lead was short-lived, however. The Yanks, realizing they were in a battle to the finish, forgot their aches and pains and, one day later, a Sunday at Yankee Stadium, they beat Philadelphia in both ends of a doubleheader as George Pipgras pitched a shutout in the first game and Bob Meusel hit a home run with the bases loaded in the nightcap. Monday was an open date, but on Tuesday they hurled the A's further back as the Babe hit a big one in the clutch.

Down the home stretch, the Cobb spirit was as fierce as ever. One day, a situation arose when a hit could win the game for Philadelphia. Cobb was the scheduled batter. Mr. Mack called him back to the dugout. "Ty," he began, as gently as he could, "you've been in a slump and I was just wondering . . ." Mr. Mack paused, gulped hard, and then went on: "I was just wondering if I sent in a pinch-hitter . . ."

Cobb never let him finish.

"No one ever hits for me!" he roared. Angrily he walked to the plate and hit the first pitch for a single to win the ball game.

Years later, Mr. Mack frequently told that story as an example of what true pride is. "Ty had pride," he would say, "and pride is the hallmark of the champion. He resented my implication that he was no longer able to deliver in the clutch. So he reacted like the proud man that he was. He got the hit."

Playing shortstop and second base in 102 games for the Yankees that summer was Leo Durocher, twenty-three, as hot-tempered as Cobb. It was inevitable they would clash. Leo the Lion took almost fiendish delight in razzing Cobb.

"Why don't you give yourself up?" Durocher would shout at him when the Yankees and A's played. "What are you waiting for them to do—cut your suit off?"

Cobb's reaction was to snarl and shake his fist at Durocher, but Leo only laughed. "Go home, Grandpaw," he'd yell. "Get wise to yourself. If you keep playing with us young fellows, you might get hurt." Cobb would stare over at him, red-faced, but usually he went back to the dugout.

One afternoon, Cobb was on first base with two out, and the next hitter singled to right center. Cobb, running as the ball was hit, set out for third. But as he rounded second, Durocher, standing near the bag, gave Cobb the hip. Ty stumbled, caught himself, kept running—and was thrown out at third by a yard. Durocher laughed and, tossing his glove back of him, started for the dugout. Cobb was furious. He stopped Leo on the third base line.

"The next time you try that," he raged, "I'll cut your legs off!"

Durocher wasn't laughing now.

"You'll cut nobody's legs off!" he shouted back. "You've been bulldozing ballplayers in this league long enough, but you don't frighten me! I'll give you the hip every time you come around second base, if I can! And if you try to cut me, I'll stick the ball down your throat!"

It took both teams to break them up.

Quentin Reynolds said he saw Cobb play only one game for Philadelphia, and that one game was responsible for starting him on a career as a short story writer.

On that particular afternoon the A's were leading the Yankees, 2–1, going into the last inning. Cobb was playing right field. He had had a typical Cobb day at the plate—three hits and a stolen base—but in the top of the ninth, with two Yankees on base and two out, a fly ball was lifted to Cobb. It should have been an easy out, but forty-one-year-old Ty could not quite get to it. The ball hit his glove, bounced out, and both Yankees scored what later proved to be the winning runs. The crowd laughed. They laughed at the great Ty Cobb. Reynolds watched from the press box.

"I felt sick," recalled the noted magazine writer and World War II combat correspondent. "I thought to myself, 'Why, that's like laughing at *God*!' "

The Yankees went on to clinch the 1928 pennant in late September, 2½ games ahead of the A's, and then swept the Cardinals in four straight to win the World Series.

Both Cobb and Tris Speaker had just about run out of time in 1928, and the third member of baseball's only Hall of Fame outfield, Al Simmons, must have felt it was sheer hard work to be out there with two overaged glamour boys. Cobb could still hit, but by his own admission he had lost much of his quickness. Speaker could neither hit (.267) nor run any more; and Simmons, in full vigor at twenty-five, not only had to patrol left field but had to chase the long drives that got away from Speaker and Cobb in left or right center.

"If this keeps up," he growled one day, "by the end of the season I'll be an old man myself."

Age was creeping up on Cobb. The strain of the game was making him more nervous and jumpy than usual.

"People pester me a great deal," he explained. "I can't sit down and talk for fifteen minutes to a friend without an interruption. Those things weren't even worth mentioning before, but now they are unpleasant realities. I know what the trouble is. I'm thoroughly exhausted and need a long rest."

Now that he had come to the end, was there anything in his career he would change?

"I suppose I'm leaving a lot of enemies behind me," Ty said. "That's because I tell the truth. If I know a guy has no guts, I say so. I don't expect him to love me for saying it. Possibly I have been too blunt and candid in my comments. Probably

I would have gotten along better if I had used more tact and diplomacy. But such things are foreign to me. That isn't my way."

Cobb started his career in 1905 against the old New York Highlanders, as a substitute. He ended it the same way on September 11, 1928, against a New York team in Yankee Stadium. There was a difference. Nobody knew who the kid at the plate was on that August 30 in 1905. But nobody had to be told who it was stepping up there to pinch hit for Jimmy Dykes of the Athletics on that day in 1928. For a quarter of a century they had watched, in anger and fascination, the man with the peculiar grip on the bat, left hand high, right hand low. They had watched him stand with neck thrust out, body crouched over the plate, showing them an angry, determined, scornful, and fighting face.

Yes, there was a difference. This time he grounded out.

At the end of the 1928 season Cobb made his retirement permanent. Admirers urged him to come back in 1929 for one more season to round out twenty-five years in the big leagues. It would have been a nice, easy number to remember, but Ty said no.

"Once upon a time," he told them, "it would have been irresistible. But now, in a baseball sense, I am too old, too weary of the daily strain. I have lost my ambition. I'm through. I have played my final game."

Cobb confessed at a news conference that it was a puzzle even to him why he stayed on the active list for so many years. During the last ten years of his career, he revealed, there were many times when he privately intended to quit baseball.

"I was serious, too," he said. "But, somehow, I never could quite do it when I came right down to it. Baseball was too much in my bones. It's damn difficult to eat baseball and sleep it and study it, year after year, and then suddenly stop just like that. It's in the bloodstream. You crave it. You can't live without it. I was hooked."

While the name Cobb would never again appear in an American League box score, it did show up in Tokyo later that fall. Ty was paid $15,000 and all expenses to manage a team of American All-Stars traveling to Japan to conduct baseball clinics and play a series of exhibition games. Babe Ruth and Moe Berg went with him. Ty assigned them to the same room. Babe enjoyed himself enormously. Booze and girls were plentiful, and there were no curfew restrictions to hinder Babe the Playboy. "Babe's never in the room," Berg said. "It's like rooming with a suitcase."

The stadium where the clinics were held was shaped like an American football arena, with upwards of 60,000 people on hand. The Japanese had an interpreter for Cobb, and he lectured on the fundamentals of batting, throwing, fielding, baserunning, and sliding. Everybody had cameras and notebooks to record everything Cobb said and did.

Twenty-seven years later, Ty still talked about his Japanese experience.

"For a model," Ty told me, "I picked out a slim little sliver of a guy from one of the Japanese professional teams and gave him a batting lesson for the benefit of the crowd. Through an interpreter, I showed him how to hold the bat, the correct stance, and the proper swing. The whole session lasted about an hour, and then I went back to the hotel where we were lodged. I napped until early afternoon and then went back to the stadium to play an exhibition game against the Japanese All-Stars. The fans, all 60,000 of them, were still in their seats, where I had left them. They hadn't budged an inch. And out on the field the Japanese ballplayers continued to practice the fundamentals I'd talked about in my lecture that morning; this despite the fact they had to play us in the afternoon."

The game itself was novel. The Japanese attack was built around a set pattern. The Americans could anticipate every move they made.

"We trounced them simply by doing the unexpected," Cobb recalled. "They were flabbergasted by such simple little tricks as the drag bunt, hit-and-run, and swinging at the 3-and-0 pitch. That was not the way they had been taught, and they were confused and frustrated to death by our strategy. I hit about .600 during the entire series, and I even pitched a couple of times. I went the full nine innings in one game and relieved in two others. In eighteen innings, I gave up only one run. I wasn't much of a pitcher, but I got by with a pretty fair kuckle ball, curve, change-up, and a fastball. It was like dangling candy in front of a child. The moment I tried anything unorthodox, the batter went blank.

I tried a quick-pitch on one of them and you should have heard the cackling on their bench and up in the stands. You would have guessed they had seen a ghost. If I threw a fastball when the batter figured curve, they panicked. They had no sense of strategy or psychology. They were blank, lost. I beat them by pitching *backwards*. They had only one game plan. Mess it up and they were dead ducks. They played the same way on defense. The Japanese pitchers had only one style. If the count was 1 and 0, expect a curve; 2 and 0, a curve, and so forth. We called every pitch in advance. We rolled up football scores on them."

11

The Passing Show

Sports were becoming Big Business. In 1929, with the repeal of Prohibition, came the legalization of betting on the horses in most states in America. College football was approaching a day when it could say farewell and good riddance to poverty. The kids in shoulder pads, fired up by stories of Rockne, the Four Horsemen, Red Grange, and Bronco Nagurski, would soon be coming into their own. The day of high-pressure recruiting was just around the corner.

In prize fighting Max Baer, Jack Sharkey, and Max Schmeling slugged heavyweights around the ring. Baer brought a flash of color to pugilism, but he never came anywhere near living up to his fantastic potential, and he faded out quicker than a three-dollar gingham dress in a cloudburst. Jack Sharkey had everything but consistency, and he was in and out of the kingdom like the thread in a loom. Schmeling was good, sometimes, and he at least had a knockout punch, but he was a plodding, methodical workman who didn't often stir up frenzied excitement. That was it. Excitement. The boxing world would have to wait a little longer for Joe Louis, alias the Brown Bomber, to make his appearance.

With the deadly accuracy of "Calamity Jane," his famous putter, Ty Cobb's old friend Bobby Jones nailed down all the major golf championships of the world in one spectacular year, 1930.

Meanwhile, what was happening in baseball immediately following Cobb's retirement? Depression nothwithstanding, Joe Fan managed to scrape together four bits for a bleacher seat. Miller Huggins died in 1929, and Joe McCarthy succeeded him.

On June 3, 1932, John Joseph McGraw left the Giants for the last time just as he had found them thirty years earlier—in last place. That same day, Lou Gehrig astonished the baseball world by hitting four home runs in one game in Philadelphia, the first player of the modern era to do it.

The scene was changing at Yankee Stadium. Murderer's Row gave way to the Bronx Bombers, and during the transition, 1929–31, Connie Mack won three straight pennants. But in 1932 it was the Yankees once more. The batting order now read: Combs, Sewell, Ruth, Gehrig, Lazzeri, Dickey, Chapman, Crosetti. That October, Gehrig led the Bombers to four consecutive victories over the Cubs in the World Series as the Babe's power began to wane. After taking up the habit in 1921, the Yankees were by this time falling into something of a rut, just pennant after pennant, championship after championship, season after season—twenty-one times in thirty-four years!

By 1935 Lou Gehrig had the Yankees all to himself. The Great Man was gone. Wear and tear and time had tapped the Babe. The Golden Era of Sport was at an end, buried in the limbo of beautiful dreams.

Life went on for Ty Cobb. His violent struggles appeared to have ended with his retirement from baseball's active roll call. In 1929 the Cobbs packed off to Europe. Shortly before they left, Ty offered $275,000 for the purchase of the near-bankrupt Cincinnati Reds, but his bid was rejected. Just as well. A few weeks after he made the bid the stock market crashed on Wall Street. Ty heaved a sigh of relief. He had almost gotten himself stuck with a big league ball club during the Great Depression.

When the Cobbs returned to America from the Old World, Ty moved them to California. He thought that perhaps a change would be good for his family. The summer of 1930 at Augusta had been sweltering, more than Ty could stand. As a ballplayer, he had always missed the South's summertime heat. But after that summer of 1930—whew! The Cobbs ran electric fans in their home for fifty-three straight nights. The experience convinced Ty it was time to move the family to Northern California, where the moderate climate appealed to him immensely. So did the schools for his children. During the Depression, the schools in Dixie felt the pinch, forcing teachers to be paid off in script. Ty wanted his five growing youngsters to have the best education possible. Menlo Park, California, near San Francisco, was the answer.

Ty might have been out of baseball now, but that old competitive zeal still burned inside of him. He hunted, fished, played golf, and trained his hunting dogs. He even tried playing polo. He had been watching a polo match, and something about the speed and fury of men on horseback galloping down each other's throats greatly excited him. In no time at all he was in the saddle and riding with blood in his eye. One of the first things he wanted to do, after he got the hang of it, was change the polo rules. Instead of three men to a side he wanted to play it one against one! Nobody wanted any part of him—including the ponies.

"That Mistah Cobb's a madman on a horse," muttered an old black groom. "He don't ride over you. He rides *through* you!"

He carried the same spirit onto the golf course with him. One day at Pebble Beach, California, Cobb teamed up with Grantland Rice in what was supposed to be a friendly four-ball match against Hal Sims, the bridge expert, and Mysterious Montague, the trick shot artist, the strongest man Granny Rice ever knew.

Sims was in excellent form, and when he was playing well there was no better, or worse, needler. Before the match began, Sims looked at Cobb and said, "Ty, I've always admired you. As a ballplayer you were in a class by yourself. But tell me this if you will. Why did you have to spike so many men?"

Cobb, of course, always angrily resented the slightest insinuation that he was a dirty baserunner. His eyes blazed, but he managed to control his temper.

The four golfers teed off. Cobb, normally a good player, was still seething and lunged at the ball as if to kill it. The team of Rice-Cobb lost the first seven holes. Sims, on the other hand, continued in championship form, while his partner, Montague, could have spotted them all ten strokes and still won handily. Granny, meanwhile, tried to soothe Cobb. But it was like throwing water on burning oil.

On the eighth tee, Cobb pushed his drive almost out of bounds and was obliged to hit a provisional. Both balls landed in a bunker, so Ty played his first ball. He scrambled to a bogie five. Sims was keeping the scorecard.

"What did you have, Ty?" Sims asked.

"A five," Ty said.

"A five?" questioned Sims.

Cobb exploded.

"Listen, Sims!" he snarled, grabbing Hal's arm in his viselike grip, "no one questions my word or score!"

Montague bolted between Sims and Cobb. Holding each at arm's length, he advised both of them to act their ages or he would bash their heads together. Hal was visibly upset, but Cobb settled down and characteristically shot fine golf for the rest of the round. Sims played like a Sunday duffer. Granny said later it reminded him of that time when Cobb faked that act with Shoeless Joe Jackson to win the batting championship.

All his life, Cobb's moods were quick-changing. There were times when he would be fierce, a man to be afraid of; times when he would lay great and compelling stress on small things, too trivial for others to consider at all; times when he would be tolerant, even solicitous, and a friendly, approachable human being; times when he would suddenly turn rude, biting, and flaunt all the rules of conventional association with his friends.

In 1935 Rice and Ty were having dinner at the Detroit Athletic Club. Nig Clarke, who used to catch for Cleveland, spotted them and came over to their table and sat down. They were having a great visit, enjoying themselves, when Granny turned to Nig and asked, "Remember that trick you had of tagging a runner out fast and then quickly tossing your mitt aside to let the umpire know it was the third out?"

Nig Clarke chuckled.

"What's so funny?" Ty wanted to know.

"I have a confession," Clarke said. "Actually, I *missed* a lot of those runners who were called out at the plate."

Nig gave Ty a playful little nudge.

"I missed you, too, Ty," he said. "I missed you at least ten times. Times you were called out."

Blood rushed to Cobb's face. He pounced on Nig like an eagle on its prey.

"You bastard!" Cobb roared, shaking him viciously. "You cost me ten runs! Runs I earned! I'm going to kill you!"

It took all Grantland Rice's strength to pull Cobb off Clarke and calm him down. Nig left the room, shaken. Cobb was still fuming an hour later.

Several years later, Cobb played golf at the California Country Club with Lefty O'Doul, manager of the San Francisco Seals, and Torchy Torrance, vice-president of the old Pacific Coast League's Seattle Rainiers. "Cobb was a terror that day," Torchy said. "He charged through two foursomes, insulting everybody and making all the members back in the clubhouse mad because he just wouldn't wait for those ahead of him to play their second shots. He charged right through them, yelling at them to get out of the way so he could finish *his* game."

For thirty-five years, the administrators of baseball felt that their game deserved its very own shrine to house the credentials of the giants of the ball diamond. To pick Cooperstown, New York as the site for the first Baseball Museum, claiming historically that that was the birthplace of baseball and start things off, the Baseball Writers Association of America held a national election among its 226 members in February 1936 and chose five players to be the first of the Hall of Fame. Each man elected had to receive more than 75 per cent of the first ballot. Ty Cobb led with 222 votes, followed by Babe Ruth and Hans Wagner in a tie, with 215, Christy Mathewson with 205, and Walter Johnson with 189. Such great stars as Nat Lajoie (168), Tris Speaker (165), and Cy Young (153) were not elected until 1937.

At the formal dedication at the Baseball Hall of Fame, in July 1936, Cobb traveled all the way from Menlo Park. His son Howell, seventeen, and daughter Beverly, nineteen, accompanied him. Another of his daughters, Shirley, stayed at home in California. She once confessed that she knew very little about her famous father's baseball career until one day when she went to work and pasted up his scrapbook.

Ty was the man of the hour at Cooperstown. Old rivals and

former teammates rushed to congratulate him. There was moisture in Ty's eye as he hugged Connie Mack. He was besieged by autograph hunters. As Larry Lajoie signed his name for a young fan, he pointed across the room at Cobb and said, "Now, son, go over there and get the champ."

In a news conference following the dedication ceremony, Connie Mack reiterated his admiration for Cobb. "Ty Cobb," he said, "could do more to upset a pitcher and a whole team than any player I ever saw. He could upset a crowd, too. Our crowds in Philadelphia were often very hostile to him, but it didn't deter or discourage him. Deep down, I know our fans admired him tremendously, as we all did, and it was a thrill to hear the great standing ovation Philadelphia fans gave him when he walked onto the field in one of our uniforms for the first time."

Following the Hall of Fame inauguration, Cobb and Walter Johnson took the long train ride together back down to New York City. They talked about the good old days.

"Shucks, Walter, I wasn't much of a hitter when I first broke in," Ty said.

"That's when I should have known you," Walter said.

"I never hit much against you," Ty said. "I had to resort to tricks to get on base."

"I'll admit you never hit me hard at first, but once you caught on to me you never let go," Walter said. "I can't complain, though. I wasn't the only pitcher you abused."

"Walter," Ty said, "I never abused you or anybody else. I just figured a way to get a base hit off you once in a while. But, as I was saying, I wasn't much of a hitter when I was a kid. For one reason, I played with boys older and bigger and stronger than I was, and I had to use their bats and they were too heavy for me. I had to learn to swing them and I finally did. People have asked me many times where I got that unusual grip that I used, with my hands about five or six inches apart. Here, let me show you."

Ty looked to the far end of the club car, forming an analogy in his mind.

"Look," he said, finally. "If you had a long pole and you wanted to touch that end of the club car with it, how do you think you could manage it best? By holding it away down on the end with both hands? Or by putting one hand down here and the other up here to give you better leverage? Well, that's what I did with a bat. Then I could get it around on a ball. Once I was able to do that, I might have been a good hitter right away, but I wasn't."

Through the years, just about everyone with whom Cobb came in contact saw him in a different light. Some, such as Mickey Cochrane and Ernie Lanigan, worshiped him. Hendrik Van Loon admitted once that a sliding demonstration by Ty in his living room was as uplifting a show as the best Russian ballet he ever saw. Knute Rockne said that every time he looked at Cobb he visualized him in football pads, a "swivel-hipped All-American halfback." It was never wise to speak disparagingly of Cobb *anywhere*, because the odds were that there would be within earshot some burly character who had been the recipient of Ty's spiritual or monetary benevolence. Others, who never happened to bump into the finer side of the man, blanched at the mention of his name.

In the summer of 1940, during a visit to New York, Ty dropped in on Babe Ruth at his home on Riverside Drive and challenged him to a series of golf matches. Babe had ballooned up to 240 pounds and looked like Humpty Dumpty on matchsticks. His massive girth filled a big easy chair, and he liked to sit with his feet parked on an ornamental beer keg from Jake Ruppert's brewery. Ty and Babe drank from oversized tumblers, and Claire Ruth, Babe's wife, kept them steadily refilled. Puffing on a big cigar and sipping his scotch, Babe suggested a best-of-three series with the proceeds going to charity. The sportswriters tackled the story with gusto and ballyhooed it as a battle between baseball's two greatest stars. The first match was set for Boston, the second for Long Island, and the third, if necessary, for Detroit. Bette Davis, the screen actress, would present a trophy to the winner.

After splitting the first two, they stopped in Cleveland and then took the boat to Detroit. On the way over, Babe was all smiling confidence, and he killed a good part of a quart of scotch. Cobb kept sober. The next day was steaming hot, causing the Babe to sweat ferociously, and Ty won the final match.

In 1947, when the Dodgers went against the Yankees in the World Series, Cobb was invited by the American League to be a guest at the games. On opening day, he stood beside Babe Ruth near home plate while the photographers took their picture. The Babe stared out at right field. Ty noticed that he had tears in his eyes. If Cobb felt anything that day, it didn't show on his face. But what he was thinking was, "I bet I could still get out there right now and show these young punks a thing or two." And he probably could.

During the Series, Cobb visited the Yankee locker room to talk to his old friend, Joe DiMaggio. Joe was sitting in front of his locker when Ty came in. Ty asked him what he usually did right after a ball game.

"What else?" Joe said, looking up at Cobb a little surprised. "I take a shower, get dressed, and go back to my hotel."

Ty looked at Joe in a sort of anguished astonishment.

"Just like that," Ty said. "You take a shower, you dress, and then you go down to the hotel."

Joe laughed.

"Sure, Ty," he said. "Then I have dinner."

"You should have said that in the first place," Ty said. "In other words, you run into the shower, run out, get dressed, run down to the hotel and have dinner. Is that about it?"

"Yes," DiMaggio said. "There's nothing to do around here after the game and I'm hungry. What's wrong with that?"

"Just this," Ty said, with a gusty, mortified sigh. "A ballplayer is on the field only so many hours. He spends most of his time away from the field. Those are the hours in which he stays healthy—or he doesn't. Don't get me wrong. I'm not preaching. I'm only telling you. Joe, because you play ball every day, you don't realize the strain it puts on your nervous system. If you don't check it, it can take years off your life as a big league player. All the things I'm telling you I had to learn the hard way, such as what to do after a game.

"When you come into the clubhouse after playing, you're all sweated up. Sit down—in your uniform. Sit down and have a can of beer if you want to. Let the other fellows run into the shower. Let them take as long as they please. No matter how long they take—and they won't take long—there will always be plenty of soap and water left. Then you take your shower. Afterward, sit down or lie down and cool out. Then get dressed and go down to your hotel. But don't go to the dining room. Go to your own room. Read the papers or listen to the radio or look out the window for an hour or so. By that time, your stomach is ready for food. Keep doing this and you won't suffer from colds or nervous indigestion."

Cobb always had a special place in his heart for DiMaggio. He considered him a great ballplayer. Joe could run, hit, throw, and field, and if it hadn't been for injuries there is no telling how much greater his career would have been. "But how can you put Joe or any other modern outfielder alongside Tris Speaker, Joe Jackson, or Babe Ruth?" Ty asked. "If DiMaggio had kept moderately active during the off-season by fishing and hunting or working out in the gym at least once a week, he wouldn't have been troubled by bad knees or a sore heel. He would have been in shape for spring training, that time of the year when he often injured himself. But he lounged around too much, permitted himself to get fat, and when he showed up in camp in March he had to train extra hard. His muscles and bones were not yet in shape. They were susceptible to injury.

"I agree with the consensus that DiMaggio was probably the most natural ballplayer in history. He had everything—speed, grace, agility, a good eye, long and strong arm muscles. But Joe will never know how great he might have been. He will never know how many more years he might have played, if he had kept himself in shape during the winter months."

Cobb's personal life fell apart in 1947. After thirty-nine years of marriage, his wife, Charlotte, divorced him. Ty was embittered. He accused her of alienating their children from him. Details of how much the divorce settlement cost him were not revealed.

The breakup of his marriage was yet another blow to the fragile dignity of this roistering old man. He yearned for respect, but just when he seemed likely to achieve it he would get into a fight or commit some other egregious indiscretion.

Cobb was entertaining friends one evening at his Atherton home. The guest list included some very prominent physicians, attorneys, businessmen, and their wives. At dinner, Cobb, who had been drinking heavily, sat at the head of the table, growing more foul with each drink. One of the ladies said something he did not like, and Cobb retaliated by calling her an "old whore." The lady started to cry. Her husband demanded an apology. "Take that back, Cobb, or I'm going to bash you!" Cobb stood up and, swaying on his feet, eyes blazing, worked his way around the table toward the man as if to throw a punch. The man, a giant of a fellow, seized a chair and smashed it over Cobb's head, opening an ugly cut on his scalp and sending him crashing to the floor. Cobb lay there, not moving. Blood oozed out of the wound and down the side of his face.

"You've killed him," somebody whispered.

"We'd better call the police."

A call was made to the local station house to report the incident. The desk sergeant wanted to know what the trouble was.

"I think I've just killed a man," he was told.

"What's his name?"

"Ty Cobb."

The sergeant began to laugh.

"What's so funny?"

"It's about time someone killed that old sonofabitch," the sergeant said, and hung up.

When Cobb revived, all his guests had gone home.

Cobb had a vocabulary all his own. To "salivate" something meant to destroy it. Anything easy was "soft-boiled," to out-smart someone was to "slip him the oskafagus," and all doctors were "truss-fixers." People who displeased him—and this included just about the whole universe—were "fee-simple sonsofbitches," "mugwumps," or (if female) "lousy slits."

In 1949 he remarried. His second wife was Frances Cass, the daughter of Dr. John Fairbairn, a prominent Buffalo specialist and long-time friend of Cobb's. The couple divided their lives between Atherton, California, and Lake Tahoe, Nevada, where Ty had an isolated ten-room, $75,000 lodge at the end of a steep 21-mile, 7,000-foot passage from Carson City. His winter residence at Atherton, 250 miles away, was an eighteen-room, two-story, richly landscaped, $90,000 Spanish-California mansion at 48 Spencer Lane, an exclusive neighborhood. You could have held a ball game on the grounds, they were so expansive.

Cobb kept up his interest in baseball. He wrote long letters to George Weiss, by this time the general manager of the New York Yankees, offering advice on young ballplayers, on making trades, and on dealing with rookies, and sizing up the Yankee pennant prospects. Young ballplayers often came to him for tips. Sometimes he went to them. One day before a game between the Yankees and the Red Sox in New York, a mutual friend introduced Ty to Ted Williams. Ted's eyes brightened at the sight of Cobb, and he said warmly, "Hello, Ty, I've been wanting to ask you a question for a long time."

"Is that so?" Ty said.

"Yes," Ted said. "How do you hit to left field?"

Cobb told Williams it was only a guess, but he went on to explain how he would hit to left if he were Ted Williams. Ted seemed to appreciate the advice.

Ty didn't know why or how, but in one of the New York newspapers the next morning there was a two-column story reporting, in effect, that Williams thumbed his nose at the little lesson Cobb had given him. "Oh, Cobb!" Ted was quoted as saying. "What does he know about it?" The truth was, Williams had said absolutely nothing. He had been very attentive, to be perfectly factual. Cobb was hurt by the article. "So was Ted," Ty said later. "How can a responsible publication print such lies?" He had always admired Ted's great skill and believed in him. "I know he wouldn't say anything for publication to put me in a bad light," Cobb said.

In 1951 Cobb spent three weeks as a guest instructor at the Ozark Baseball Camp, held in the midst of a state park in Missouri's southern Ozarks. He was then sixty-five, a somewhat mellow and tired old man, and from the first moment he was introduced to all the kids, he became a wise grandfather to them all. "Mr. Cobb is tired, now, so don't bother him with too many questions," the students were told privately after the formal introduction.

One of the teenagers was Paul Hemphill, now the fine columnist for *Sport* magazine. From what Hemphill had read about him, Cobb had once been hell on wheels, but now he was only a sports legend turned out to pasture. "The old man seemed to sincerely enjoy hanging around us kids each night at dusk, sitting on the steps to the dining hall and regaling us with stories about the beanball fights and the sharpening of spikes and the other vendettas which had punctuated his career," Hemphill recalled.

His most singular memory of that Ozark Baseball Camp occurred toward the end of the second week. The youngsters had played an intrasquad game and then, at dusk, were going off to their cottages to clean up for dinner. Shyly, young Hemphill approached Cobb as he walked across the infield, and Paul worked up the courage to ask him about sliding.

"How do *you* do it?" Cobb asked.

There were only the two of them, and Paul tried an impromptu hook slide into third base. Ty told him to stand aside.

"This used to work pretty good for me," he said.

Suddenly there he was, at sixty-five, wearing khaki work trousers and sneakers and a white Ozark Baseball Camp T-shirt, backing up and making a quick 10-foot run and viciously tearing into the bag with a sharp *whump*. Paul had a lot of books with old pictures of Cobb in his prime, but the thing he remembered most about him was the brief flicker of greed and hatred in his eyes at that moment when he triumphantly sat sprawled in the Ozark dust—*safe at third*—trying to recapture the good old days before it was too late.

A year later, Cobb traveled up to the State of Washington for some sport fishing. While he was there he attended a Pacific Coast League ball game at Sick's Stadium as a guest of the Seattle Rainiers. Before the game, Ty went down to the Seattle dugout to sey hello to the ballplayers and watch them finish batting practice. Suddenly, someone inside the cage turned to Ty and shouted, "Hey, Ty, wanna hit some?"

"No chance," Ty called back.

"Com'on, Ty, get a bat," a chorus of players urged.

Everybody waited silently. Then Cobb, sixty-six, walked slowly into the batting cage and took the bat from the batter. He took his position at the plate and settled in the classic Cobb stance. He held the bat with hands spread about five inches apart, his feet spread comfortably, and, when he took a cut at the first pitch, there was still that smooth follow-through, the blurred bat whipping all the way around. He connected solidly with five pitches in a row. Whang! Sock! Bing! Whump! Whack! He just met the ball easily, smashing it squarely on the nose. The crowd greeted the impromptu exhibition with loud applause. It was a rare treat. No one enjoyed that brief moment more than Cobb himself.

Later that summer, Ty traveled to New York on some business. Harry Grayson and I took him over to Ebbets Field to watch a game between the Giants and Dodgers. We rode in a cab across the bridge to Brooklyn and weren't in the ball park twenty minutes before Cobb was down in the right-field bullpen volunteering advice to one of the Dodger catchers.

"Son, let me give you a little tip," Ty told him. "After you give the pitcher the sign, reach down and grab a handful of dirt, as if you're drying off the sweat. Now, just before the ball gets to the plate, drop the dirt on the batter's feet. Get the picture? It'll distract him just enough to make him flinch and take his eye off the ball."

Harry Grayson and I stood at the side, watching the lesson.

"Look at the old devil," Harry whispered. "Nearly sixty-seven years old—and still showing ballplayers how to cheat!"

After Cobb left town, I talked to Bucky Harris about him. The former Boy Wonder Manager of the Washington Senators was by this time managing Detroit, and the Tigers were in New York to play the Yankees. While the Tigers took batting practice, we sat in the Detroit dressing room under Yankee Stadium and pushed back the years.

"Cobb made a believer out of me," Bucky said. "He was terrific. Once he got to first base, he was always dangerous, a constant threat. If his legs were slowing up, his headwork wasn't. He was still the best slider in baseball. Oldtimers who played against him when he was at his peak told me that he worked twice as hard as anyone else on the Tigers. He never loafed. His energy was fantastic. He was a polished ballplayer most of his career. He was master of almost every facet of play. If you gave him half a chance he was certain to outguess you. Mentally, he was always a jump ahead of you. George McBride, who managed the Senators in 1921, told me to keep my eyes on Cobb if I wanted to learn something about baseball. I was still pretty wet behind the ears, and McBride said, 'Bucky, watch

Cobb run the bases and pick up some tricks. He has a variety of slides, get them down pat. Copy him. He'll show you what fight and spirit can do when it's mixed with natural talent.' McBride was right, of course. He had been a star shortstop in the American League when Cobb stole all those bases. He knew what he was talking about."

In the spring of 1955 Cobb invited me to his lodge at Lake Tahoe to discuss a book collaboration with him. Close friends had been urging him to write his life story to set the record straight. "I might say that I have reserved quite a few matters pertaining to my early life and later which no one knows about," wrote Ty in a letter to me. "There are many things that should be corrected. For many years, now, book publishers and motion picture companies have hounded me with lavish offers to do my story. I have shunned the picture people because I know enough, dumb as I am, that if they filmed my life, the first thing they would want would be for the actor playing my part to jump just as hard as he could with flying spikes in some infielder's face. I solemnly say to you, such as this never happened."

The meeting was arranged and I flew out from New York to Reno a month later. Ty was at the airport to meet my plane, and for the next several weeks we talked. The rest of the time I followed him around unobtrusively while observing him in revealing situations, noting his reactions and the reactions of others to him. My aim was to absorb the whole scene, to capture the private Cobb, his dialogue and moods, the tension, drama, conflict, and then to jot it down in a diary for future reference. In this way I kept a personal daily log on him. Because he guarded his privacy so intensely, I seldom took notes in his presence. Often when he saw a pencil clutched in my hand he'd admonish me: "There will be no talk till you get rid of that pencil—this is *off* the record." Other times he would say, "Put this down in your notebook." Thus he was a very unpredictable subject. When he was sober, he could be a very charming host; when drinking, there was the devil to pay. Unfortunately he drank most of the time.

Cobb kept a memorandum booklet, which he called his private sonofabitch book. It was filled with names of people he didn't like, and he was forever adding to the list. Once, in a bar in Carson City, a fellow Ty knew passed him and did not speak. Ty made a note of this seeming snub, and the man's name went into the sonofabitch book. After that, if ever the opportunity arose for Ty to take a crack at that guy, he took it. Ty grew cantankerous when drinking and held cosmic grudges.

High on Cobb's sonofabitch list were most New York sportswriters; Hub Leonard, who in 1926 had accused Ty and Tris Speaker of "fixing" that Tiger-Cleveland game in '19; Ban Johnson, the old American League president long dead; the late John J. McGraw; feisty Leo Durocher, whom Cobb couldn't intimidate; and all those people who intimated that Cobb ever used his gleaming spikes on another player. Cobb seldom got through a single day without adding a new name to his private S.O.B. book. Eleanor Roosevelt was on the list, too, for purely personal reasons, and so was his butcher, telephone company, his first wife, the Democrats, certain doctors and judges, and a coin machine that wouldn't return his nickel.

Tears slid down Ty's face one day as we sat alone on the sunporch of his lodge and talked about his boyhood. That was a strange sight, because the image I had of him was of a taciturn and hardened man. "The Cobbs cry easy," he said. It was the first time I ever asked him a direct question about the mysterious death of his father, and the silent bitterness he still held against his mother after all those years showed through. "My father had his head blown off with a shotgun when I was only 18 years old—*and by my own mother*," he said. "But I've never talked about it, because the sobsisters would have a picnic at my expense if they knew." He quickly changed the subject, but I had to wonder if this lonely and emotional man, who could be so gentle and compassionate, and yet who could battle with his fists with a ferocity which was frightening, might now have wept many times in the secret hours of night.

Many times, during his baseball career, Cobb had been quoted as saying that "my children mean everything to me." Their names were Ty, Jr., Herschel, Shirley, Beverly, and Howell. None of the boys played baseball. As a matter of fact, Ty, Jr., *despised* baseball, but he loved tennis. Ty, Sr., managed to overlook this sacrilege, however, when Ty, Jr., settled down and graduated from medical school, after flunking out of several Ivy League schools. He was practicing medicine when he was cut down by a brain tumor in the early 1950s.

Cobb was in a particularly quiet mood as he talked about those private matters he held so dear. Lake Tahoe served as the perfect retreat for him. "This is the only place where I can relax," he said. "I do my deepest thinking up here. I used to feel this way about California, but that's all gone now. The drifters have ruined California. They come in waves from the anemic farm-lands of the South and the slums of the East, looking for jobs and fresh air and room for their children to grow. Yet their very presence is destroying what they seek, replacing it with noxious fumes and bungalow ghettos."

Ty's lodge sat hidden among tall pines overlooking Lake Tahoe, like a scene in a Technicolor movie. The snowy peaks and catwalk ridges of the Sierra Mountains accentuated its rugged beauty. When the sun started to dip in the West, causing magic colors to fade to pale blue, Ty watched quietly. "There is some-thing fascinating about sunsets," he said. "Each one is different. Each is magic. Each makes a beautiful climax to the bustle and hustle of the day. The whole world seems to sink to rest."

The far-off, forlorn quaver of a bullfrog echoed his sentiments.

On the subject of baseball, he had some very definite opinions. "Baseball today is putrid," he said, "and you can blame it on the lively ball and the home run. There are too many lopsided scores. What's happened to those grand old one-run, last-inning finishes? Only the other day Brooklyn and the Phillies played a 16–2 game that took 3 hours 50 minutes. In May, 1920, the Dodgers and Boston went twenty-six innings to a 1–1 tie that was stopped by darkness—and the whole thing took only 3:50, and Joe Oeschger and Leon Cadore pitched all the way. I think most fans would have preferred the 1–1 marathon to the 16–2 slaughter."

Ty had little respect for modern managers. He said they were a lot of bunk.

"They've destroyed the players' initiative," he said. "A batter ought to have more freedom up there at the plate. Ask any player today. He'll tell you how confusing it is to be so tightly controlled from the coaching line or the bench. They've turned players into robots. They tell 'em what to hit, when to hit. Some balls come over the plate big as a balloon but the hitter is ordered to lay off of them. How about belting a few of those cripples? It'd be interesting to know what would happen if a player was free to hit on his own. Kids don't learn the fundamentals anymore. Most of them don't practice. They don't even train. I can't think of one player in the majors today who is a first-class baserunner. Nor of any pitchers and catchers who know how to stop a good baserunner. Science is out the window. Baseball has degenerated into a slugging match."

It was a theme I heard Cobb repeat over and over again.

During the time I was a guest at his lodge, Ty continued to rise early each morning to phone his stockbrokers in San Francisco and New York and wrestle with the stock averages. With a mind that read behind the fluctuations of a dozen different issues, he made money consistently. He admitted to me one day that, during the few weeks I lived with him, he made $375,000 on his investments.

An example of how his financial mind worked can be shown in the following anecdote. One day while staying with Ty I got a call from a woman friend in New York. She was an associate producer of the long-running television show, "What's My Line?" Would Ty be willing to appear as the Mystery Guest on the program? She asked me to talk to him.

"We'll pay him $350," she volunteered.

I passed this information along to Cobb, provoking a snort.

"What's the top fee they pay?" he wanted to know.

"She says $750 tops," I said.

Cobb was plaintly irritated. "Then I want $750," he snapped.

I passed the information along to the woman caller.

"I'll have to talk to my boss," she said, nervously.

She called back from New York fifteen minutes later.

"Okay," she said, "tell Mr. Cobb he can have it."

By now, Ty's wheels had been turning. There were dollar signs in his eyes. He had changed his mind again. The ante had just gone up.

"I know what I'm worth," he growled. "The price has just doubled. I want $1,500. I don't want a penny less."

Cobb was a hot item at the time. He had a magazine series (fee, $25,000) running in *Life,* and it was attracting lots of national attention in the press. All the major TV and radio talk shows were after him. He knew he could command the top buck.

Though the whole sequence would have kept him on "What's My Line?" for only about six or seven minutes, Ty said it was worth a fee of $1,500.

"They didn't pay that much even to Marilyn Monroe when she was on," I told him.

"I know I don't look as good in a bathing suit as Monroe," Cobb said. "But, then, she didn't hit .367, either."

"And you don't have a 40-inch bust," I quipped.

The producers back in New York said $1,500 was too much. But a few days later they phoned Ty back. He got his $1,500, which he promptly turned over to his pet project, the Ty Cobb Educational Foundation.

"Well," he said to me as he hung up the phone, "I won that round."

Some writers called Cobb "the world's champion pinchpenny."

He averaged 150 fan letters each month, requesting his autograph. Many of them enclosed return-mail stamps. Cobb used the stamps for his own outgoing mail. The fan letters he burned. "Saves on firewood," he'd mutter. In my own dealings with him, he often phoned me coast-to-coast, *collect.* If he couldn't reach me on the phone, he telegraphed—*collect.* One day when he reversed the charges, I said to him, "What's the matter, Ty, are you down to your last $10-million dollars?" He didn't think it was funny. He swore at me and hung up.

Over the years Ty's wealth was the subject of much conversation and conjecture. He was called "the world's richest baseball player." In a particularly candid mood one day, he frankly told me that his personal fortune was worth between $6 million and $10 million. "But I'm not telling you exactly how much," he quickly added. "Only I know—and I'm keeping it to myself." (I learned later that he fought off calling in his attorneys and drafting his last will and testament until just before he died.)

Although branded a skinflint by his enemies, there were contradictions that embellished the Cobb legend. He built and endowed a first-class hospital in the name of his parents in Royston. When his spinster sister, Florence, was crippled, he tenderly cared for her until her last days. The widow of a one-time American League batting champion would have lived in want but for Cobb's steady monetary support. A Hall of Fame member beaned by a pitched ball and enfeebled came under Cobb's wing for years; and regularly he mailed dozens of anonymous checks to indigent old ballplayers, relayed by a third party—a rare act among retired tycoons in other lines of business. While money was his idol, from his multimillion dollar fortune he assigned large sums to create the Cobb Educational Foundation, which financed hundreds of needy Georgia youngsters through college. His father was the inspiration of the Foundation.

"My original idea," Cobb said, "was the Lincolnesque characters, boys and girls out of the fields and the mountains, boys and girls who otherwise would not have the opportunity of college."

Ty set demanding standards for applicants. All beneficiaries of the fund had somehow to get through their freshman year of college to prove their devotion to education before they could qualify.

At the time he discussed his foundation with me, thirty-one students in Georgia colleges were drawing aid from it. Only one student had ever been dropped. She got married. The foundation frowned on any such distracting influences.

"We want stars," Cobb said. "We want stars in medicine, in law, in teaching, and in life. We want to be identified with their success. Here, let me show you some of my students."

He went to a closet in his study and came back with a stack of index-file jackets. He picked his way through them and singled out some with pride. There was a boy from Blairsville, Georgia, who was "bound to become famous"; another boy who had already fought his way to Johns Hopkins University.

"I like young people who are willing to fight for their education," Ty said, gritting his teeth and clenching his fist.

Then there was the son of a house painter's widow from McRae, Georgia; a disfigured boy, only four-feet-eight, who overcame his handicap; and a boy who worked on a farm all summer to be able to go to college.

"The Lincolnesque characters," Cobb repeated, "out of the fields and the mountains."

Earlier that year a number of the Cobb scholarship students were invited to meet Ty at a session of the foundation board in Atlanta. Seven of them showed up, well scrubbed and barbered and in their Sunday best. They lined up to meet Cobb. The first student shook Ty's hand and began to express his appreciation.

"Mr. Cobb," the awed boy said, "I just want to thank you . . ."

The boy could go no farther. He broke into tears. Ty himself broke into tears and hugged the boy. Then the six other students broke into tears, and there wasn't a dry eye among the board members, either. No planned ceremony of appreciation could have so soulfully rewarded Ty Cobb, himself a country boy.

"For the past five years," Cobb said, returning the files to the closet and closing the door, "every fee I have made for public appearances and testimonials has been put into the Cobb Foundation. I tell them, 'I'll come, but it will cost you. I'm not worth it, but I will charge you what you are paying the others, the check to be made out to the Cobb Educational Foundation.' What I want to do is get into my car and drive around to the colleges and meet them, see them at their work, show them that I am personally interested in them.

"These young people have filled to some extent a void in my own life. In April, 1951, my son Herschel, a Coca-Cola distributor in Santa Maria, California, died suddenly of a heart attack at thirty-three. In September, 1952, Tyrus Junior died at the age of forty-two of a brain tumor. Tyrus was a practicing physician in the little town of Dublin, Georgia, and had become the doctor in my life. If I had been a doctor I could have had the companionship of my son. I could have been the beacon that pointed him the way. We could have grown up together in our profession. But I was a ballplayer, and my sons had no inclination toward baseball."

The Cobb personality was filled with contradictions. While on the one hand he could be ultra-conservative with his nickels and dimes, he often was a high-roller at the Nevada dice tables. At the Riverside Hotel casino in Carson City one night he won $12,000 in three hours. In another spree, he pocketed more than

$3,000 at the dice tables. A scientific craps player who had won and lost huge sums in Nevada over the years, he often bet $100 chips, his eyes constantly alert, not missing a play around the board. If he decided that a table was "cold" he would move to another casino down the street, then another and another. Sometimes he would play all night.

"Gambling is the roughest business in the world," he told me, "and to survive you must establish your own rules and then live by them. Work out your own limits, know the rules, and never overextend. The trick is to recognize that luck is a tremendous factor. You need luck to beat those house odds. Over the long run, those odds are going to beat you. Bet modestly. Use the thing for entertainment. When you're winning, for god's sake don't press. Winning can make for a helluva good time. Have the good time, remember the odds, and walk away. The plain fact is that to play against the house odds long enough is to be a loser," he said. "All odds in every game favor the house. The trick is to remember to leave the game before you've lost too much."

One evening Ty felt I should see a casino. "You can't go back to New York without seeing one of our casinos," he said. His lodge was only a mile from the nearest gambling house. Ty offered to drive me.

When we arrived, he didn't get out of the car. He told me to go in alone.

"Aren't you coming?" I asked.

"No," he said, "it wouldn't look right. What would the kids of America think if they knew that a member of the Baseball Hall of Fame was frequenting such a place? It's my duty to protect the good name of baseball."

I thought of that moment several years later when reading in the paper that Ty Cobb had been tossed out of a Reno Club for accusing a stickman in a dice game of cheating.

Before I left Ty to return to New York, he asked me to do him a favor. By now he was treating me like a long lost pal. I should explain that a new book of mine, *That Kelly Family,* the authorized story of Princess Grace Kelly and her Philadelphia family, was being published later that summer. Like millions of other movie fans, Ty was smitten by the beauty of Princess Grace.

"Do you think," he asked me, "that you could get Grace to send me an autographed picture? I saw her in *Rear Window*. I sure do admire that girl. I knew her father, Jack, the old sculler, when I played ball in Philadelphia."

I promised Ty I would do what I could for him.

A month after I left him, Ty wrote me the following letter:

Dear John:

Thanks to you, received picture from Grace Kelly, autographed to "the champ," me. Just like her paw—she's a real thoroughbred.

The beautiful lake is still out there and to be here seems to be where I am most happiest. I am planning a trip East; to Atlanta, then New York, and Cooperstown. I'll be stopping at the Ambassador Hotel, or, if I decide to change, at the Ritz Towers. I expect to arrive in New York about 22nd August. Mr. Keating, president of Chevrolet, says I can borrow a car from them in New York to drive to Cooperstown. I'd like you to go with me. You look up the maps and proper route to take. I will be here so drop me a line. I am fine.

As ever,

Ty

I wrote back assuring Ty that I would take care of reserving a double room for us at Cooperstown. I also mentioned that I was seriously thinking about buying a certain stock he told me about while I was with him in Nevada. Within four days, Ty replied:

Dear John:

I hasten to say do not invest in anything I talked to you about. I can see where a young fellow can with study and wisdom make himself independent; I see it, but you would have to learn it and at times restrain yourself and hew to certain lines. I could not help or interest myself in your behalf. I have the urge to have my friends participate in what I feel sure of; I have the desire to share and it makes me feel happy. I have in the past underwritten losses, it's a mistake I suffer.

Now, John, the stock I told you about was a tip I got from a *big man*. I bought 200 shares. I do not like it and am getting out; don't know if I lose or what, but he is a fellow who hasn't the feeling I have (or think I have) for people. You must remember, *I* did not myself advise you to buy this stock. I told you about it but stated you should have your broker look into it for you first.

If I wanted to tell you of some 3 or 4 or more stocks that would take much money to buy, I could have. In the last few days, they have done *so well,* but I could not be your financial adviser and be responsible for you. I do not gain and would not. I think I told you of Coca Cola—well, it has *gone up* again, and still others have made me so much money in one day, it is pitiful. But I could not "tout" you. I can stack the chips up high, but could not see you take the same chances. So please forget anything I told you about investments—your business is your business.

Your friend,

Ty

In late August, Ty traveled to New York as planned and borrowed a car from President Keating of Chevrolet (Ty owned 7,500 shares of stock in the company), and together we left for Cooperstown, New York. On the drive upstate, we were only about an hour from our destination when Ty suddenly asked me to make a right turn off the Thruway, taking us 25 miles out of our way.

"Why are we going this way?" I asked him.

"We need gas," he said.

"But there was a gas station just a mile up the highway from where we turned off," I pointed out.

"I know that," he said, sharply, "but they give *Green Stamps* at the station down this road. I save them!"

We drove down a country road and finally found the station. Ty had stopped there before. While the attendant filled our tank, we got out of the car to buy soft drinks. Cobb, known in the soft-drink trade as "Mr. Coke," automatically bought a bottle of Coca-Cola. The nickel he dropped into the slot would later come back into his own pants pocket by way of the thousands of shares of stock he held in the company. Just to be different I dropped my coin into the 7-Up machine. That was a mistake. All I heard for the rest of the journey to Cooperstown was a tirade against the diversion of the five-cent proceeds that Cobb felt I had personally taken away from him. At first I thought he was kidding. He wasn't. He meant every word of it. Moral to that story: Never drink a 7-Up in the company of a person who owns 20,000 shares of stock in Coca-Cola!

There were no dull moments while we were at Cooperstown. On the first night we were invited to the summer home of a noted Johns Hopkins surgeon, a long-time friend of Cobb's and a native of Georgia. The doctor had been looking forward to showing Ty off to his friends at a private dinner party. When we arrived, several dozen guests of all ages were overcome with excitement upon meeting the old Georgia Peach; few sports figures I have ever known produced such an effect upon people.

During dinner, Ty sat at the head table drinking his meal and answering questions about his baseball career. At first he appeared to be enjoing himself enormously, but as the evening wore on and the Scotch took hold, he grew more and more tipsy, until finally his eyes became sleepy and his head fell on the table. The host came over to me and whispered, "You'd better take him back to the hotel. I don't want my friends seeing the great Ty Cobb this way."

After a good night's sleep, Cobb recovered his poise with the same unbelievable speed he'd shown in baseball. In his heyday, trainers often sewed up deep spike cuts in his knees, shins and thighs on a clubhouse bench, without anesthetic, and he lost few innings. That night, we attended a big banquet hosted by the Baseball Hall of Fame committee. On the way, Cobb advised me to circulate among the other guests and make myself at home. "You won't be able to sit at my table," he said, "because they've set aside a place just for us Hall of Famers. I'll have to be with them."

A cocktail hour preceded the main dinner, and while Cobb touched up old times with Connie Mack, Ed Walsh, Cy Young, Frankie Frisch, George Sisler, Joe DiMaggio, and others, I shared a table with some of the sportswriters from New York.

Later, as the food was being served, I suddenly looked up from my salad plate and found myself staring into the cold, whisky eyes of Cobb. He didn't say anything at first, just stared.

"When I travel all the way up here with a man—and he's my guest—I expect him to sit at *my* table," he said icily. He ignored the other writers with me.

"But you said I'd have to shift for myself—that only the special guests could sit at your table," I reminded him.

The waiter had just placed a plate of roast beef in front of me. Cobb picked it up and dumped it in my lap.

"From now on," he snorted, spitting the words out the side of his mouth, "you are on my sonofabitch list," and he took out a little black book and wrote my name in it. Then he wheeled around and went back to his table. No one at my table spoke, until Harry Grayson grunted, "The old sonofabitch!"

That night, in the bed next to mine, Cobb slept the sleep of the just and innocent. If he had a conscience, I failed to find it. It was not his nature to suffer pangs of remorse.

On the way back down to New York the next day, Cobb was in a reflective mood. "I'm tired," he said. "I'm old and I'm tired. I don't like to say I'm old, but I am. It has been a tough life—twenty-four years of fighting off Nap Lajoie, Joe Jackson, Eddie Collins, Tris Speaker, and Babe Ruth, trying to stay ahead of them. I had to do that year after year. I've used myself up since I was seventeen. I don't believe any player had a tougher time than I did. Now I'm sixty-nine and I'm tired."

Cobb dozed for the next hundred miles as I drove. He awoke only once, and what he said struck me as pure hypocrisy, in view of the record. He was talking about what religion meant to him. "My father always told me to live on the side of right," he said. "He said that when I'm faced with a problem I should try to solve it as if I were kneeling in front of God. Sometimes your decision will be unpopular, but you have nothing to fear if you know you are on His side."

Cobb had convinced himself he lived that way. The hell with what the world wanted to make of it.

He went back to sleep and didn't awaken again until we crossed the George Washington Bridge. I was just starting the car down Riverside Drive to take him back to his room at the Ambassador Hotel in midtown Manhattan, when Cobb suddenly straightened up.

"Slow up—not so fast," he said. He placed his hand on my arm and pointed to the east side of the street. "There it is," he said, and he told me to stop the car. "That's where the Babe lived." He was silent for a moment. His eyes were misty. "The memories I have of that place. What a guy. He was the most natural and unaffected man I ever knew. God, how I miss him."

The very sight of Babe Ruth's old home had a profound effect upon Ty.

"Whenever we'd play in New York," he said, "I'd come up

here after games and sit with Babe and enjoy a drink or two and some small talk. My, how that man loved to eat. He was a physical freak. He defied all the laws of nature. If he'd ever been sawed in half on any given day, I think three-fourths of Stevens's concessions would have been found inside him. Nights, after a ball game, he'd send out for five or six club sandwiches —those huge triple-deckers with all the fixings—and then sit in bed and polish them off before going to sleep. And, yes, between each sandwich he'd puff away on a big, black cigar. I know, because I was with him. I'd love to have seen a daily logbook of his life. No other ballplayer could have done what he did to himself and lasted so long."

As Ty waved me on down the highway, tears welled up in his eyes again.

Before we parted, I asked Ty Cobb one last question. It was a question he had been asked many times before, but he always dodged it.

"Well, what about it, Ty, do you think you were a better ballplayer than Babe?"

"Why pick on Babe and me?" he asked. "Why not ask Connie Mack? Let him be the judge. He has seen all the great ones."

"I'm asking you," I said.

"All right, I will tell you what I think," he said, finally. "Yes —of course—I think I was better than Babe on the ball field. I *know* I was. The record book says so. It shows I was a better all-around player than Babe. I will go along with that."

12

"Where's Baseball?"

In the latter years of his life, spring training time often found Cobb ensconced in a $30-a-day suite at Scottsdale, Arizona, close by the practice parks of the Red Sox, Indians, Giants, and Cubs. There, each March, Cobb held court. He didn't go to see anybody. Commissioner Ford Frick, Ted Williams, Joe Cronin, and other baseball notables came to *him*.

It was no secret that major league owners and league officials hated to see Ty coming, for he thought their product was putrid and he said so, incessantly.

"Ballplayers today hit for ridiculous averages, can't bunt, can't steal, can't hit-and-run, can't place-hit to the opposite field—and you can't call them ballplayers," Cobb droned on. "I blame Frick, Cronin, Bill Harridge, Horace Stoneham, Dan Topping, and all the others for wrecking the game's traditional league lines. Nowadays, any tax-dodging mugwump with a bankroll can buy a franchise, field some semipros, and get away with it. Where's their integrity? Where's *baseball*?"

No one could shut him up. After all, who else had a lifetime batting average of .367, made 4,191 hits, scored 2,244 runs, won twelve batting titles, hit over .400 three times, and stole

892 bases, 96 in one season? Who was first into the Hall of Fame at Cooperstown? Not Babe Ruth, not Honus Wagner, not Walter Johnson, not Christy Mathewson—but Tyrus Raymond Cobb, by a landslide vote. So Cobb held an open forum wherever he went.

We were sitting on the porch of his Nevada lodge one afternoon when Ty got it off his chest.

"You'll recall the two articles I wrote for *Life* magazine recently," Ty began. This was not an angry Cobb, just a Cobb who wanted to set the record straight. "In them I was harshly critical of modern baseball. My remarks stirred up a hornet's nest, as you know. Yet what I said still goes. I blasted these modern ballplayers for their utter disregard for conditioning. I told how some of them refuse to hit to all fields, and I picked Ted Williams as a prime example. Ted has improved since the *Life* articles were published, but that doesn't excuse him for not hitting to left field before.

"I also said that both Ted and Joe DiMaggio possessed great natural ability, and that Phil Rizzuto and Stan Musial are the types who'd have been big stars in any era. With the exception of Hans Wagner, there never has been a greater shortstop than Rizzuto. He is my kind of athlete, always thinking, always beating you. Phil is typical of the shortstops you find on so many championship teams. You'll remember him for the games he's saved rather than for the ones he's *won*. At his peak, how many times did you see him bail a Yankee pitcher out of a tight jam with an impossible stop which started the desperately needed double play? You can't count them. Rizzuto started to slip about two years ago [1954], and the wear and tear are beginning to show now. This will probably be his last year [it was], and it may be more than coincidence that '54 was the year the Yankees lost the pennant."

Ty suddenly reached down and fished a newspaper clipping out of his shirt pocket. His eyes smoldered as he glanced at it.

"This writer quotes me as saying there are no modern ballplayers who would have been stars in my time," Cobb said. "Can't he read right? I never said that. If anyone got that impression from my *Life* stories, I can't help it."

Ty wadded up the clipping into a ball and disgustedly dropped it over the side of the porch.

He said, "As a matter of fact, there have been quite a few modern ballplayers who could have beaten our brains out. The *Life* editors simply didn't give me enough space to name them all. Run down the list. There's been no greater catcher than Roy Campanella, and few better shortstops than Pee Wee Reese, and you can't forget Red Schoendienst, the Cardinals' second baseman. I could also name the Giants' Don Mueller, whose hitting has always impressed me, and Willie Mays. As for Ted Williams, I've always felt he had great hitting ability. It's just too bad he didn't come along in my time. We'd have taught him to hit to all fields—or else. With the stiff measures of discipline we had, Ted would go down as maybe the greatest hitter of all time, despite my .367 lifetime average. As it is, he ranks pretty high on the list. Ted illustrates the modern attitude. When he first came up to the Red Sox from the Pacific Coast League, he really hustled. He hit .406 in his third season (1941). He was *trying* to make good then. But then came fame and fortune, and he obviously began to relax somewhat, as later averages seem to show. His stretch in Korea on those bombing missions quite naturally brought him back a little apprehensive about resuming his baseball career in a flourish. Evidently his age also worried him. So what does he do? He starts hustling as he never hustled before. He's made an enormous comeback. And that proves my point: Ballplayers with the potential, but lacking the natural desire, will never know how great they could have been. As custodians of baseball to keep the true game alive and up to the standards it should be, what are the players doing? Very little. They have the ability but not the honest reverence for our national game. They aren't putting out.

"Imagine three big stars—Ted Williams, DiMaggio and Ralph Kiner—stealing a combined total of only three bases one year [1951]. That's criminal. You prove to me there aren't many times in a season when in the late innings a sacrifice isn't the wisest and most valuable play, or the squeeze play. And yet you seldom see this strategy any more. It isn't right to let baseball deteriorate this way. Batters stand at the plate and practice for their own enjoyment and amusement, swinging from their heels for the bleachers. They are all trying to copy Babe Ruth—but there was only one Babe. Yes, and he'd hit to opposite field, too. And bunt—and beat them out. And, yes, steal, too. We worked harder at baseball. One spring, I remember, we were locked in a tight practice game with the Giants, and one of their players was trapped off second base and didn't maneuver very well in the rundown. So he was tagged out and McGraw was furious. It was only an exhibition game, mind you, and yet at 10 o'clock the next morning McGraw had his entire squad out on the field for special practice. The guy who'd been picked off second ran until his tongue hung out. McGraw was teaching him how to take a lead and how to return safely to the base. Then he showed him how to dance back and forth in the rundown. While he was doing that, he was also polishing up the other players, telling them how to nail a baserunner in a rundown. Everybody was learning something and improving their game. McGraw took advantage of every waking hour. Why, he held practice almost every day at 10 A.M.—only a few hours before the regular ball game. Nowadays? Managers can't even get their prima donnas into uniform much before noon. And if a play goes haywire, the manager says the equivalent of 'naughty, naughty!' and let's it go at that. Ballplayers just don't work at baseball the way we did. So until they revive the zest, the hustle, the inside strategy, and that old driving desire to excel, I have to insist that the game we played was superior to what we see today."

That reminded Ty of an anecdote he heard from Connie Mack. One day the Athletics went to Chicago for a doubleheader with the White Sox and Rube Waddell, that nutsy old character, was picked by Mr. Mack to pitch the first game. The game lasted seventeen innings before Philadelphia scored a run to win it. Waddell, a genuine workhorse, was still in there at the end and struck out fourteen batters along the way. There were no lights, so the managers agreed to limit the second game to five innings. Because Waddell had appeared so strong and relaxed in the seventeenth inning of that first game, Mr. Mack was reluctant to retire his star for the day.

"Rube," Mr. Mack said, "do you think you're strong enough to pitch the second game?"

Waddell felt his arm.

"I can't tell yet, Connie," he said, innocently. "Let me warm up first and see how my arm feels."

Ty said that's what he meant by *dedication*.

Baseball skill relates inversely to age. The older a man gets, the better the ballplayers of his generation were when young. With that in mind, I believe Cobb was too harsh on modern ballplayers. I told him so, and he just glared at me.

"I still think you're too rough on them," I persisted.

Ty had been sharpening a hunting knife on a whetstone. He paused, ran his thumb over the blade edge—then abruptly flung the steel across the room. It stuck into the wood floor at my feet.

"Who the hell asked you?" Ty growled, and the subject was closed.

Later, Joe DiMaggio replied to Cobb's attack on modern baseball. Now, he and Ty were good friends, and Joe, being Joe, never let himself get into a shouting match with the old warhorse. Joe had too much class for that. But he admitted he had some very definite opinions about himself as a ballplayer.

"I think I had the drive and I worked at being a ballplayer every day of my life," Joe said, quietly. "I never let myself get out of shape during the off-season. With me, it was always pride. Ten days of spring training and I was ready to play the schedule. For most of my career, I never thought much about anything else except hitting a baseball or catching one. But since spring training lasted six weeks, I used the time to improve myself. We had a coach with the Yankees by the name of Earle Combs who would give you as much time as you wanted. I'd get Earle to hit ground balls to me in center field just as hard as he could, and then I'd charge them like a shortstop and try to throw a ghost runner out at the plate. Weeks later, when I'd make that same play at Yankee Stadium—cutting down a runner trying to go from second base to home plate on a sharp grounder into center field—people would wonder how I could do it. Combs knew how I did it. I don't think you'd find many young guys now who'd voluntarily put themselves through some of the things I did. But I must admit this: I liked practice. It was never a bore."

In 1955 DiMaggio was elected into the Baseball Hall of Fame. Cobb arranged to be at Cooperstown for the ceremony. He asked me to go with him. Ty flew in from the West Coast, and the next day I picked him up in my car at the Ambassador Hotel, on Park Avenue, and started crosstown toward Riverside

Drive. At Fifty-eighth Street and Sixth Avenue, we stopped for a light. Suddenly a shiny black Cadillac convertible with the top down drove up next to us and stopped, waiting for the light to change. Two men and a woman sat in the front seat. The fellow on the right had his head turned so we could not see his face. It was a hot afternoon and he was in shirt sleeves. Then he turned and gave our car a casual glance. When he saw Ty, his mouth fell open.

"W-w-why . . . hey, Ty!" he cried, leaping out of the car.

Ty had been staring straight ahead, paying no attention. At the mention of his name, he snapped his head around, startled to hear it spoken right there in the middle of a busy midtown Manhattan street. Then he recognized the face.

"Wal, dawgone," Ty drawled. "Joe!"

That's who it was—Joe DiMaggio.

Despite the fact that the light had turned green, Ty Cobb and Joe DiMaggio held a reunion then and there in the middle of the street.

"Where are you headed?" Joe asked.

"To Cooperstown—to see you into the Hall of Fame," Ty said. "Congratulations."

Joe grinned.

"It has been a long climb, Ty," he said. "But I finally made it. I'm proud to be in there with a champ like you."

Watching them, I thought to myself, here's Ty Cobb, the first man to be elected to Baseball's Hall of Fame, bumping into Joe DiMaggio like this—the newest member of the shrine. And both on their way to Cooperstown this very moment. It was, indeed, a very small world.

13

The Curtain Comes Down

There's a wind of airy suspicion
That falls before old fans
And rips a tide of indecision
Not like that of any man's.

There are those who say he's death
And curse his every stride and hit
And leave the flowers to springtime
And claim his fame's unfit.

They say that all of fame is fleeting
And his was luck of sorts
But here's a toast to fearless Cobb
The man who put hell in sports.

—DAVID STIDOLPH

Although the story of Ty Cobb really ended for me the last time I saw him, he lived on for five more years, and perhaps the story of how he lived what time was left to him is the saddest chapter of all.

It is sad that the baseball public remembers him mostly for his violence, his bitterness, and his wild ways. He was one of those to whom had been given the faculty of living much of his life in the spotlight. He had a natural affinity for headlines. Long after I left him, a rash of stories about his troubles continued to make news. There was a court dispute over income taxes with the State of California; a piece in the paper telling how he flattened a heckler with one punch in a San Francisco nightclub brawl; a story announcing he was being sued for assaulting an ex-ballplayer; front-page headlines spotlighting his divorce from his second wife, Frances, who once told me, "When he's drinking, I'm afraid of him. I'm afraid he might kill me." There was a run-in with a traffic cop; another story of how he knocked a prominent business magnate into a fish pond for suggesting Ty had ever been a dirty baserunner; an account of how he took a baseball bat to a member of his own family, breaking her nose; another about how he had to pay $1,500 damages for breaking up a butcher shop, because he hadn't liked the meat he had bought.

There were still other altercations at such places as a Reno gambling casino, a Carson City restaurant, and a Virginia City saloon. Trouble trailed him everywhere. If someone wasn't suing him, he was suing them. His pet litigation was against his gas and electric company at Atherton, claiming he'd been over-charged $16 in his monthly statement. He stubbornly refused to pay the bill and consequently was forced to live by candlelight when the company shut off his power.

Whenever anyone threatened to sue him, he would growl: "Get in line, Bub, there's a hundred others ahead of you." He courted trouble almost gleefully. In Phoenix he threw a salt-shaker at a waiter; in Scottsdale he tried to punt a cabdriver like a football when the man stooped to pick up the fare that Cobb deliberately dropped.

He was desperately ill. Everything that hurts had caught up with him, but still he refused to act like a man on his last legs. He drank heavily. His consumption of whisky averaged a quart a day. He ignored his doctor's warnings and continued to make the rounds of saloons. He carried a loaded Luger wherever he went. One night he fired three shots at a party of drunks outside his motel window for disturbing his sleep. He saw nothing strange in his wild behavior.

"I'm an honorary sheriff of California and a Texas Ranger,

ain't I?" he grunted, as if those titles were the only explanation required.

During the final year of his life, Cobb had grown even more eccentric. Wherever he traveled he carried with him, stuffed into an old brown bag, more than $1 million in stock certificates and negotiable government bonds. The bag never was locked up. Cobb assumed nobody would be foolish enough to rob *him*. He tossed the bag recklessly into any handy corner of a room, inviting theft. In Scottsdale, Arizona, it turned up missing.

Cobb hit the ceiling. He narrowed the suspects to a maid and a cook he'd hired. When questioned, the maid broke into tears and the cook quit. Hours later, the bag was discovered under a pile of dirty laundry.

Cobb fancied himself something of a Sherlock. He was always playing detective, preparing traps. When an epidemic of thefts swept through Lake Tahoe, Ty was concerned. His lodge was furnished with priceless trophies, guns, fishing equipment, and other personal valuables. This called for unique measures. One of his precautions was to hang several bedsheets on a backyard clothesline before leaving the lodge.

"It gives the appearance of freshly-washed laundry drying in the sun," Cobb explained to me. Then, in large, bold letters he printed a note and pinned it to one of the sheets: "JOE—BE BACK IN 15 MINUTES—TY."

"It really works, too," beamed Ty. "The thief comes snooping around here, sees the note, and thinks I'm coming right back. Go into his mind. He knows I wouldn't go away for very long and leave my laundry hanging on the line. I can go away for months at a time knowing my lodge is safe."

It is suspected that Cobb reached the end of his patience long before the final hour approached. His health had slipped rapidly and he grew more irascible. His three living children (two were dead) had long ago withdrawn from him; he could not boast one intimate friend remaining in the wide world. His weight had dropped from 206 to 178, and he suffered from cancer, a leaky heart, aching back, infected bowels, hypertension, and diabetes.

On May 1, 1961, Cobb accepted an invitation to be a house

guest of writer Al Stump at Al's beach house overlooking the ocean at Santa Barbara, California. Cobb was failing fast by this time. He was having trouble getting around, was given to fainting spells, and was taking massive doses of cobalt radiation, the ultimate cancer treatment. He hurt all over. Two doctors had examined him and gave their opinions: Ty had only a few more months to live, no more. The cancer had spread so far that it had infected the bones of his head. The pain was intense and unrelenting, requiring heavy sedation. Yet, with teeth bared and sweat pouring down his face, Ty fought off medical science.

"They'll never get me on their damned hypnotics," he swore to Stump. "I'll never die an addict . . . an idiot."

Stump was sure that Cobb had reached the end of his patience. All the signs pointed to self-destruction. Ty was dangerously close to suicide.

What a sharp contrast with the death scene of Babe Ruth in 1948. When The Babe was dying, his once great, mortal bulk emaciated by cancer also, thousands congregated outside the high walls of the hospital and looked anxiously up at the window of the room where he lay. The newspaper presses lay in wait with pages of obituaries, and editorials announced the impending catastrophe as a national calamity. Even in England, the penny papers watched for the news.

And now it was Cobb's turn to go. Except for Stump, he was all alone. "Do I die a little at a time, or all at once?" he wondered aloud. "I think Max had the right idea." He referred to Max Fleischmann, a wealthy friend who had cheated cancer by putting a revolver to his temple and squeezing the trigger. Then he mentioned Babe Ruth. "If old Babe had known he had cancer, he could've got it over faster, too."

Stump sat next to Cobb's bed for the rest of the night. He was afraid to leave him alone. Tucked inside of Cobb's pants on a nearby chair was the Luger, which he carried with him everywhere. Stump was sure that Cobb would have pulled the trigger on himself that night at the first chance. They talked out the night together and prayed, and finally sleep came.

It was late morning when Al lifted Ty into a car and drove him home to his big, gloomy estate at Atherton. Few words were spoken during the long drive.

One of Cobb's last ambitions was to see an American League team on the Pacific Coast. It finally happened with the formation of the Los Angeles Angels in 1961. Fred Haney was General Manager of the Angels, and when their new spring training tour took them to Phoenix, where Ty had gone for the sunshine, Haney found him in bed, gaunt, emaciated, in terrible pain. But, as sick as he was, Ty said, "Fred, don't worry about me. I'll be in Los Angeles to throw out the first pitch."

"Of course you'll be there," Haney told him. In his heart, though, he knew better.

But when the season opened, Ty was in Los Angeles to help the Angels open at home. He sat in a box near home plate and threw out the first ball—and threw it hard, too. Then he put his hand on Haney's shoulder and said with immense satisfaction, "I told you I'd make it."

"He was able to stick it out for two innings," Fred Haney said. "Those words—'I told you I'd make it'—were the last I ever heard Ty Cobb speak. And in their pride and indomitability was a true reflection of the man."

After that it was all downhill. On June 5, Ty was admitted to Emory University Hospital in Atlanta. In addition to cancer, he was also suffering from diabetes, bursitis, and a back injury sustained in a hunting accident in Idaho. He would not come out alive. Ty knew it. He wanted to die in his native Georgia and be buried with his parents and sister in the family mausoleum he had built for them on a hillside overlooking the Royston cemetery.

Despite his discomfort, Ty remained alert and as ornery as ever. A nurse stood by the foot of his bed, ready to anticipate his every mood. Everything was being done that could be done.

On July 7, Ty took a turn for the worse. On the tenth he was definitely worse. Under the strain of cancer and all his other ailments, his strength had failed steadily, and Ty seemed resigned to death. He offered little resistance now. There was a definite breaking down of the will to live. This was indicated in a gesture he made to Al Stump nine days before the end came. On a photograph of his mausoleum he mailed to Al were scribbled the words: "Any time now."

On the morning of July 17, Ty closed his eyes and dropped

off into a deep sleep. The mantle of death seemed to descend and hang over him. The old spike-scarred legs no longer stirred, and those rasping breaths grew silent. At 1:20 P.M., on July 17, 1961, the great Ty Cobb was dead.

The next day Ralph McGill, publisher of the Atlanta *Constitution,* wrote that for most of Ty's life he was in competition with life, but chiefly with himself. "For the last dozen years he had been trying to go home again," McGill observed. "He could never quite make it, and it angered him that here was something with which he could not come to grips and have it out. Try as he would, Ty Cobb could not find the old dream in the hills of north Georgia where he was born. But he made it at last. He went to sleep for the last time on the sunny afternoon of July 17 just about the time the players of his day would have been taking the field for batting practice. He died in a coma-like sleep. He went home as quietly as if his father had come and taken him in his arms and carried him away."

Now, at last, weary and old and lonely, Tyrus Raymond Cobb had gone home to stay.

One of his final gestures, before lapsing into the coma, was typically Ty Cobb. He opened that old brown paper bag he always carried with him, piled $1-million in negotiable securities on the night table beside his bed—and placed his Luger on top of them.

To the very end, Ty Cobb remained in character.

14

Cobbian Baseball

For such a shrewd realist, Ty Cobb was unusually superstitious. During the days when he was having success at bat, he always walked to the ball park over the same route, wore the same clothes, ate the same food. He always hung his towel on the same peg in the dressing room, believing it brought him luck. When a clubhouse boy absentmindely moved it one day, Ty flew into a rage and threatened to annihilate him. He never allowed a hat to be placed on a bed. This man who hated to be called "lucky" believed in luck.

The Tigers needed all the luck they could get. During the years from 1912 up to the war, the highest they finished in the standings was a second in 1915, after a fourth place finish the year before. They were third in 1916, four games behind the championship Red Sox, and fourth in 1917, a mere 21½ games behind the White Sox.

In the years 1913–18, Cobb was a model of consistency. His batting averages, in order, were .390, .368, .369, .371, .383, and .382.

"When I was streaking for a batting championship, it was always a big strain," Cobb said later. "In 1913, for example, my eyes bothered me and I didn't expect to finish first. But I got hot in the final weeks and finished on top with .390. My wife was the only member of my family who felt I could do it. She insisted all the way that I'd win the title. I lost twenty pounds that season."

Baseball was still in the Cobbian era, with its tight-to-the-vest strategy, tight pitching, tight fielding, and slick strategic concepts. Teams still played for one run at a time. This was "inside" baseball, where the steal, the squeeze bunt, the sacrifice, the place-hitting, and other deft manipulations were designed to break through rigid defenses. It was defensive baseball in its ultimate form. Cobb, of course, was the leading exponent.

No game in the world was as dramatically neat as when the Tigers were a run behind and Cobb was on first. Baseball suddenly took on a new meaning. It was now as full of surprises as a mystery play. The plot and its ending may have been perfectly apparent up to the ninth inning and the last man at bat, and then with stunning suddenness it would change entirely and go on to a new ending, as Cobb circled the bases on a puny dribbler by the batter.

"Full speed ahead!" was the Cobb motto as he raced for the extra base. He frequently went from first to third on an infield out. It sounds unbelievable, but in 1915 against the Athletics he scored all the way from first on an *infield out*. Impossible? It is in the records. The next day, manager Connie Mack called his players together to review their signals. He turned to Wally Schang, his spunky catcher, and said, "Now, Wally, suppose Cobb was on second and you knew he was going down to third on the next pitch. What would you do?"

Schang brightened.

"Why, Mr. Mack," he said, "I'd fake a throw to third, hold the ball, and tag the sonofabitch when he came into the plate."

Cobb often did things that appeared utterly foolish to the untutored eye. He had a reason for every move he made, though. Many times he stretched singles into doubles, figuring it out this way: He knew precisely how long it took him to run two bases. There seldom was any variation, not more than half a step. On a hit to center, right, or left field, he estimated that any of six possibilities existed: The fielder might fumble the ball as it took a wild bounce; it might slip from his grasp as he went to throw; he might make a bad throw; he might make a perfect throw that took a bad bounce; he might make a perfect throw that the second baseman dropped; the second baseman might make a perfect catch of a perfect throw and the baserunner still could escape the tag.

Ty constantly planned ahead. When the Tigers led, 7–1, and the victory no longer was in doubt, Ty did what he called "establishing a threat." He figured that with a six-run lead and the Tiger pitcher going well, one out, more or less, was not going to fracture the Tigers. He could afford to be thrown out. In the back of his mind, Cobb knew that on a hit to the outfield he usually got about halfway down to second before pulling up. He could get back to first base before the ball, because experience taught him that the outfielder almost always threw to second. Cobb's point was that the fielders were on the defensive. The runner was the attacker. If the runner had any speed at all, all that hindered him from advancing to second was the remote chance of stumbling over the bag or on the base lines. "But the runner still has those six chances to make it safely to second," Cobb said.

He activated his theory and let himself be thrown out a few times when Detroit had a big lead. The damage was done. He had already established a threat in the minds of the fielders. They had watched him race for second and miss by the narrowest of margins. Now in a close game, a few weeks later, Cobb would once more attempt to stretch a single into a double—only this time the fielder would tighten up and hurry his throw ahead of Ty. One of the six mischances usually happened, and he was safe.

"But the play wasn't made then and there," Cobb said. "It was really made weeks before when I tried to stretch a base hit into a double and was thrown out."

On the field, it always seemed to fans as though Cobb's daring, slam-bang slides gave him deep, physical pleasure. They didn't. They could not have, particularly early in a season, when his hips were covered with raw sliding sores. But he learned to hit that dirt as though he loved it. By midseason, when his hide had toughened up, he was thankful that he had forced himself to take the punishment earlier in the season.

Another Cobb trick was to watch a baseman's eyes. He always

made up his mind on which side of the bag to slide by glancing at those eyes. Once he had made his decision, he never changed it. "Too many baserunners have been injured because they changed their minds at the last instant trying to decide which side of the base to hit," Cobb said. "The runner is likely to sprain an ankle or break a leg. I always stuck to my original decision and never suffered worse than some gooseberries or a minor spike wound."

Cobb felt he sometimes was given undeserved credit for his feats. He would get an extra base on a bobble or a wild throw and . . . well, everybody was very kind to him, he said. "That Cobb," they would say. "What a hair-trigger mind he has. He has only a split-second to think but he always knows what to do. And that speed!"

Cobb claimed it wasn't split-second thinking at all. It might have looked that way, but what he did at the moment actually was planned weeks before. He told himself that if such-and-such happened he would do one thing, and if the other thing happened, he would do something else. Speed? Sure, he could run. His best time in the hundred-yard dash was 10.1 seconds, but there were other American League players faster than Ty. He said he looked faster than he really was because he got a good jump. He told Mickey Cochrane, the great catcher, that once he got a jump on the pitcher not even the greatest of catchers could throw him out at second, regardless of how strong and accurate his arm was.

Early in Cochrane's career he was catching for the Athletics against Detroit, and as Cobb came up to bat he nodded to Mickey and said, "Mick, the hit and run is on. I'm hitting the first pitch." Cochrane could not believe his ears. There was the great Ty Cobb tipping him off. He was sure Ty was only kidding. But playing it safe, Mickey signaled for a pitchout. That still did not stop Cobb. He reached across the plate and stroked the ball into center field for a base hit. Mickey took off his mask, stepped in front of the plate, and gave Ty a deep bow. Ty stood on first base laughing back at Mickey. Cochrane turned to the umpire and said, "That Cobb isn't even human."

Mickey Cochrane said it was almost impossible to stop Cobb from scoring: "All he needed was four inches of the plate."

With Cobb in the league, those oldtime catchers were always

practicing getting the ball out of their padded gloves fast and snapping their arms into throwing position. That was part of the pregame ritual, a catcher springing into position after each warmup pitch. Most of them possessed uncanny quickness. One of the best was Billy Sullivan, who caught for the White Sox during the years 1900–1914. For a while, Billy gave Cobb plenty of trouble. Then one day Ty stepped into the batter's box and said, "Billy, if I get on first base I'm going to steal on the very first pitch." Billy only grunted. Ty did get on base, but Sullivan just ignored him. Cobb was only bluffing, he thought. But on the first pitch to the next batter, Ty stole second as the astonished Billy Sullivan was caught flat-footed.

In the fifth inning, Cobb batted again. "Billy," he said, "if I get on base I'm going down again on the first pitch." Once more, Ty got on base, only now Sullivan wasn't taking any chances. He called for a pitchout. On the first two pitches, Cobb remained rooted on first base as the count on the batter reached two balls and no strikes. Now the next pitch had to be over. This was the situation Cobb had been waiting for and he stole second. "I never had much trouble after that running on Billy," Ty said.

Psychology was also at the bottom of a play that provided Cobb with one of his most satisfying moments in baseball. The victim was Hal Chase, the great New York first baseman who had a slingshot arm and could whip the ball across the infield with blazing speed. Sportswriters referred to Chase as "poetry in motion," one reason why Cobb was so proud to have tricked him.

One of Chase's favorite plays was to throw out runners from second who rounded third base too far on infield plays at first. If the man rounded third by just this much, Hal fired the ball over to his third baseman and caught the runner before he could get back to the bag.

Cobb spent part of the season setting up Chase. He would round third base and dive back, always just ahead of Hal's throw. What Ty was doing was waiting for the exact moment when he felt Chase was trapped in this cat-and-mouse game. The day finally arrived. Ty was on second base and the ball was hit to the second baseman. Ty dashed to third on the play at first and rounded the bag. Chase, after the putout, fired the ball to third.

The third baseman whirled around to tag Ty, only Ty wasn't sliding back—he was on his way across the plate. The startled third baseman didn't even bother to throw home. Once more, Cobb had demonstrated his genius for performing the unexpected. He never wanted any infielder, pitcher or catcher to enjoy a moment's rest. He wanted them so badly scared they would still be shaking the following day. Another of his pet maneuvers was, with a runner on third and himself on second, to race around third for the plate after tagging up on a fly ball, following so closely behind the baserunner ahead of him that the catcher was what you might call bewildered.

One day Cobb was on first base in a game against the Athletics and Claude Rossman hit a low line drive into left field. Socks Seybold played the ball like an infielder. Ty rounded second in full flight heading for third. Home Run Baker anchored himself at third with his back to the plate, waiting for the throw from Seybold. Baker knew Cobb was coming—he was *always* coming. As the ball slammed into Baker's mitt, he whirled around to his right to tag Ty—but Ty wasn't there. Anticipating Baker's move, he thundered into third on the dead run and at a 45-degree angle. His toe touched the bag in stride, and he kept right on for home without once breaking stride. Typically, Cobb slid away from the catcher's tag but got a piece of the plate with his hand to score. He was so obviously safe the catcher didn't even bother to argue.

Billy Evans, umpiring behind the plate, gasped at Cobb's daring. He said, "That looked like pure suicide, Ty."

"Suicide nothing!" Cobb snorted. "Didn't Baker have to uncross his legs, turn around—and then throw? He was in no position to get me."

All of which was very true. Home Run Baker did a good imitation of a pretzel trying to tag the phantom Cobb. That play demonstrated four parts of the Cobb personality: his quick mind, power of concentration, sublime courage, and his ruthless determination to win.

Though they never got along off the field, Cobb and Sam Crawford were a winning entry on the bases. Ty would often be on third base when Wahoo Sam drew a base on balls. As Crawford started down to first base he would sort of half-glance at Cobb across the infield. Ty would make a slight move that let

Sam know he wanted him to keep going on to second. Two-thirds of the way down the first-base line Wahoo, without any warning, would suddenly turn on the speed and fly around first as fast as he could go and tear for second.

"Now Cobb was on third," Crawford recalled. "They're watching him, and suddenly there I go, and they don't know what the devil to do. If they try to stop me, Cobb goes home. Sometimes they'd nail him, and sometimes they'd catch me, and sometimes they didn't stop either of us. Most of the time they were just too confused to do anything, and I'd wind up at second, on a base on balls."

The personal duel between Cobb and the opposing battery was a thing of beauty. Every inch of ground that Cobb could chisel by increasing his lead off a base brought him that much closer to victory. The contest developed into a battle of wits between Ty and the pitcher. Those seemingly endless throws that the pitcher made to the base to hold Cobb close were not made for exercise or to annoy the customers, but to reduce those inches. Those inches otherwise would have been translated into hundredths of a second around the next base and spelled the difference between safe and out. Runs depended upon those infinitesimal measurements. One pause, one tiny mistake, and Ty was off with the speed of a bullet.

Cobb upset infields as he upset batteries; scoring from first on singles, going from first to third on sacrifice bunts, scoring from second on infield outs and sacrifice flies, stealing, making delayed steals, purposely getting himself trapped between bases. And he usually got away with it.

Ty said he found it easier to steal third base than second. The only reason he didn't do it more was that the gain didn't warrant the risk. When he was on second he was able to take a wider lead because the pitcher then had to turn completely around to watch the base. If he wanted to nail Cobb, he had to whirl and throw without looking, taking his signal from the catcher. He also had to depend upon his shortstop or second baseman to cover. That didn't leave the pitcher much of a target. His shortstop and second baseman were on the run. Often the throw was poor and caused a mixup. But, generally speaking, Cobb found very little advantage in stealing third. He reasoned that a clean hit

could score him from second just as easily. He said he tried to
steal third only when he was going for base-stealing records. "I
had a personal philosophy about stealing second and third bases,"
Ty said. "The way I saw it, I stole second for the *team* and third
for *myself*."

On close plays at third base, watching the baseman's eyes was
most important. When the throw came in from right field, Cobb
lined his body up with the ball near the base so that it would
hit him. If he was lucky enough for it to carom off him, then he
frequently dashed on home to score. Even if the ball missed him,
at least he got in the third baseman's line of vision. The third
baseman usually just stood there wondering where the ball was,
and often he dropped it after finally getting a glimpse of it.

Cobb added a new dimension to baseball. Before his time, the
baserunner was the natural prey of the team in the field. He was
a hunted creature with nine men trying to collar him. In this
sense he was on the defensive. It was his responsibility not to
get caught. Cobb changed all that. Once he reached first base,
the whole infield was on the defensive, in blind terror of what he
might do to them. Ty's main purpose was to make them throw
the ball. He knew that if they juggled it among themselves long
enough, in their nervousness they would throw it away.

Cobb made life much simpler for the Detroit batters who followed him in the lineup. The pitcher, catcher, and infielders
had something else on their minds, with Ty on base. His spirit
rubbed off on his teammates. One day, for example, Davy Jones
led off the inning with a walk and went to third on a single by
Germany Schaefer to right field. Schaefer was a gifted baserunner,
a master at timing. With the double steal on, Schaefer got a fast
break and was well on his way to second before the pitch crossed
the plate. Davy Jones, meanwhile, did not budge off third. The
fact that Davy was taking no chances tickled Schaefer. "Hey,
Davy, we'll try it again," Schaefer shouted, and he turned around
and ran back to first base. The Tigers were playing the Indians,
and pitching for Cleveland was a rookie. He was so frustrated by
Schaefer's antics that he held on to the ball too long when
Germany took off for second again and allowed Davy Jones to
score the winning run. Afterward, Schaefer argued with the official
scorer, claiming he was actually entitled to *three* stolen bases on
the play: second, first, and then back to second again.

Oldtime sportswriters hinted in their articles that there was an element of black magic about Cobb, that he must have had a pact with the devil. Nonsense. What Cobb had was much more useful. What he had was a mixture of nerve and imagination and courage, all in preposterous amounts. He probably conceived, with difficulty, of the possibility that he might be killed, but it was a small and insignificant thing compared with his lust to win. He knew he could be hurt, because at one time or another he was bruised and cut from one end of his body to the other, but injuries he considered mere nuisances. He also had a fantastic skill based on psychology and nothing more mysterious than abnormally, almost freakishly fast reactions. Cobb himself claimed another attribute: an incredibly fine intuition.

"I could tell to the second what my opponents would do on almost every pitch," he said. No one who ever saw him sail around the bases, breaking every law of nature, obviously anticipating the behavior of infielders in tenths of a second, his body a blur as he flashed by, would doubt it.

Jimmy Austin, who played third base for New York, never forgot the day when Cobb was on first and Wahoo Sam Crawford drove him around to third on a base hit to right field. Jimmy just stood at his station, nonchalant, as though nothing was happening. At the last instant the ball came just as Cobb hit the dirt, and Jimmy caught it and in the same motion pushed Ty's foot off the bag and tagged him out. For a moment, Cobb didn't move a muscle. He just lay there on the ground. Finally he gave Jimmy the eye. "Mister," he said, in a soft, Southern accent, "don't you ever dare do that again."

Jimmy got the message.

"When Cobb was on a ball field, watch out," Austin said. "He could be really nasty. He was nobody's friend then. He was out to win, regardless."

Cobb admitted he got almost as much satisfaction from stealing bases as he did from batting. He never stopped working at baserunning, even after he reached superstardom. He often stayed on the field until nightfall, alone, running short wind sprints between the bases. In those exercises he concentrated on sharp cuts around each base, touching the bag just so, and zig-zagging back and forth, the way football halfbacks practice dodging tacklers. He even practiced a fake limp.

Sometimes he would "limp" onto the field at the start of a game as though he were suffering from a Charley horse. He would keep it up, limping and complaining within earshot of the other side about how much his leg hurt him. Then, at the strategic moment, the "pain" conveniently disappeared and Ty would be off to the races. He also discovered that it was a big help to stumble deliberately at first base and get up apparently lame, or to pretend to hurt himself sliding into second base. He figured if he was a good enough actor the pitcher and catcher would relax and grow careless, and then it was a cinch to steal on them. He even thought up a play in which he could stumble at third base and sort of limp down the baseline toward the plate, gingerly rubbing his leg and indicating he might be getting ready to call time out. The plan was to limp close enough to the plate so that a sudden burst of speed would enable him to score. "But that was one trick I never got a chance to try," Cobb said.

While American League pitchers disposed of mighty Babe Ruth and other renowned hitters by walking them, they didn't walk Cobb if they could help it, because he was even more dangerous once on base. He gave catchers fits. It was almost mandatory for them to throw a base ahead of Cobb to head him off. One afternoon Lou Criger of the Red Sox aroused Cobb's antagonism by boasting to reporters he would would stop Cobb easily. "He'd better not try any steals today," Criger said. "I shot him down on the bases the last time we played the Tigers, and I'll do it again." Cobb was furious.

Cobb singled to right field the first time up. "Hey, you big baboon, I'm going down on the next pitch!" he shouted back at Criger. He promptly stole second, and then third. At third, Cobb put his hands contemptuously on his hips. He cupped his hands and cried down the line toward the squatting Criger behind the plate, "Out of my way, ice wagon, I'm coming home on the next pitch! If you try to stop me I'll cut you to pieces!" Cobb stole home. He had rounded the bases on three straight pitches.

Cobb was supposed to have sharpened his spikes with a file before a game in New York one day. The act was supposed to have sent shivers down Yankee spines, allowing Ty to run wild on the bases that afternoon. It makes a good story, but Cobb told me there was one thing wrong with it: It never happened. That is, it never happened to *him*. Or so he claimed. Cobb said the incident involved two of his teammates, neither of them regulars. The Yankees had been beating the brains out of the Tigers, so the two subs decided to practice some amateur psychology. As the Yankees came onto the field at the start of the game, there sat the two Tigers on the bench, filing their spikes. Neither of them played in the game. "The press had to have a name to make it a good story, so they chose me," Cobb said later. "They made up other stories about me, too."

Cobb was always super-sensitive about his image as a base-runner. Just before World War I he hit the roof when Larry Lajoie, who retired in 1916, told a sportswriter that Cobb once deliberately spiked him while he was covering a throw at second base. Cobb's blood pressure rose. His eyes flashed. He sprang out of his chair at his informant as if to throw a punch at him. "Larry's a goddamned liar!" he yelled. "I never spiked him in my life! I never purposely spiked anyone, except maybe one or two who deserved it!" Cobb denied the charges vehemently, but Larry later pulled up his pants leg and pointed down to row after row of neat, jagged scars from ankle to knee. "Cobb," he said. "Cobb made those. There's the evidence. Look at it."

When this was reported back to Cobb, he said, more rationally now: "Look, I tagged a base with my shoe up, and there are no spikes in the toe of the shoe. I couldn't have made those scars on Larry, no matter what he says. I'm supposed to have spiked a lot of players, but no one ever bothers to check my scars. I'm carrying some evidence, too." His legs were, indeed, scarred from his ankles to above his knees, jagged scars and neat ones. He was pockmarked with them. But that was not surprising. He might have come from the Southern aristocracy, but in a baseball uniform he was strictly a roughneck, a mean, provocative competitor. He had asked for those scars.

One of Ring Lardner's favorite stories was about the rookie pitcher who asked his manager for some advice on how to get Cobb out. The manager said it was easy. Easy? "Sure," the manager told the youngster, "just get a gun and shoot him."

Among the most fascinating spectacles from the standpoint of sustained suspense and nervous anticipation was Cobb hunched over the plate waiting for the ball to leave the pitcher's hand. The drama that was packed into the activity at home plate seemed tremendously magnified when fans considered the ballistics and forces under which Ty and the pitcher dueled. The distance between the rubber and home plate was 60 feet, 6 inches. The batter had between three-tenths and four-tenths of a second to make up his mind whether to swing or let a pitch go by. Cobb's bat was only about three feet long, and his arms extended it another foot or so. Actually the ball was in position where Cobb could get a whack at it for only three feet of its journey. This brought the time element in which the ball remained in a position where Cobb could reach it with his club to somewhere around .02 second. That was cutting it pretty thin. Yet despite the odds, his lifetime batting average for 11,429 times at bat was .367!

A perfectionist, Cobb often complained that a lifetime was too short to solve every detail of hitting. The longer he lived, he said, the more he realized that batting was a mental problem. The ability to grasp a bat, swing at the proper time, take a proper stance—all those things were elementary. Batting was a study in psychology, he said, a sizing up of the pitcher and catcher and watching out for all those little details that could tip off the batter. "It's like the study of crime, the work of a detective as he picks up clues," Cobb said. All his playing career, Ty argued that hitters are made, not born. Billy Evans, the old umpire whom Cobb often fought, did not agree. He believed that hitting is a gift. A batter either has it or he doesn't.

"It is seldom, if ever, acquired," Evans told a writer in 1917. "Cobb is a natural, the greatest all-around ballplayer I have ever seen. He does everything well. He has the speed and knows how to use it. He has a keen mind and always takes advantage of any slip. He can bunt, he can drag the ball, he can place-hit; when he wants to, he can go for distance. He hits at few bad balls and gets a lot of walks. His great alertness and quickness drives the other team nuts. He's a constant threat. He developed the fallaway, or fadeaway, slide, which gives a baseman handling the ball little more than the spikes to touch when Ty comes sliding in."

Considering the nice, neat rows of championship batting figures after Cobb's name in the record book, sportswriters seldom talked to him about the problem of slumps. But he had them. And like most batters he couldn't tell anyone why. "It is even more difficult to find solutions for ending them," Cobb admitted. "Illness and injuries often cause them. Illness destroys your physical resistance. I know when I'm not feeling well it causes me to press in an effort to make up for the lack of zip in my swing. And injuries to either arms or legs often cause me to lose my timing. If I have to favor an injury I throw myself off stride unconsciously."

Cobb felt that worry also started him off on a slump. For three or four days he would hit the ball right on the nose—but straight at some fielder. He just couldn't buy a base hit. Since he was hitting the ball squarely, but with no luck, Ty told himself he shouldn't give the problem any serious thought. But with every day's failure he saw his batting average tailing off, and he started worrying about the problem. "That's mistake number one," Ty told Hugh Fullerton. "Now that I'm thinking about my slump, I'm also starting to think about how to overcome it. This is when my trouble begins. In my effort to overcome it, I'm changing my stance, my swing and stride, and this further handicaps my timing. When I first went into the slump, I tried my best to keep from worrying. I killed off the desire to press by gripping the bat with my hands spread apart. This helped me to control my bat better. It also kept me from going after bad balls, which always happens when you're pressing. So my best bet for ending a slump is not to worry and go right on batting in my regular style. Another remedy is to hit the ball right back at the pitcher, and that's what I'm going to do."

Cobb blamed only himself when he was in a batting slump. He knew it couldn't be the pitchers, because some of them had been his "cousins" for thirteen years and now were getting him out; striking him out or making him pop up or hit the ball into the dirt. It was his own fault, and instead of thinking it out properly, he would walk up to the plate and try to powder the ball. When he misfired and didn't connect, he reached the point when he asked his teammates what they thought he was doing wrong. He always got answers. Plenty of them. "The trouble is," Ty said at the time, "the answers are all different. One guy says I'm standing too close. One says my feet arc too far apart. A fourth says I shouldn't try to outguess the pitcher, and still another says I should guess because I'm hitting at too many bad balls and should wait and make the pitcher come in with what I want. Nobody ever tells me how I should let the pitcher know what I want or what to do if I have two strikes on me and the pitch I don't want is over the plate."

Fortunately, not many of Cobb's teammates were speaking to him, so he mostly had to figure his problems out for himself, and this was what he finally decided: He could hit those pitchers, but now he wasn't hitting them. They didn't have any more stuff on the ball than they had the last time he faced them. His eyesight still was good and he could see the ball as well as always. He used the same stance, and he gripped the bat the same way. The reason he couldn't hit the ball was because his stroke was off. He discovered he was hitting just under the ball, or just over it. So what was the solution then? "To meet the ball squarely in the middle," Cobb said, after he broke out of his slump. "I know it sounds so simple, but that's what I've done. All I had to do was flatten out my swing, so that when the pitcher throws I can hit the ball back to him. That's all I did for the first few days. Now I'm hitting it where he can't reach it. I tell other slumping batters to do the same but they don't believe me. But it works, so help me." Cobb always blamed slumps on batters who lost their heads over home runs.

Cobb sometimes didn't take batting practice or, if he did, hit only a half-dozen balls. If he met the ball solidly, he knew his timing was right. "What can I possibly gain by sweltering in the hot sun?" he asked one day. "I'm doing more good for myself and my team by storing up energy than using it up in too much batting practice. If I'm in a slump, then that's different. Then I take extra practice to regain my timing. I go back to the fundamentals and concentrate on hitting the ball squarely. To do this I ask the pitcher to lob up soft stuff to me and I bunt the ball back to the mound. I gradually lengthen my swing until I'm lacing line drives to center field again."

Ty classified his batting style as something between the free swinger and the choke hitter, but definitely closer to the choker. His method of gripping a bat kept infielders constantly in a state of anxiety. They had to guess what he was going to do. Ty was one of the few batters to use the sliding grip. Power hitters like Sam Crawford caused place-hitters to all but disappear. Yet when Cobb met up with Hans Wagner in the 1909 World Series, the two men discovered to their amazement that they both gripped the bat the same way.

Batters of the Cobbian Era had a lot to think about, including trouble with their bats. Moisture often got into the wood, especially during spring weather, and this caused cracks. That practically amounted to a tragedy, since team owners worked on slimmer budgets and were less generous about buying new ones than today. The ballplayers, including Cobb, spent a lot of time rubbing their favorite bats with neat's-foot oil or tobacco juice to keep out the dampness. Cobb's special prescription was a chewing tobacco called "Nerve navy-cut," the juiciest kind he ever found, rubbed in by the hour with a piece of bone. The bone he used, the hollowed-out thigh of a steer, was anchored to a table in the Detroit clubhouse for forty years.

"Once, in Detroit, a fan introduced himself to me and said he had an idea for treating bats," Cobb recalled. "He said that he worked in a plant that manufactured hammer handles, and the company used special machinery to treat the wood with oil under pressure. That formula didn't make much sense to me, but I gave the man some old culls on which to experiment. When he brought them back to me they were so saturated with oil I could hardly swing them. But I took them home with me and left them hanging next to my furnace to dry that winter. The excess oil drained out and those bats turned out to be the finest I ever had. Unfortunately, the man must have died or moved away, because I never saw him again.

"My favorite bat was a Louisville Slugger. Except for the weight, I never had to revise it in any way. It was 34½-inches long—a length easy to handle—had a medium small barrel with a slight taper to medium large handle, then flared out slightly to a medium shallow knob.

"My bats weighed 40 ounces right down to the last several seasons of my career, when I went to 35- and 36-ounce clubs.

"I was very particular about my bats. They were my meal-tickets. I had them tailor-made for me. The Hillerich & Bradsby people assigned their best lathe man to make them for me. I insisted on a special kind of wood, no green stuff. Whenever this special wood arrived in their plant, the order came down: 'Put it aside, that's for Ty Cobb's bats.'

"Toward the tail end of one important season I ran out of bats up in Detroit, so I called Hillerich & Bradsby.

" 'You've got to help me,' I told them. 'I'm fighting for the batting title and I have nothing left to bat with.'

"By this time, the old lathe expert who always made my bats for me had been promoted upstairs to a top executive position, but he put on some coveralls and went down into the machine shop and personally carved me out a dozen of the slickest bats you ever saw. I was forever grateful to him. He saved my batting championship for me.

"The following year I ran into a similar pinch. I called Hillerich & Bradsby.

" 'I'm down to a couple of old culls,' I told them. 'Can you help me?'

"They checked their inventory.

" 'Sorry, Ty,' they said, 'we're all out of your kind of wood.'

" 'What am I going to do?'

"The president of the company got on the phone.

" 'Don't worry, Ty,' he said. 'I think I've got the solution. We'll get your bats to you.'

"I didn't know this, but the bat company was in the process of organizing and stocking a trophy room in its office. Among its exhibits were some prized autographed bats formerly used by famous hitters. That didn't discourage the company executives. They bundled up an armload of those trophies, bats containing my special wood, and instructed their No. 1 lathe man to whittle them down to my size. That's what you call loyalty beyond the call of duty."

Bats were sacred to ballplayers in Cobb's day. There used to be a great hitter named Billy Bottenus who played for Cincinnati, and Billy believed religiously that there were just so many base hits in each bat. He would never allow any of his teammates to borrow his private weapons. "I'm not going to let anybody else use up the hits in my bats," Billy would say.

As the man said, them wuz the days.

Postscript

Ty Cobb was never quite sure of his place in American history. "Do you think they'll remember me?" his voice comes down the years. Immortality was important to him. The thought that his baseball reputation might be forgotten tormented him. "I don't want to be remembered just for my records," he said. "I want people to know about the sweat and the blood and the hell it took to get me there."

Cobb wondered aloud to me one time just what impact he had made on modern baseball. "I'm not sure my brand of baseball will even survive," he said. "Baseball has changed. The old game is gone forever."

Time has proved Cobb wrong. The stolen base is back. Cobb missed by a season seeing his record of 96 stolen bases broken by Maury Wills. Among other similarities, both Cobb and Wills concentrated on one-base hits. Ty had 3,052 lifetime singles and stole a total of 892 bases. In 1962, the year he smashed Cobb's record, Wills led the National League in one-base hits. In fact, he led the league four times in singles, tying a record. The year he stole 104 bases he made 208 hits—and only 13 of them were doubles.

Wills, who added to his knowledge by studying old Cobb films, agreed with Ty's thesis that the worst thing a champion base-stealer can do is try for extra-base hits. Ironically, Lou Brock, whose 118 stolen bases in 1974 was a new record, kept doing precisely that—hitting doubles, triples, and home runs. In 1968 he led the National League with 46 doubles. Even worse, he picked up the habit of hitting home runs. He hit as many as 21 in a single season, or more than Wills hit in his entire career. (Maury managed 20.) As for Cobb, he hit more triples than he did homers, which gives you an idea of how Ty tried to hit the ball.

Jim Murray said he didn't think Brock brings much at all to the art of base-stealing. The Los Angeles *Times*'s star columnist observed that he "looks like a guy trying to go straight. He doesn't slide. He doesn't get much of a lead. He won't steal home. He hates to steal third. He doesn't intimidate the opposition."

Most of Brock's career, he has been indifferent to base-stealing tactics. He doesn't choke up on the bat, rarely bunts his way aboard. "He generally acts more as if he's going after Henry Aaron's record than Ty Cobb's," Murray added.

Lou Brock shrugs off the criticism. He says he was in the majors three years before he found his career going in the direction of base-stealing. "I thought to be able to stay in the majors you had to throw, run, hit, and hit with power," Brock said. "We all get caught up in that syndrome. I've been accused by my critics of not having baseball science. How do they figure? For instance, I know that I've got to get down to second base in 3.5 seconds and thirteen and a half strides to make it safely on a bang-bang play, but I don't pretend to study the craft so intently as Wills and Cobb did. Maury told me to take a longer lead. So did such other great baserunners as Papa Bell, Max Carey, and Frankie Frisch. But as I told Carey and Bell—and I'm sure I'd have had to say the same thing to Cobb, too—I am not quite as tall as they were. I'm five-eleven and weigh 175. So I have to rely on a quick start and a short, hard pop-up slide. It isn't quite so rough on you as Wills's whole-body slide. I have slowed up since I first got to the big leagues. Formerly, I could cover the distance between the plate and first base in 3.4 or 3.5 seconds. Now it's more like 3.8 or 3.9. I've lost a step or two."

At his peak, Maury Wills was often compared favorably with

Cobb for intelligence, speed, fast acceleration, and baserunning science. Both of them made a deep study of pitchers. Wills, for instance, studied them when he was on base or in the dugout, or even when they pitched in batting practice. He made a mental note of every mannerism, every detail. What he looked for most were giveaways, tipoffs that told him if a pitcher was going to throw to first base in an attempt to pick him off.

"He may have shifted slightly or moved his feet or twisted his head or something else," Wills recalled. "An expert like Warren Spahn of the Braves was the toughest of all to steal on. He had no tipoffs. But if a pitcher telegraphed his intentions, I was usually a couple of steps in full stride before he even released the ball to the plate. I had such quick acceleration that I sometimes knew I had the base stolen even before I made my break for the bag."

During the years 1947–61, Earl Torgeson, a big first baseman with the speed of a deer, earned his pension with the Braves, Phillies, Tigers, White Sox, and Yankees. He was in three World Series. Torgeson grew up down the block from Hall of Famer Earl Averill in the little town of Snohomish, Washington, 30 miles north of Seattle. Torgeson was weaned on Cobbian baseball. He read everything of Cobb's he could get his hands on. A great deal of the battle of wits centered on the steal in those days, and that was the angle from which Earl studied baseball.

Recently, Torgeson, a county commissioner, told me what Cobbian baseball meant to him.

"Kids ask today, why take chances on smart baseball just for one run?" Torgeson said. "What good is one run any more? The idea now is to get a whole flock of them at a time. They play for the *explosion* inning. When they see the pitcher begin to weaken, they pounce on him like wolves ganging up on a prairie rabbit.

"I was a Cobb man, loved to run the bases. They say you can't outrun a thrown ball, but you can. A lot of guys do. The most fantastic emotion alive is the race between a baserunner and the outfielder's throw to second or third base. When you can see the ball coming and you know you can beat it to the bag— well, it's a great thrill. In my rookie year, I stole 16 straight bases before Walker Cooper of the Cardinals stopped me.

"I met Cobb once and spent hours talking baserunning with

him. We both agreed that the old Brooklyn Dodgers (1947–56) was the greatest base-stealing ball club in history. They had Roy Campanella, a great slugger, home-run hitter, and steady behind the plate. He averaged about 14 stolen bases a season. But he'd steal those 14 out of only 15 tries. Duke Snyder averaged about 23—but 23 out of 25. They were all stolen when they needed them, too. Carl Furillo would pick up another 15 out of 16 or 17 attempts. Then, of course, there was the great Jackie Robinson, he'd get you 35 and only get caught once or twice all season. Now, we're talking about two different things: intimidation and the surprise element. Campanella was the surprise factor. Opponents said he couldn't run, but he could, he was quick. Robinson represented the element of intimidation. Cobb was intimidation, so were Wills and Brock. Intimidators usually are given a free hand. The managers I played for always told me: 'Steal whenever you think you can make it,' and that's what I did. But there's a time to steal and a time to stay put. In a tight game, for example, you're the runner on first in the ninth inning, with one out. The batter then hits a long foul that misses by inches, shaking up the pitcher. He's edgy now, careless. Suddenly he isn't holding you so tightly on first. Most of his concentration is on that batter who nearly poled that last pitch over the fence. That's the psychological time to steal."

Cobb still holds the record (32) for the most times stealing home. Paul Castner, the old Notre Dame football-baseball-hockey All-American who played under Knute Rockne (1920–22), told me recently that he was responsible for $\frac{1}{32}$ of that record. Paul, now seventy-seven, lives in Saint Paul, Minnesota.

"It happened in 1923, and I was pitching for the White Sox straight out of Notre Dame," Castner recalled. "The Tigers had a rally going, and I was sent into the game in relief to try and stop it. Ray Schalk was the catcher, and he told me to throw only fastballs. The idea was for me to master my control first before I tried any breaking stuff. That didn't make much sense to me, but I did what I was told. After all, I was only a rookie— and rookies, in those days, didn't talk back to veterans.

"Imagine being ordered to throw only fastballs at Ty Cobb. He knew I was fresh out of college and he went to work on me immediately."

Cobb stalked to the plate, giving Castner the eye. The first pitch was a called strike. Cobb thought the ball was low and squawked to the umpire. On the next pitch, he dug in and pickled it into right-center for two bases. Then he advanced to third on an infield out. Fatty Fothergill, a .315 hitter, was the next batter. Paul's first pitch to him was high and wide. Out of the side of his eye Castner saw Cobb flapping his arms and making half-threats to steal home. He had a reputation for being rough on rookies, but Paul didn't let him get his goat. You old rascal, Castner said to himself, you know you are only bluffing.

Castner's next pitch was in the dirt. Schalk blocked it with his body to avoid a wild pitch. Once more, Cobb broke with the pitch but pulled up sharply down the line and retreated back to third. Now Fothergill had Castner in a hole, two balls and no strikes. Paul told himself, Cobb is only acting, he has no intention to steal home. There was no reason for him to steal. Fothergill had a hot bat, Castner was restricted to fastballs, and the odds were that Cobb could score easily on a hit or long fly.

Castner decided to ignore percentage baseball and take a full windup instead of the customary stretch. "I just wanted Cobb to know he wasn't upsetting me," Paul said later. He was just at the top of his windup when he saw Cobb break for the plate. Paul quickly threw the ball to Schalk—a good throw, too, about eight or ten inches off the ground. The ball got to the plate a fraction ahead of Cobb, but Ty, a slashing slider, avoided the tag and was called safe. The great Ty Cobb had stolen home on rookie Paul Castner.

Castner finished the inning, but when he returned to the dugout, Manager Kid Gleason blistered his hide. On his way in, Paul had left his glove near the coach's box and Gleason, pointing to it, shouted, "Go back and get that glove before you stumble over it—then get the hell out of my sight!" Gleason disturbed Castner more than Cobb had. "He was among the legion who hated Cobb and had fits anytime Ty did something big," Castner told me. "So he took it out on me by banishing me to the showers."

Cobb once explained to me that he could not go along with those who claimed they could actually follow a pitched ball until it struck the bat. "What really happens is that your eye picks up the ball about six feet in front of the plate, telegraphs the warning to the brain, which in turn directs your wrists, and you either hit or miss it," Cobb said. "You can see the curve break, but it is too late by then, for your arms are already moving to hit the ball. The roar of the crowd in the stands makes no difference. If you concentrate, you hear nothing. All you think is, 'I'm going to hit the ball, I am going to hit it, I *can* hit it.' "

Earl Averill, who was elected into the Baseball Hall of Fame in 1975, had a .318 lifetime average. He told me recently he had to disagree with Cobb. "Not only could I see my bat make contact with the ball," Averill said, "but sometimes I could even see the ball *flatten out* upon contact."

Cobb picked Babe Herman, of the Dodgers, as the most mysterious .323 batter he knew. "Bill Klem told me that every time he'd call a strike on Babe," Ty said, "the big first sacker hollered bloody murder and kicked up a storm. But every time he swung and missed he'd turn to Bill and ask if the pitch was good or bad."

Moe Berg said Babe Ruth was just as big a mystery. Moe caught in the majors behind him many times. "Babe was the only hitter I ever saw who didn't shorten his grip with two strikes against him," Berg said. "The normal procedure, of course, was to take the precaution of moving the hands up a little on the bat handle. I never found out whether Babe didn't know he had two strikes on him, or whether he didn't care."

On the great Brooklyn Dodger teams of the 1950s, I had a deep attachment to Clem Labine, their star relief pitcher. Crewcut Clem belied Cobb's contention that the modern ballplayers were not dedicated, inventive, or willing to pay the price for success. Fifteen minutes with Labine and you knew Cobb was wrong.

A relief pitcher, in Cobb's day, was a sub who went into the game when the regulars were worn out, or took a turn when someone developed a sore arm. He was "insurance," and cheap insurance at that. But Labine, and young pitchers like him, revolutionized baseball. Now they were specialists and enjoyed far more prestige and pay. Their responsibilities to the team grew hugely. In times of trial they were the firefighters and never the least bit surprised that most of the situations they walked into were crucial.

I covered the Dodgers for the NEA Syndicate during the Labine years, and Clem sometimes came over to my apartment in Brooklyn Heights for a beer. One night I asked him what differences he saw in modern baseball from the Cobbian era. I had just returned from Lake Tahoe and a visit with Ty.

"Cobb can't figure out these starting pitchers," I told him. "He's mystified by the necessity of so many relief pitchers. He wants to know what's happened to the Iron Men."

"In the first place, there's the juiced-up ball," Clem said. "Every pitcher who goes out there ought to be entitled to wear an insignia such as that prized by combat infantrymen. You toss the ball up to the plate and it comes back at you like a mortar shell. Make one mistake and it's possible to lose a leg. No one argues about the ball being livelier. The bat boy might sneak into the lineup and knock the left field stands down with a line drive. As an example, take my own case. It is a very well-known fact that I can't hit my hat size. Last year [1955], I amassed the amazing total of three hits during the entire season—all *home runs!* The point I want to make is that the ball in use today is practically jet-propelled and leads to other problems. To begin with, pitching has one thing in common with such other sports as golf, tennis, bowling: The *follow-through.* It's the sweep of the arm—that carrying of the motion through to its logical conclusion—that gives a pitcher his rhythm. Now, you might have the proper rhythm, a smooth motion, but you can no longer use it very much. You're just too busy wondering if that high-power projectile once called a baseball isn't coming back to take your head into center field.

"It used to be that a pitcher was taught that as soon as he finished his motion—that follow-through I was talking about— he was supposed to drop back, plant himself on the balls of his feet like an infielder, and he was ready to move in any direction after a batted ball. Now you merely try to prolong your life by whatever means seem necessary at the moment. If you throw the wrong pitch, the ball is over the fence before you've finished your motion. This forces you to bear down on each and every pitch. You can't relax. Wild Bill Donovan, Rube Waddell, Cy Young, and all those other pitching greats of yesterday that Cobb is always talking about—well, they weren't made to feel they were being shot at each time a ball left their hands. They could relax now and then.

"Another factor working against us today is that from five to six dozen balls are now used in each game. Compare this with Cobb's era, when, if three or four balls were used up in one afternoon the owners asked the auditor to make an investigation. Under modern rules, a ball goes out of the game the moment it gets a spot on it. If the cover gets even slightly rough or dirty it is tossed out of the game. This is somewhat different from the old game. Then, the pitcher had all the best of it. He could deliberately blacken one side of a new ball with tobacco juice or licorice and create an optical illusion to fool the batter. Clark Griffith, they tell me, used to stand in the box and tap away at the ball with his spikes. No wonder they called him the Old Fox. Another common practice back then was for the pitcher to get on his knees and rub the ball on the grass and dirt to give it 'wings.' Imagine trying to get away with that today. Every ball must be as smooth and as clean as a billiard ball. The fans want hitting, so the pitcher gets few breaks.

The records show that Labine saved 96 big league games other men started, and won only 77 himself. But one of those wins was a sensational ten-inning shutout to beat the Yankees in the 1956 World Series, tying a long-standing record held by Christy Mathewson. Clem was thirty then and at his peak.

"I was never a superstar, never a Feller or a Koufax," Clem said recently, "but I could get the job done. Somebody who'd counted told me I got Stan Musial out forty-nine times in a row. I'd curve him and jam him with the sinker. But Henry Aaron—I never got him out. My best pitch was the curve. It worked like a lefthander's. Warren Spahn asked me how I threw it. I bent my thumb under a little. They call that cheating— *cunnythumb*—but, hell, all the good curveball pitchers cheat a little nowadays. My best pitches were the overhand curve and the sinker. I discovered my sinker quite by accident. Back in 1950 Brooklyn sent me to Caracas, Venezuela, to pitch in the winter league. Warming up before a game one Sunday, I experimented with—well, let's call it a dry spitball. That is, I threw the ball the exact way a spitball is thrown, only I didn't apply saliva. Ken Staples, my catcher, made a gallant attempt to spear the ball. It seemed to sail, taking a crazy flip-flop, and then hitting Ken squarely on the side of the head.

" 'For the luva Mike!' cried Ken, rubbing his crown, '*what* was that? How'd you throw it?'

"I said, 'The same as a spitter—with the fingers gripping the bare part of the ball.'

" 'Well,' Ken said, 'let's use it in a game from now on.'

"My sinker ball was difficult to control at first, but I worked on it until I could count on it in the pinches. I also tried to master the spitter. Someone showed me how to throw it and I worked on it, but I couldn't control it. The first time I threw it, I hit the catcher in the throat. I just didn't have a spitball."

Perhaps the most successful of the modern spitball pitchers was Gaylord Perry. In his first dozen years in the big leagues he loaded up the ball well enough to win 183 games, earn $100,000 a season, and gain the distinction of being the best pitcher in the American League in 1972.

When Perry greased the ball just right, it looked like a fork-ball. His techniques were so refined it was almost impossible to tell for sure what he was throwing.

"Modern batters never had to bat against the spitter as I did," Cobb said once.

"The hell we didn't," retorted John Pregenzer, who was on the same San Francisco pitching staff as Perry in 1963–64. "At least half the pitchers in the National League were throwing spitballs without restrictions whatsoever in the 1960s. They were using just about everything to wet the ball down—Vaseline, slippery elm slop, baby oil, even vaginal jelly. When the ball is greased just right, it dances like a forkball and is practically impossible to hit. I don't know the dynamics of why the spitball, or grease-ball, does what it does, but in that distance of sixty-feet, six-inches it makes only one break. It rotates like a fastball, but when you hold up the slippery spot on the ball, it will break sharply downward, and when you hold it down it will sail or move away from a right-handed batter. Some spitballers claim they can move the ball either way, depending on how they load it up.

"Some guys are a lot more sophisticated about cheating than the Cobb gang was. I knew one pitcher who substituted Vaseline for spit and got the same sort of spin on the ball. When he was on the mound, he had grease hidden on nearly every part of his body—in his belt buckle, in the rolls of his socks, underneath the hatband, under his arms, in the heel of his glove. Every place he touched, he got Vaseline. There was no way umpires could stop him.

"When I was with the Giants, Gaylord Perry was just experimenting with the spitter. He still had a lot to learn. Tom Haller, our catcher, complained in the middle of one game of the way he was wetting the ball. 'Gay,' he said, 'please cut down on the load. I'm getting drenched.'

"Pitchers today cheat just as much as they did in Cobb's time. A few years ago, Jim Bunning [Detroit] and Jack Fisher [Baltimore] were locked in a tight pitchers' battle for seven innings—and the plate umpire had to toss eighteen balls out of the game because he spotted nicks and cuts on them. The Orioles claimed Bunning was the culprit, and the Tigers said it was Fisher. Wes Stock, then with Baltimore, said he didn't want to pass judgment—but sure as hell someone out there on the field was cutting baseballs!"

In his prime, Wes Stock, my neighbor, was pure pitcher. He stood 6 feet 2 inches and weighed 190, and there was a fluidity to his motion you seldom see with such sinews. He played with dedication and he played in pain, before a shoulder injury finally drove him off the active list. In five years at Baltimore and four at Kansas City, the former Washington State University star appeared in 321 big league games (ERA of 3.60), mostly in relief. Now he is the pitching coach of the World Champion Oakland Athletics.

Wes believes a lot of managers have trouble with modern ballplayers because they make the mistake of treating them the way athletes were handled in Cobb's era.

"People and times change," Stock told me. "They are far more mature now, and have been subjected to a lot more formal instruction. As a coach, I have to adjust to them, not they to me. I size them up carefully, then must make intuitive, unshakable decisions as to how to fit them into the pitching roster. When a rookie is first brought to me, I talk to him, watch him practice for a while, and then decide one of two things: (1) He's a starter, or (2) he's going to be a relief pitcher. I don't spend a lot of time making up my mind, either. I first look for body coordination—arms, legs, torso—and then size up his arm-speed and delivery. I wish it were also possible to probe into his head and stomach and know if he's *coachable*. I'd love to see what his gut-feeling is when the dam is dangerously close to breaking."

When Coach Stock first joined the Athletics prior to their three straight World Championships (1972–74), he was warned to expect trouble from Vida Blue, who was having contractual problems with Owner Charley Finley and had sat out part of the season. There was tension in the air. Wes accepted the fact he had to win Vida's confidence—to make him believe in him, a member of the Finley staff.

"Part of the credit goes to my fourteen-year-old son, Jeff," Stock recalled. "Vida liked him; they were on very cordial terms. So after school was out that summer, I put a uniform on Jeff, a fine little athlete, and let him shag balls for the team. Vida often played catch with him. Through this association, Vida started warming up to me. It finally dawned on him I was not his enemy, not a spy for Finley, but a friend hired to help him become a better pitcher.

"I read once that Ty Cobb claimed modern ballplayers don't work very hard. Well, I run my *starting* pitchers sixteen laps a day, *every* day, and that covers three-quarters of the outfield grass from foul line to foul line. I make the relief pitchers run ten laps. Every relief man runs ten, every starter sixteen—unless he's pitching that day, and then he's excused to prepare himself mentally for the game. I never monkey with a starting pitcher; he's on his own before the game.

"Cobb also faulted the modern game, claiming the science has gone out of it. I wish Ty could have seen our Dodger scouting report before the 1974 World Series. Al Harnsworth scouted Los Angeles for us, and prior to the Series opener I asked him three basic questions: (1) Did the Dodgers like inside or outside pitching? (2) Were they high- or low-ball batters? And (3) did breaking stuff bother them? After studying Al's report, I figured that Steve Garvey was probably going to hurt us the most, because he had fattened up his average all season on pitchers who pitched like ours. Before the World Series started, I told my pitchers to hold Garvey to a minimum, if possible, because he was going to get his hits regardless. I cautioned them to keep the bases clear whenever Garvey came to bat—to concentrate on stopping the rest of the Dodger attack—and if they did that, I was sure we'd have a good chance of winning the Series. Fortunately, that's the way it worked out."

The philosophy of physical conditioning has changed immeasurably since Cobb played ball. Melvin Durslag, for example, thinks spring training is too long. "Baseball usually takes the position that if it was good enough in Cobb's day, it is good enough for the upstarts of the Space Age," said the Los Angeles *Herald-Examiner* sports columnist. "The only difference is, the upstarts are in better shape than the Cobbs."

Durslag points out that the number of big league ballplayers who abuse their bodies during the winter nowadays is small. Many of the athletes volunteer for weight- training programs. They run. And they hold down their bulk. "You check with your trainers," Durslag said, "and you will find how few players report to camp noticeably heavy."

Following up on Durslag's suggestion, I talked to Gary Nicholson, team trainer of the Chicago Cubs for the past ten years. Gary, out of Indiana University, spends the off-season as trainer at Pacific Lutheran University in Tacoma, Washington.

"Baseball goes in cycles," Gary told me. "You've always had pitchers, for instance, experimenting with the game and training habits. An example is Mike Marshall. He's probably one of the best-educated pitchers in history; surely, his approach to baseball is every bit as scientific as Cobb's was. Remember what Mike did a couple years ago when baseball officials lowered the pitching mound from 15 to 10 inches? Like Cobb would have done, he figured that the change gave him an advantage with his curve ball over the batter, something like 2½ inches closer to the plate. Cobb always studied the game, so does Mike. He tackles his job from all angles—velocity, stride, windup, the whole anatomy of pitching. Mike and Cobb were a lot alike. Cobb was a loner, so is Mike; Cobb was arrogant, so is Mike; Cobb was an individualist, so is Mike; Cobb was always improving his play, so is Mike.

"Mike Marshall trains in his own fashion, as Cobb did. He ignores the rules of baseball conditioning, rules which were developed even before Cobb's time. Both of them were inventive in a game that hasn't seen very much invention in a hundred years. Baseball is still terribly backward. When I first became a trainer, oldtimers scoffed at the new practice of applying post-game ice packs on a pitcher's arm. They had never heard of such a thing. The old method was to *milk down the arm*—that is, suspension of the arm above the head, rubbing it with lotion or alcohol, and then *pushing the blood back to the heart*. But then we started packing elbows and sore muscles in ice, a half-hour at a time, and you should have heard those oldtime pitching coaches holler. They claimed that the athletes would catch cold in their muscles, but we knew better."

Nicholson, who was chief trainer of the 1974 National League All-Stars, researched the subject and discovered that a training room in the Cobbian era was nothing more than a bare table at one end of the clubhouse. Over the years, there was very little improvement in this phase of baseball. One of the storied trainers was Andy Lotshaw, who occupied the dual role of trainer for both the Cubs and Chicago Bears for thirty-five years. Andy wasn't a college man, but everyone addressed him as "Doctor." Doctor Andrew Hemingway Lotshaw.

When Dizzy Dean was sold to the Cubs in 1938 for $185,000, sore arm and all, the Chicago management had him X-rayed and diagnosed by several distinguished surgeons. Diz still complained of a bad arm. "Get me away from them big sawbones," he cried. "Lemme go back to Andy." Dizzy went back to "Doctor" Lotshaw, who soaked, rubbed, and massaged the lame arm daily, until finally Dean was able to pitch and win a game. "Jes' ol' goose greese and turpentine," Dizzy said when asked to describe old Andy's magic tonic. "It ain't goose grease, Diz," Andy said. "It's olive oil, turpentine, lemon, and some other things I ain't tellin'."

"Doctor" Lotshaw had a special brand of liniment for Pat Malone, who pitched for the Cubs in the 1930s. Pat wouldn't allow Andy to use anything on his arm except this particular tonic. Malone was scheduled to pitch against the Giants one day and came to Andy for the customary pregame rubdown. Andy could not find Pat's pet liniment. There was a bottle of Coca-Cola on a bench, and Andy grabbed it. He poured it into an empty liniment bottle and went to work on Malone. When he finished, Pat said he had never felt better after a massage, and then went out and beat the Giants.

Old Andy Lotshaw was the Cubs' Number One cheerleader. He would sit on the bench and raise the devil. "Gotta keep up the *morals* for my men," he would say. "Gotta make 'em into an aggression club."

The Andy Lotshaws of baseball are gone now. A new breed is in command. In 1975 more than 75 per cent of the chief trainers in the majors had college degrees, with several master's degrees among them.

"We have to be smarter," Nicholson said. "There are many more college men in the big leagues today, whereas there were only a handful when Cobb played. Today's athletes are much more complex. They are more scientific. Pitchers come to me regularly and ask me to outline a muscle-building program for them. They want to build up their strength. They want exercises that will help add speed to their fastball and exercises that will give them more endurance.

"Some of them ask if there is a magic pill they can take, but when you mention pills—well, that's a naughty word around baseball. We have gone through the Era of the Greenie—uppers and downers—the whole gamut. But that seems to be over. In Cobb's day, it was beer and hard booze. On the Cubs we have an oldtimer in charge of equipment, and he took me into the back room and showed me some old trunks that had been tailor-built fifty years ago just for the purpose of carrying booze bottles on road trips.

"In the early 1950s, rookies came to the majors actually convinced that pep pills helped them throw harder and run faster. I have personally seen ballplayers *bomb out* and be so high on greenies they couldn't hit the broad side of a barn with a cannon. Years ago, when I was trainer for the Tacoma Cubs of the Pacific Coast League, I caught one of the players dumping liquid amphetamine into the clubhouse coffee pot. His teammates were unaware of it, and they accused me of making a terrible-tasting brew. It made them real high, and for a while Tacoma was the *happiest* ball club in the minors."

Cobb told me that he lost about twenty pounds each season.

He said it was a terrible strain on him when he was battling for the batting title. Slumps were especially hard on him and made him more than usually superstitious. When he was going well at the plate he always tried to do everything exactly the same way day after day. If he had a particularly good day at bat, the next day he tried to remember which sock he put on first. If it was his left sock, then he put that one on first. He also made it a point to hang his towel on the same peg.

One day a loud, shouting argument cropped up between Ty and the Tiger trainer. Ty had gone 4 for 4 the day before and had carefully hung his towel on the same peg where it had been before the game. But when he came into the clubhouse the next day, it was hanging on a different peg. Cobb went wild. "Who moved my towel?" he cried. He was sore. The trainer confessed he did it. "Your towel fell down and I picked it up and hung it there," he explained. Ty asked him why he didn't put it back on the same peg where it had been hanging, and the trainer said he didn't know which one it was. That afternoon, Cobb went hitless and blamed his performance on the trainer for moving his towel. So Ty put the towel back up on his lucky hook, and the next game he went 4 for 4. "You figure it out," Cobb told me.

Cobb's old friend the late Lefty O'Doul sported the most famous superstition of all. When he was manager of the San Francisco Seals he wore a green suit for luck. It didn't always bring it. One day, an impostor purchased a green suit and went around San Francisco representing himself as Lefty O'Doul, signing checks, running up bills, living it up. O'Doul was contacted and disowned the man.

"Listen," said Lefty, who was not exactly esteemed for his fielding when he was a player for the Giants, "the next time a man in a green suit comes around and says he's Lefty O'Doul, take a bat and hit a fly ball to him. If he catches it, call the cops."

O'Doul attended a baseball dinner in San Francisco in 1960 at which Leo Durocher, the featured speaker, told the audience how great Willie Mays was. After Leo sat down, Lefty got up and spoke. He said that while he agreed with Durocher that Mays was brilliant, he certainly didn't think he was the greatest ballplayer of all time.

"Apparently Mr. Durocher never saw Mr. Cobb or Mr. Ruth or Mr. Joe Jackson or Mr. Harry Heilmann," O'Doul said. "Willie Mays is a great fielder and he can run bases pretty good, but he couldn't carry the bat of Mr. Cobb. Not a chance. Mr. Cobb would have been in his glory in modern baseball. He'd steal first base every night."

A small boy sitting in the audience wanted to know what O'Doul thought Cobb would have hit against modern pitching.

"Oh, about the same as Mays," O'Doul said. "Maybe .340, something like that."

"Then why do you say Ty Cobb was so great?" the boy asked. "An average of .340 with today's lively ball ain't so great."

"Well," Lefty O'Doul said, "you must remember that Mr. Cobb is nearly seventy-four years old."

While Cobb admitted that the oldtimers were probably rougher than the modern players, he also felt that today's "polite" game has produced the most bruising single play he ever saw. I mean, the football scrimmage commonly tolerated when a base-runner hurtles into second base in an attempt to break up a double play by banging into the pivot man and sending him crashing to the ground. "That isn't baseball as we played it," Ty said, "and I am amazed that the infielders of today put up with it. An infielder subjected to that sort of hostility would have calmly made his throw to first base in the exact direction of the runner's face. Or he'd have come down with gleaming spikes planted none too gently in the runner's ribs. No runner would have tried it twice. No, sir, I have often thought that today's players, with their awkward sliding and those rough blocks at second base, actually do more damage than we did for all our fierce tactics."

The late Chuck Dressen, when he managed the Brooklyn Dodgers, lamented that one of the things wrong with modern baseball was that the players were too *courteous* toward their opponents.

In a club meeting, he demanded, "What is it with you guys? Is knighthood back in flower or something? Or are they your lodge brothers? Take a simple little thing like picking up the mask for their catcher. Sure, it's not important, but there's something behind it. You pick up the mask, wipe it on your clean uniforms, and hand it back on a tray to the catcher. Why, I'm expecting any day one of you'll go sliding into a base and a guy from the other team will borrow the ump's whiskbroom to brush you off."

Times change. Players today are far more considerate of the enemy than they were in Cobb's day, when, for instance, brushing back or knocking down the hitters was an accepted part of a pitcher's strategy. The only time a hitter really worried was when they *didn't* dust him off. It made him think he was through!

In 1934 Casey Stengel, a Cobb favorite, was asked by a reporter to enlarge upon the kind of team he expected to have in Brooklyn that season.

"It will be a fighting team," Casey said, "but at the same time it will be a very polite team. Whenever one of my pitchers hits a .400 hitter in the head with the ball he must apologize. He must walk up to the man and say, 'My dear fellow, I'm awfully sorry. Please view this regrettable incident as an accident.'

"If my men are not courteous to the men they hit, I will have no part of them. I am constitutionally opposed to low, vulgar tactics."

Before the Dodgers took the field against the Giants in an exhibition game that spring, Stengel delivered a locker room lecture:

"I don't want any handshaking out there today. If any of you guys have friends on the other side, wait till next October to become sociable. I don't want any talking, either. If you feel you must say something, be sure to say it with a snarl. A ball game ain't a junior prom. Get what I mean?"

One of the rookies didn't. He wanted details.

"What's a junior prom?" he asked.

"You don't know what a junior prom is?" thundered Casey. "A junior prom is a prom that ain't old enough to be a senior prom!"

One spring Abe Pollock, having refereed prizefights, thought he would combine refereeing with baseball umpiring. He started in the bush leagues and didn't survive the first season.

"I stood for everything," Abe mourned. "They stepped on my feet with spikes, they kicked me on the shins, and they bumped me around. One day, in Fort Wayne, the crowd was after me. I didn't mind what they said or did, how many pop bottles they threw, or anything. But right in the middle of the game this big dame walked down the aisle carrying a bull terrier on a shawl strap, dropped it over the front of the grandstand railing, and yelled, 'SIC HIM!' That's when I quit."

And so we finally come to the $64,000 question. How many bases can a man possibly steal in one season, or a lifetime? Lou Brock began in 1965 a record string of ten straight seasons of 50 or more stolen bases. The 118 he stole in 1974 fattened his lifetime total to a National League career high of 753, which was only 140 shy of breaking Ty Cobb's all-time career record of 892.

Does Brock think he can top Cobb over the next couple of seasons?

"I don't set goals," Lou Brock said. "Playing the game, loving the game, the head-to-head competition, the psychological warfare —those are the factors that motivate me."

He sounded just like Tyrus Raymond Cobb.

Appendix

Lifetime Record of Ty Cobb

(Many of the statistics in this section were generously provided by the baseball historian Ernest J. Lanigan.)

COBB'S BEST YEARS

In	Record	Year
Batting	.420	1911
Games	156	1915
At bats	625	1924
Runs	147	1911
Hits	248	1911
Doubles	47	1911
Triples	24	1911
Home runs	12	1921–1925
Sacrifices	27	1922
Steals	96	1915
Runs batted in	144	1911
Walks	118	1915
Slugging	.621	1911
*Strikeouts	2	1926

* Fewest

TY COBB'S RECORD

Height 6' ¾". Weight 175. Batted left, threw right.

Managed Detroit Tigers, December 1920 to November 1926.

Year	Club	League	G	AB	R	H	HR	SB	RBI	BA
1904	Augusta	So. Atl.	37	135	14	32	1	4	—	.237
1904	Anniston	S.E.	22	—	—	—	0	6	—	.370
1905	Augusta	So. Atl.	104	411	60	134	0	40	—	.326
1905	Detroit	American	41	150	19	36	1	2	—	.240
1906	Detroit	American	97	350	44	112	1	23	—	.320
1907	Detroit	American	150	605	97	*212	5	*49	*116	*.350
1908	Detroit	American	150	581	88	*188	4	39	*101	*.324
1909	Detroit	American	156	573	*116	*216	*9	*76	*115	*.377
1910	Detroit	American	140	509	*106	196	8	65	88	*.385
1911	Detroit	American	146	591	‡147	*248	8	*83	‡144	*.420
1912	Detroit	American	140	553	119	‡227	7	61	90	*.410
1913	Detroit	American	122	428	70	167	4	52	65	*.390
1914	Detroit	American	97	345	69	127	2	35	57	*.368
1915	Detroit	American	156	563	*144	*208	3	*96	95	*.369
1916	Detroit	American	145	542	113	201	5	*68	67	.371
1917	Detroit	American	152	588	107	*225	7	*55	108	*.383
1918	Detroit	American	111	421	83	161	3	34	64	*.382
1919	Detroit	American	124	497	92	‡191	1	28	69	*.384
1920	Detroit	American	112	428	86	143	2	14	63	.334
1921	Detroit	American	128	507	124	197	12	22	101	.389
1922	Detroit	American	137	526	99	211	4	9	99	.401
1923	Detroit	American	145	556	103	189	6	9	88	.340
1924	Detroit	American	155	625	115	211	4	23	74	.338
1925	Detroit	American	121	415	97	157	12	13	102	.378
1926	Detroit	American	79	233	48	79	4	9	62	.339
1927	Phil.	American	134	490	104	175	5	22	93	.357
1928	Phil.	American	95	353	54	144	1	5	40	.323
Major league Totals			3,033	11,429	2,244	4,191	118	892	1,901	.367

WORLD SERIES RECORD

Year	Club	League	G	AB	R	H	HR	SB	RBI	BA
1907	Detroit	American	5	20	1	4	0	0	0	.200
1908	Detroit	American	5	19	3	7	0	2	3	.368
1909	Detroit	American	7	26	3	6	0	2	5	.231
Total			17	65	7	17	0	4	8	.262

* Led league.
‡ Tied for league lead.

OTHER OUTSTANDING COBB RECORDS

Led the American League outfielders in 1924 in fielding percentage, made most putouts in 1911 and assists in 1908. Had 30 assists in 1907. Tied league record for highest batting average for 100 or more games, season— .420 (1911); played 3,033 games in 24 years; most times at bat, league— 11,429; most runs scored, league—2,244; most stolen bases, league—892; most base hits, league—4,191; most times five hits in one game, season—4 (May 7, July 7, second game, July 12, and July 17, 1922); six base hits in six times at bat—May 5, 1925; set major league record with most total bases, league—5,863; tied league record with Lou Gehrig for most total bases, game—16, May 5, 1925; made most one-base hits, league—3,052; most three-base hits, league—297; hit three home runs, game—May 5, 1925. Received Chalmers Award (automobile) for leading all American League batters, 1910. Elected to Baseball Hall of Fame, 1936.

COBB VS. RED SOX PITCHERS °

Pitchers	Games	At Bats	Hits	2B	3B	HR	Pct.
Arellanes, Frank	1	6	1	0	0	0	.167
Burchell, Fred	3	11	1	1	0	0	.091
Bedient, Hugh	2	8	2	1	0	0	.250
Bush, Joe	5	20	2	0	0	0	.100
Barry, Ed	1	4	3	0	1	0	.750
Cicotte, Ed	5	20	7	0	1	1	.350
Collins, Ray	21	76	23	2	3	1	.303
Collins, Warren	3	7	2	1	0	0	.286
Dinneen, William	3	8	3	1	0	0	.375
Ehmke, Howard	8	26	7	2	1	0	.269
Foster, George	8	26	5	0	0	0	.192
Ferguson, Aleck	4	12	6	1	0	0	.500
Fullerton, Curt	3	12	7	1	1	1	.583
Fuhr, Oscar	2	7	1	1	0	0	.143
Gregg, Vean	3	10	6	1	1	0	.600
Gibson, Norwood	1	4	0	0	0	0	.000
Glaze, Ralph	1	4	2	0	0	0	.500
Harriss, Bryan	1	4	2	0	0	0	.500
Hall, Charles	2	8	4	2	0	0	.500
Hoyt, Waite	3	13	1	0	1	0	.077
Harper, Harry	2	8	2	0	0	0	.250
Harris, Joe	3	12	4	0	0	0	.333
Jones, Sam	9	32	9	3	0	0	.281
Karr, Ben	1	4	1	0	0	0	.250
Karger, Ed	8	30	9	4	0	0	.300

* These records and those following show Cobb's performance against opposing pitchers who pitched at least one complete game against Cobb's team; totals are his complete records against the teams' pitching.

Pitchers	Games	At Bats	Hits	2B	3B	HR	Pct.
Leonard, Hubert	10	32	12	1	2	1	.375
Lundgren, Delmar	1	5	3	1	0	0	.600
Morgan, Harry	2	8	1	0	0	0	.125
Musser, Paul	1	3	2	0	0	0	.667
MacFayden, Dan	1	4	0	0	0	0	.000
Morris, Edward	2	8	2	2	0	0	.250
Mosely, Earl	3	11	4	0	1	0	.364
Myers, Elmer	5	20	6	3	1	0	.300
Mays, Carl	13	41	14	0	0	1	.341
O'Brien, Thos.	5	19	8	1	0	0	.421
Pennock, Herb	7	27	10	3	0	0	.370
Pape, Larry	1	4	1	0	0	0	.250
Piercy, Wm.	3	10	3	0	0	0	.300
Quinn, John	7	32	11	1	1	0	.344
Ruth, Babe	13	46	15	0	0	0	.326
Ruffing, Chas.	4	13	3	0	0	0	.231
Russell, Allan	3	13	3	0	1	0	.231
Steele, Elmer	2	8	2	0	0	0	.250
Shore, Ernest	7	28	11	3	1	0	.393
Thomas, Alphonse	1	5	2	1	0	0	.400
Tannehill, Jesse	4	15	4	0	0	0	.267
Wiltse, Harold	5	20	8	2	0	0	.400
Wingfield, Fred	5	15	6	0	1	0	.400
Winter, George	5	21	10	1	1	1	.476
Welzer, Tony	1	4	2	0	0	0	.500
Wood, Joseph	14	56	21	8	2	0	.375
Young, Cy	12	47	18	4	3	0	.383
Zahniser, Paul	2	8	1	0	0	0	.125
Totals	242	895	293	52	23	7	.329

COBB VS. WHITE SOX PITCHERS

Pitchers	Games	At Bats	Hits	2B	3B	HR	Pct.
Altrock, Nick	7	30	7	1	0	0	.233
Adkins, Grady	1	1	0	0	0	0	.000
Burns, Bill	2	10	0	0	0	0	.000
Benz, Joe	2	8	2	0	0	0	.250
Blankenship, Ted	6	21	5	1	0	0	.238
Connally, George	3	11	3	0	0	1	.273
Cicotte, Edward	22	79	27	5	2	0	.342
Danforth, Dave	4	17	6	3	0	0	.353
Faber, Urban	31	112	29	6	1	1	.259
Hodge, Clarence	1	4	0	0	0	0	.000
Kerr, Dick	8	33	9	0	1	0	.273
Leverette, Gorham	3	9	5	1	0	0	.556
Lange, Frank	2	8	5	1	0	0	.625
Lyons, Ted	15	55	18	3	0	0	.327

Pitchers	Games	At Bats	Hits	2B	3B	HR	Pct.
Owen, Frank	3	11	3	1	0	0	.273
Olmstead, Fred	2	6	4	1	0	0	.667
Patterson, Roy	2	9	1	0	0	0	.111
Robertson, Charles	5	18	5	0	2	1	.278
Russell, Ewell	9	28	6	0	0	0	.214
Shellenback, Frank	1	3	0	0	0	0	.000
Scott, Jim	8	25	10	1	0	0	.400
Smith, Frank	18	66	17	3	0	0	.258
Thurston, Hollis	6	25	12	1	0	0	.480
Thomas, Alphonse	4	17	8	1	0	0	.471
Wilkinson, Roy	2	6	3	0	0	0	.500
Wolfgang, Mel	3	11	8	1	2	0	.727
Williams, Claude	10	40	11	1	0	0	.275
Walsh, Ed	22	88	27	6	0	0	.307
White, Guy	26	94	26	4	0	0	.278
Young, Irving	1	4	1	1	0	0	.250
Totals	229	849	258	42	8	3	.304

COBB VS. CLEVELAND PITCHERS

Pitchers	Games	At Bats	Hits	2B	3B	HR	Pct.
Baskette, Jim	1	3	0	0	0	0	.000
Buckeye, Garland	5	16	4	0	1	0	.250
Berger, Charles	1	3	2	0	0	0	.667
Bernhard, Bill	4	16	5	0	0	0	.311
Blanding, Fred	6	25	12	2	1	0	.480
Bagby, Jim	19	70	22	6	1	0	.314
Coumbe, Fred	3	10	1	0	0	0	.100
Chech, Charles	3	11	2	0	0	0	.181
Cullop, Nick	1	3	3	1	0	0	1.000
Caldwell, Ray	3	12	3	0	0	0	.250
Coveleskie, Stanley	20	77	21	3	1	0	.272
Dillinger, Harley	1	3	0	0	0	0	.000
Edwards, James	3	12	1	0	0	0	.083
Eels, Harry	2	5	3	0	1	0	.600
Falkenberg, Fred	4	15	4	0	0	0	.267
Gregg, Vean	8	30	10	1	1	1	.333
Hudlin, Willis	2	7	0	0	0	0	.000
Hagerman, Rip	3	11	4	3	0	0	.364
Hess, Otto	9	33	10	1	0	0	.303
Joss, Adrian	20	73	17	2	0	1	.233
Karr, Ben	1	5	2	1	0	0	.400
Krapp, Gene	2	6	2	1	0	0	.332
Klepfer, Ed	2	8	2	0	0	0	.250
Kahler, George	7	25	7	2	0	0	.280
Liebhardt, Glenn	6	21	5	1	0	0	.238
Lattimore, Bill	1	6	3	0	0	0	.500

Pitchers	Games	At Bats	Hits	2B	3B	HR	Pct.
Lowdermilk, Grover	1	1	1	0	0	0	1.000
Link, Fred	1	4	2	0	0	0	.500
Mails, Duster	1	6	0	0	0	0	.000
Myers, Elmer	1	3	1	0	0	0	.333
Metevier, George	1	4	1	0	0	0	.250
Miller, Walter	5	19	5	0	0	0	.263
Mitchell, William	7	27	9	3	0	1	.333
Morton, Guy	9	33	12	1	0	1	.364
Moore, Earl	2	9	4	0	0	0	.444
Rhoades, Dusty	16	64	17	3	0	1	.266
Roy, Luther	1	4	0	0	0	0	.000
Speece, Byron	1	1	0	0	0	0	.000
Steen, Bill	1	3	1	0	0	0	.333
Sothoron, Allen	2	6	2	0	0	0	.333
Smith, Sherrod	5	16	5	0	0	0	.313
Shaute, Ben	7	27	4	0	0	0	.148
Townsend, John	1	3	1	0	0	0	.333
Thielman, John	2	8	2	1	0	1	.250
Uhle, George	20	65	24	9	2	0	.369
Wright, Clarence	2	6	1	1	0	0	.167
West, James	3	9	3	2	0	0	.222
Young, Cy	7	27	6	0	0	0	.222
Totals	233	851	246	44	8	6	.289

COBB VS. DETROIT PITCHERS

Pitchers	Games	At Bats	Hits	2B	3B	HR	Pct.
Carroll, Owen	2	7	4	0	0	0	.571
Collins, Warren	1	0	0	0	0	0	.000
Gibson, Sam	3	10	4	1	0	0	.400
Holloway, Ken	2	8	3	2	0	0	.375
Sorrell, Vic	1	4	2	0	0	0	.500
Van Gildar, Elam	1	1	0	0	0	0	.000
Whitehill, Earl	2	4	1	0	0	0	.250
Totals	12	34	14	3	0	0	.411

COBB VS. YANKEE PITCHERS

Pitchers	Games	At Bats	Hits	2B	3B	HR	Pct.
Bush, Joe	7	26	5	1	0	0	.192
Caldwell, Ray	16	54	23	5	1	0	.426
Chesbro, Jack	9	33	12	2	1	0	.364
Collins, Warren	3	7	5	2	0	0	.714
Cullop, Nick	2	9	4	2	0	0	.444
Doyle, Joe	3	10	2	0	0	1	.200
Ford, Russell	16	57	25	2	4	0	.439

Pitchers	Games	At Bats	Hits	2B	3B	HR	Pct.
Fisher, Ray	9	31	8	4	0	0	.256
Griffith, Clark	1	4	0	0	0	0	.000
Harper, Harry	1	3	1	0	0	0	.333
Hoyt, Waite	12	35	7	2	0	0	.200
Hughes, Tom	2	7	4	2	0	0	.571
Hogg, Bill	4	20	8	1	0	0	.400
Johnson, Henry	4	10	2	1	0	0	.200
Jones, Sam	7	28	8	1	0	0	.286
Keating, Ray	4	13	2	1	0	0	.154
Lake, Joe	1	5	2	0	1	0	.400
Love, Elmer	3	10	4	0	2	0	.400
Manning, Walter	10	38	12	1	0	0	.316
Mogridge, George	13	50	14	2	1	0	.280
Mays, Carl	14	47	14	2	1	2	.298
Moore, Wilcey	1	1	0	0	0	0	.000
McGraw, Bob	1	4	1	0	0	0	.250
McHale, Marty	2	9	3	2	0	0	.333
McConnell, George	4	15	5	1	1	0	.333
Newton, Eustace	3	12	2	0	0	0	.167
Orth, Al	4	16	6	1	1	0	.375
Pennock, Herb	10	41	17	0	0	0	.415
Pipgras, George	3	11	2	0	0	0	.182
Powell, Jack	1	4	2	0	0	0	.500
Quinn, John	4	15	7	0	0	0	.467
Russell, Allan	4	14	3	0	0	0	.214
Ruether, Walter	1	4	2	0	0	0	.500
Shocker, Urban	6	20	11	1	0	1	.550
Schulz, Albert	4	13	4	1	1	0	.308
Shawkey, Bob	15	61	31	4	3	1	.506
Thomas, Myles	1	4	0	0	0	0	.000
Thormahlen, Herb	4	16	2	0	0	0	.125
Vaughn, Jim	7	27	10	3	1	0	.370
Warhop, Jack	14	60	25	5	2	2	.417
Wilson, Pete	5	14	6	0	1	1	.409
Totals	235	858	309	49	22	8	.351

COBB VS. ATHLETICS PITCHERS

Pitchers	Games	At Bats	Hits	2B	3B	HR	Pct.
Adams, Jim	1	5	1	0	0	0	.200
Baumgardner, Stan	2	8	2	0	0	0	.250
Brown, Carroll	3	12	4	0	0	0	.333
Bressler, Rube	1	4	3	0	0	0	.750
Burns, Dennis	3	10	4	1	0	0	.400
Bush, Joe	7	25	9	0	0	0	.360
Bender, Chief	14	54	20	1	1	0	.370
Coakley, Andy	2	7	4	0	0	0	.571

Pitchers	Games	At Bats	Hits	2B	3B	HR	Pct.
Coombs, Jack	13	42	13	2	2	0	.370
Cottrell, Ensign	1	4	0	0	0	0	.000
Coveleskie, Stanley	1	3	1	1	0	0	.333
Crabb, Jim	1	4	2	0	0	0	.500
Dygert, Jim	5	17	5	0	0	0	.294
Grove, Bob	3	9	3	0	1	0	.333
Gregg, Vean	2	9	3	0	0	0	.333
Gray, Sam	2	9	3	0	0	0	.333
Hasty, Bob	4	18	4	1	0	0	.222
Harriss, Bryan	5	20	5	0	0	0	.250
Houck, Byron	2	8	5	2	0	0	.625
Heimach, Fred	2	8	2	0	1	0	.250
Johnson, Jing	3	10	4	0	1	0	.400
Krause, Harry	10	39	13	1	0	0	.333
Kellogg, Al	1	2	0	0	0	0	.000
Knowlson, Tom	1	4	1	0	0	0	.250
Keefe, Dave	2	8	2	0	0	0	.335
Kinney, Walter	2	9	3	0	0	0	.333
Meeker, Roy	1	4	2	1	0	0	.500
Moore, Roy	1	5	2	0	0	0	.400
Morgan, Cy	1	1	0	0	0	0	.000
Myers, Elmer	10	36	12	2	1	0	.333
Nabors, John	2	9	6	1	0	0	.667
Naylor, Roleine	9	33	16	3	1	0	.485
Noyes, Win	5	19	7	1	0	0	.368
Ogden, Warren	1	4	1	0	1	0	.250
Pennock, Herb	1	5	2	0	0	0	.400
Perry, Scott	5	20	11	2	1	0	.550
Plank, Edward	33	124	37	4	1	0	.298
Quinn, John	2	8	3	0	0	0	.375
Rommel, Ed	13	46	16	3	1	1	.348
Rogers, Tom	1	3	2	1	0	0	.667
Schlitzer, Vic	1	4	0	0	0	0	.000
Schauer, Aleck	1	4	2	0	2	0	.500
Shawkey, Bob	3	11	2	0	1	0	.182
Seibold, Harry	2	8	5	2	1	0	.625
Sheehan, Tom	3	15	5	0	0	0	.333
Vickers, Rube	2	6	2	1	0	0	.333
Williams, Malcolm	1	4	1	0	0	1	.250
Wyckoff, Weldon	5	19	6	0	0	0	.316
Waddell, Rube	5	18	7	2	0	0	.389
Zinn, Guy	1	5	3	0	0	0	.600
Totals	202	759	266	32	16	2	.350

COBB VS. BROWNS PITCHERS

Pitchers	Games	At Bats	Hits	2B	3B	HR	Pct.
Allison, Mack	1	4	2	0	1	0	.500
Baumgardner, George	2	8	1	0	0	0	.125
Bayne, Bill	3	9	0	0	0	0	.000
Brown, Charles	2	7	2	1	0	0	.286
Ballou, Win	1	5	2	0	0	0	.400
Bailey, Bill	11	42	15	2	0	0	.359
Crowder, Alvin	3	8	0	0	0	0	.000
Dinneen, Bill	2	6	3	0	0	0	.500
Davenport, Dave	5	20	5	1	0	0	.250
Danforth, Dave	7	25	5	0	1	1	.200
Davis, Frank	11	30	8	3	0	0	.267
Gaston, Milt	3	12	4	2	0	0	.333
Gray, Sam	1	4	3	0	0	0	.750
Graham, William	5	17	5	2	0	0	.294
Glade, Fred	7	23	5	0	0	0	.217
Groom, Bob	1	5	1	0	1	0	.200
Gallia, Mel	2	7	2	2	0	0	.286
George, Bill	2	8	3	0	0	0	.375
Hoff, Chester	1	4	1	0	0	0	.250
Hamilton, Earl	13	43	13	0	2	1	.300
Howell, Harry	10	39	9	2	1	0	.231
Jacobson, Al	7	23	6	0	0	0	.261
James, Bill	3	13	3	0	1	0	.231
Kolp, Ray	2	10	3	2	0	0	.300
Koob, Ernie	1	3	0	0	0	0	.000
Lowdermilk, Grover	3	10	6	0	2	0	.600
Lake, Joe	4	16	8	0	1	0	.500
Leverenz, Walter	1	1	0	0	0	0	.000
Mitchell, Roy	3	11	5	1	0	0	.455
Maple, Rolla	2	6	1	1	0	0	.167
Nelson, Al	1	5	4	0	0	0	.800
Nevers, Ernie	1	1	0	0	0	0	.000
Ogden, John	2	7	3	0	0	0	.429
Pruett, Hub	1	2	2	0	1	0	1.000
Palmero, Emilio	1	5	4	2	1	1	.800
Plank, Edward	6	20	7	2	0	0	.350
Pelty, Barney	10	33	13	0	1	0	.394
Powell, John	15	59	20	1	2	1	.339
Rogers, Tom	4	16	7	1	0	0	.438
Rose, Charles	1	3	2	0	0	1	.667
Ray, Bob	3	10	0	0	0	0	.000
Shocker, Urban	11	40	9	3	0	1	.225
Sothoron, Allan	6	21	10	1	0	0	.476
Sisler, George	1	5	0	0	0	0	.000
Smith, Ed	1	3	1	0	0	0	.333
Spade, Robert	1	4	1	1	0	0	.250
Voight, Olin	1	4	2	0	0	0	.500

Pitchers	Games	At Bats	Hits	2B	3B	HR	Pct.
Van Gilder, Elam	12	44	14	2	0	1	.318
Wingard, Ernie	2	8	4	0	0	1	.500
Weilman, Carl	17	59	14	2	1	0	.237
Waddell, Rube	7	25	6	1	1	0	.240
Wright, Clarence	1	5	2	0	0	0	.400
Zachary, Tom	4	13	4	0	0	1	.308
Totals	228	811	250	35	17	9	.308

COBB VS. WASHINGTON PITCHERS

Pitchers	Games	At Bats	Hits	2B	3B	HR	Pct.
Acosta, Jose	1	5	3	1	0	0	.600
Ayers, Yancey	5	17	5	1	1	0	.294
Brillheart, Benson	1	4	1	0	0	0	.250
Burns, Bill	4	14	3	1	0	1	.214
Braxton, Garland	1	4	1	1	0	0	.250
Brown, Lloyd	1	4	0	0	0	0	.000
Boehling, Joe	8	22	11	1	0	1	.500
Coveleskie, Stan	3	10	0	0	0	0	.000
Cashion, Carl	4	17	11	0	0	1	.647
Erickson, Eric	2	5	2	1	0	0	.400
Falkenberg, Fred	4	14	4	1	0	0	.286
Francis, Ray	3	12	1	0	0	0	.083
Gehring, Hank	2	8	4	0	0	0	.500
Goodwin, Clyde	1	4	1	0	0	0	.250
Graham, Oscar	1	4	0	0	0	0	.000
Gray, Dolly	12	41	10	3	1	0	.268
Groom, Bob	10	38	11	0	2	1	.289
Gallia, Mel	4	15	6	0	0	0	.400
Gaston, Milt	3	9	3	0	0	0	.333
Hughes, Thomas	9	32	11	2	1	0	.344
Harper, Harry	5	19	7	1	0	0	.368
Hadley, Irving	6	14	5	1	1	0	.293
Johnson, Walter	67	245	82	14	3	1	.335
Kitson, Frank	3	14	5	1	0	0	.293
Lisenbee, Horace	3	9	1	0	0	0	.111
Moyer, Charles	1	4	1	0	0	1	.250
Mogridge, George	11	44	14	2	1	0	.318
Martina, Joe	2	8	3	0	0	0	.375
Otey, Bill	1	4	1	0	0	0	.250
Patten, Case	3	12	8	3	1	0	.667
Reisling, Frank	3	12	3	0	0	1	.250
Ruether, Walter	3	10	5	2	0	0	.500
Smith, Charles	4	15	8	1	0	2	.533
Shaw, Jim	10	38	11	2	0	0	.289
Schacht, Al	1	5	3	1	0	0	.600
Thurston, Hollis	1	4	1	0	0	0	.250

Pitchers	Games	At Bats	Hits	2B	3B	HR	Pct.
Townsend, John	1	3	2	1	0	0	.667
Tannehill, Jess	1	4	1	0	0	0	.250
Vaughn, Jim	1	3	1	1	0	0	.333
Walker, Ewart	3	13	8	4	1	0	.615
Wolfe, William	1	4	1	0	0	0	.250
Warmuth, Wallace	1	3	1	0	0	0	.333
Zachary, Tom	15	55	16	3	0	1	.291
Zahniser, Paul	1	4	2	0	0	0	.500
Totals	227	825	278	49	12	10	.337